Warranty Fraud
Management

Wiley & SAS Business Series

The Wiley & SAS Business Series presents books that help senior-level managers with their critical management decisions.

Titles in the Wiley & SAS Business Series include:

Agile by Design: An Implementation Guide to Analytic Lifecycle Management by Rachel Alt-Simmons

Analytics in a Big Data World: The Essential Guide to Data Science and Its Applications by Bart Baesens

Bank Fraud: Using Technology to Combat Losses by Revathi Subramanian

Big Data, Big Innovation: Enabling Competitive Differentiation through Business Analytics by Evan Stubbs

Business Forecasting: Practical Problems and Solutions edited by Michael Gilliland, Len Tashman, and Udo Sglavo

Business Intelligence Applied: Implementing an Effective Information and Communications Technology Infrastructure by Michael Gendron

Business Intelligence and the Cloud: Strategic Implementation Guide by Michael S. Gendron

Business Transformation: A Roadmap for Maximizing Organizational Insights by Aiman Zeid

Data-Driven Healthcare: How Analytics and BI Are Transforming the Industry by Laura Madsen

Delivering Business Analytics: Practical Guidelines for Best Practice by Evan Stubbs

Demand-Driven Forecasting: A Structured Approach to Forecasting, Second Edition by Charles Chase

Demand-Driven Inventory Optimization and Replenishment: Creating a More Efficient Supply Chain by Robert A. Davis

Developing Human Capital: Using Analytics to Plan and Optimize Your Learning and Development Investments by Gene Pease, Barbara Beresford, and Lew Walker

Economic and Business Forecasting: Analyzing and Interpreting Econometric Results by John Silvia, Azhar Iqbal, Kaylyn Swankoski, Sarah Watt, and Sam Bullard

Financial Institution Advantage and the Optimization of Information Processing by Sean C. Keenan

For more information on any of the above titles, please visit www.wiley.com.

Warranty Fraud Management

Reducing Fraud and Other Excess Costs in Warranty and Service Operations

Matti Kurvinen
Ilkka Töyrylä
D. N. Prabhakar Murthy

WILEY

Published by John Wiley & Sons, Inc., Hoboken, New Jersey.
Published simultaneously in Canada.

For general information on our other products and services or for technical support,
please contact our Customer Care Department within the United States at (800)
762–2974, outside the United States at (317) 572–3993 or fax (317) 572–4002.

Wiley publishes in a variety of print and electronic formats and by print-on-demand.
Some material included with standard print versions of this book may not be included
in e-books or in print-on-demand. If this book refers to media such as a CD or DVD
that is not included in the version you purchased, you may download this material at
http://booksupport.wiley.com. For more information about Wiley products, visit
www.wiley.com.

Library of Congress Cataloging-in-Publication Data is available:

ISBN 9781119223887 (Hardcover)
ISBN 9781119239703 (ePDF)
ISBN 9781119239741 (ePub)

Cover Design: Wiley
Cover Image: ©iStock.com / 1xpert

10 9 8 7 6 5 4 3 2 1

Dedicated to

Sirpa, Joni, Saila, and Niina, I love you all,
and the memory of Marko, I miss you — MK

Susanna, Markus, and Sonja, for their understanding during
the long hours it took to complete this book — IT

Jayashree for her support — DNPM

Contents

Foreword

As warranty management has seen a significant evolution over the last 25 years—from a purely reactive/administrative task toward a strategic component within the product life cycle, and nowadays even more as an essential part of how to manage the customer experience in the customer/consumer purchase-to-repurchase cycle—it is surprising how limited the available literature on warranty management and fraud avoidance is.

Matti Kurvinen, Ilkka Törylä, and D.N. Prabhakar Murthy have now written an important book about this topic. They are addressing all major points of warranty (fraud) management and explaining many important topics and interdependencies. As it provides many practicable samples and a very pragmatic approach to many theories, this book is the perfect reading for everybody who has to deal with warranty management, either looking for new insights or as an excellent holistic overview for those who are new in the business.

The first few chapters focus on explaining the general area of warranty and associated terminology and influencing levers. In Chapter 2, there are essential insights about products and warranty concepts. The authors describe the correlation between product performance, failures, and product reliability, followed by an explanation of the nature of warranty and different types and classification of warranties.

After a general description of the topic and clarification of core terminology, Chapter 3 describes the warranty servicing process, channels and parties in a warranty service network, and associated contracts. As warranty cost is the most critical metric for most warranty owners, Chapter 4 concentrates on this topic. It describes critical factors underlying warranty costs, warranty cost metrics, and warranty cost forecasting and management.

With Chapter 5 the authors are going beyond the core descriptions and explanations. From my perspective, this chapter touches one of the most important areas, which—unfortunately—is not really managed well in most companies, as it requires true holistic business understanding and associated mandate to influence entire processes and business models. This chapter looks at end-to-end warranty management from a product life-cycle perspective, including critical key decisions to be made at different stages of product life cycle. As soon as the preparation determinations are made during the product creation stage, the focus must change toward the service life-cycle perspective and how to manage the warranty process from bringing a product to market and to customers, to how to provide warranty service, to subsequently managing the claims process and related invoicing and payments within the service delivery ecosystem.

Chapter 6 goes into details of potential fraud variants with many useful samples and cases. It introduces the different forms of warranty fraud and a structure looking at the actors, victims, motivations, and methods for fraud. Especially when looking at how to improve warranty (fraud) management in your organization, there is a holistic perspective of what could go wrong. In addition, the chapter highlights several aspects that are addressing the motivation and root cause for fraud attempts, such as underpay by original equipment manufacturers or too-high investments in required infrastructure, tools, and certification.

Although all attempts are to a certain extent unethical, there should be a difference between intentionally driven (criminal), opportunistic, using gaps in the system (criminal), and unconscious (unaware and missing knowledge) motivation. The chapter provides a deeper insight into what root cause has been "created" by the warranty provider itself or brings weaknesses of service delivery ecosystem to the surface.

As soon as warranty owners understand motivation and applied methods of warranty fraud, they are reasonably prepared and can make the first step toward initiatives on how to fight against it. Chapters 7 to 10 provide insights on how to manage or even avoid fraud, including many examples. The authors provide core understanding for how to create a basic structure for a manufacturing company, how to manage warranty fraud and more specific methods for customer fraud avoidance, and opportunities for fraud detection and management. Methods for fraud avoidance and management are given from many different perspectives and directed at all parties of a holistic warranty service delivery ecosystem. Based on their own experience and expertise, the authors share practical ways to direct focus to start initiatives against warranty fraud.

Very often, warranty (fraud) management is established as a functional entity within the service organization, with limited access and mandate to improve or change relevant processes or business models. The sphere of influence of warranty (fraud) management owners is very small and realistically restricted to information gathering, analytics, and reporting. In order to drive significant changes, they are dependent on many other stakeholders and business owners outside of their influence. Chapter 11 takes a holistic view of the customer service process and service organization—what are the mechanisms, when and where to influence warranty management in general and warranty fraud management in particular. By understanding the end-to-end picture and the associated levers where to tackle warranty fraud most effectively, this chapter gives excellent input for organization design and associated governance principles.

Closely linked to organization design, processes, and governance are the underlying capabilities for organizations, which are described in Chapter 12. Here the authors lay out an initiative to improve warranty fraud management capabilities. They describe the key considerations from understanding the as-is situation through laying the foundation for improved warranty control and developing critical capabilities and how to implement these.

Finally, Chapter 13 gives an interesting outlook toward new approaches and potential impact of new technologies.

Overall, I highly recommend you read the book if you are directly or indirectly responsible for reducing warranty fraud and improving the warranty management process in your business. There are many ways that you can positively impact the bottom-line success of your company by taking this topic seriously and approaching it in a holistic way. The shared expertise of the authors will help you avoid mistakes and improve the overall approach to warranty (fraud) management.

Maximilian Kammerer
Altaussee, Austria, December 2015

After various leading after-sales service positions at Apple and being the Global After Sales Service Executive at NOKIA Mobile Phones at its height, Maximilian Kammerer is one of the thought leaders in the after-sales service industry. In addition, Maximilian has been lecturing several years at the ISS International Business School of Service Management in Hamburg. Nowadays, as Partner at Barkawi Management Consultants and Managing Partner at 1492: \\ The Collective Intelligence, Maximilian is developing new service strategies and designing the right organizational capabilities to execute these strategies. One focus area is how to avoid fraud, or at least to properly manage warranty cost without negatively affecting the customer experience within the service delivery ecosystem.

Preface

A multinational manufacturer made an after-sales process assessment to evaluate its performance and compare it with leading practices across comparable industries. The initial focus was on operations in Europe. One of the findings was that the warranty costs across countries within the company were not consistent, taking into account the general cost levels and sales volumes per country. A closer study revealed further inconsistencies and bigger anomalies, comparing different service agents inside each country.

That triggered the need to initiate activities to understand what was going on and ways to detect problems (such as fraud) and reduce the amount of warranty costs, starting with a few pilot countries. The results were almost instant. Many service agents had, over the years, learned to work around the seemingly loose controls of the manufacturer, and significant levels of fraud were detected. The manufacturer decided to accelerate the work and widen the focus to other European countries, which yielded similar results.

After the successful European implementation, the regional service heads of the manufacturer were approached for targeting the same improvements at the global level. There was a high level of skepticism, as indicated by the statement of one of the senior managers: "Yes, the European results were impressive, but Europe was crap. You are welcome here, but you won't find anything. We know our service agents, and our controls are watertight."

After less than two weeks of analytics on the regional data in another region, there was enough evidence of fraud (and high warranty costs) leading to the implementation of improvement programs similar to that in Europe. This was then followed up with other regions of the globe. During the implementation, many of the local customer service managers were shocked when they noticed the scale of fraudulent activities done by their long-term partners. "I have been playing golf with this guy every Sunday for the past five years. I can't believe he has been doing this to me," said one customer service manager. Not to talk about the incidents, where the employees of the company were also part of the scheme, working in collusion with the local service agents.

WHAT HAS CHANGED DURING THE PAST TWENTY YEARS?

The first two authors have seen a number of similar cases and diverse ways that fraud occurred in the servicing of warranties and maintenance service contracts as part of their consulting activities. The imagination and ruthlessness of some of these companies/individuals in creating fraud has been very impressive—sadly, their behavior can only be described as unethical and antisocial. The surprising thing is, we have seen and heard many similar stories when working and discussing with our clients. The strategic importance of warranty management and the general maturity of the warranty profession in the industry have improved during the past 20 years. In the same way, the development of technology (mobility, cloud, analytics, social media, industrial Internet) has enabled new and more effective information system support for warranty management. Still, one hears and reads about people or companies (often accidentally) getting caught for cheating leading global brands. In the client discussions, the two most common statements are still (i) we believe there might be something wrong, but we don't know who, where, and what is the scale of the problem, and (ii) this is not a problem with us. Depending on the source, the estimates of warranty fraud are between 3 and 15 percent of the warranty costs. At the low end of the range, this translates to several billion US dollars globally.

WHY IS IT SO DIFFICULT?

Why is it so difficult for companies to recognize or do something about it? Why do we see the same gaps in control and same tricks applied we saw 15 years ago? In our opinion there are three fundamental reasons:

1. Lack of awareness of the problem
2. The sensitivity of the issue
3. Lack of skills

Lack of Awareness

If you don't have the right tools, processes, and skills to manage warranty fraud, you typically won't detect it. In many cases, the first two authors have seen companies having these in place at the high level, but the small flaws in the details have a critical impact. When you don't detect fraud, you think it is not a problem, or if you believe it is a problem, you don't have a picture of the magnitude of the problem.

A magazine article explaining that this is an industrywide issue won't necessarily convince companies that it is their issue as well.

This leads to the vicious circle—not believing it is an issue leads to not investing in the capabilities, which leads to the issue staying under the radar. Although huge amounts of money are lost, it stays as a part of the total warranty expenditure and "the mandatory cost of doing business."

Sensitivity of the Issue

"We don't want to talk about warranty fraud, since the term *fraud* implies intent, which is an overly harsh statement," said one client executive. Although the methods discussed in this book are also effective in detecting and avoiding incidents resulting from sloppy procedures or unintentional mistakes, the main focus is on warranty fraud with criminal intent.

It is a challenging topic because people want to believe the best in others. Someone's word is generally respected, so accusing the other party of fraud or even asking for further evidence to clarify unclear issues is very difficult for most people.

Also, as the matter is so sensitive, companies are not willing to discuss it in public, so people can't hear and learn from the experiences of others. For this same reason, we have chosen to keep every case example anonymous (in many cases, that has also been a specific request from the people interviewed) unless the case example originates from a publicly available source.

Lack of Skills

Typically, most of warranty management training happens by participating in conferences, seminars, workshops, and learning on the job. All three authors have lectured at various conferences and conducted several workshops around the world. One of our interviewees (responsible for a global warranty management team in a global industrial equipment manufacturer) was quite frustrated about the lack of a solid training curriculum for a warranty management professional. "I am not looking for a one-day intro on a warranty management topic, but something more comprehensive—something like the PMI (Project Management Institute) certificate on warranty management. If I could have that, I would instantly sign-up my whole team."

NEED FOR A BOOK ON WARRANTY FRAUD

There is vast literature on warranty management topics, but very little on warranty fraud management. The first two authors had been thinking about writing a book on warranty fraud since April 2014. In October 2014, they contacted the third author (as he had written four books and edited one on various aspects of warranty) to explore the possibility of writing a book jointly. The motivation for this was to combine the deep understanding of warranty management and warranty fraud of the first two authors with the broader perspective of warranty of the third. In addition, it brought two different perspectives—theoretical and practical—together. This is important, as theory and practice are two sides of the same coin.

During that time, we also teamed up with Bill Roberts from SAS Institute and Maximilian Kammerer from Barkawi Management Consultants and 1492:\\ The Collective Intelligence.

FOCUS OF THE BOOK

The focus of the book is to assist manufacturers and other extended warranty (maintenance service contract) providers to effectively manage warranty fraud through detection and avoidance.

As mentioned earlier, the topic is sensitive and will stay sensitive. Our objective is to demonstrate the ways of dealing with this topic without offending honest business partners (which should be the majority) while still being fact based and determined to identify dishonest partners and initiate actions to improve.

Our focus is to provide practical ways to control warranty fraud through effective detection and avoidance methods. The book aims to develop the skills of warranty professionals working in this area. More specifically, it addresses the following issues:

- What is the topology of the most common fraud scenarios, who are the actors, what are their motivations, and who are the victims?

- What are the methods to tackle the known and also the unknown scenarios?
- What are the building blocks required for structured warranty fraud management?
- How can organizations get started, and how can you implement a warranty fraud reduction initiative?

We hope that this book will increase awareness of the topic. We also hope that the practical examples and methods described will help warranty professionals to analyze their data and processes from the fraud perspective, thus finding concrete evidence and facts of the situation in their own company and using that to increase the awareness, where necessary.

TARGET AUDIENCE

This book is primarily intended for after-sales professionals in general and warranty management practitioners in particular. Due to the scale and impact of the problem, it could be of interest to finance and control professionals as well. As a secondary target group, we see the academic community and hope that this book will serve as a bridge to reduce the gap between academia and industry and for the blending of theory with practice. The book can also be used as a reference book for graduate-level programs in various areas such as operations research, operations management, supply chain management, and after-sales services.

Acknowledgments

Many people and companies have contributed in this effort. We thank Maximilian Kammerer for his insight and comments across the book, and his contributions to Chapter 11 and the Foreword, and Bill Roberts for his insight on advanced warranty analytics and for establishing contact with John Wiley & Sons. We would also like to thank Eric Arnum from *Warranty Week* for his insights on warranty costs and fraud, Kim Vestman from Wärtsilä Corporation and Marko Niinistö from Philips HealthCare for their insight and experiences shared, Mark Nagelvoort from PCMI on updates on warranty management software capabilities, and Marko Ylä-Autio for his advice on warranty cost management. We thank Springer Verlag for granting the permission to use material in Appendices B and C. We also want to thank the many people whom the first two authors interviewed who have chosen to stay anonymous.

Espoo, Finland: Matti Kurvinen
Klaukkala, Finland: Ilkka Töyrylä
Brisbane, Australia: D. N. Prabhakar Murthy

About the Authors

Matti Kurvinen (Espoo, Finland) is a management consultant focusing on service strategy and operations, warranty management, installed base management, and product/component traceability as key enablers of new industrial Internet-based service offerings. Prior to starting his own consulting company, he had a 23-year career with Accenture, where he has held various leadership positions (leading the Finnish Management Consulting practice 2009–2014, Global Lead of the Accenture Warranty Management offering 2006–2014) and worked as the responsible project director or content expert in several supply chain and warranty cost reduction initiatives across clients in industrial equipment, automotive and electronics, and hi-tech industries. He holds an M.Sc. (Industrial Engineering and Management) degree from Aalto University/Helsinki University of Technology. Matti Kurvinen can be reached through LinkedIn at fi.linkedin.com/in/kurvinen.

Ilkka Töyrylä (Espoo, Finland) is a management consultant with over 20 years of experience from Nokia, Accenture, and Midagon. Service operations, outsourcing, warranty management and traceability are among his key areas of expertise. He has managed and/or been a subject matter expert in various warranty cost reduction projects. At Accenture, he was one of the key global subject matter experts in warranty management and fraud reduction. He is a coinventor in the US patent on Warranty Management System and Method issued to Accenture in 2011. The patent includes proven methods to identify fraud in warranty repair data. For the last seven years, Ilkka Töyrylä has been a visiting lecturer at Aalto University, Helsinki, on warranty chain management and fraud reduction. He holds Dr.Sc. (Industrial Management) from Aalto University/Helsinki University of Technology and M.Sc. (Economics) from Helsinki School of Economics. His doctoral thesis on traceability studied utilization of serial number data, warranty management being one of the application areas. He can be reached through LinkedIn at fi.linkedin.com/in/ilkkatoyryla.

D. N. Prabhakar Murthy is an Emeritus Professor in the School of Mechanical and Mining Engineering at The University of Queensland. He has held visiting appointments at 15 universities in the

United States, Europe, and Asia and has carried out joint research with several research groups around the world. He has researched various aspects of reliability, maintenance, warranties, and service contracts over the last 40 years. He has authored or co-authored 25 book chapters, 170 journal papers, and 150 conference papers, and co-authored 10, and co-edited 3, books. He has given several keynote lectures at various international conferences and given over 200 research seminars at several universities around the world. He has served on the advisory boards for 30 international conferences on reliability and technology management, on the editorial boards for 12 journals, and reviewed papers for over 30 international journals. He has consulted for several businesses in Australia, Europe, and the United States on various topics on warranty and reliability. He obtained B.E. and M.E. degrees from Jabalpur University and the Indian Institute of Science and M.S. & Ph.D. degrees from Harvard University.

CHAPTER **1**

Overview

Warranty costs are a significant burden for manufacturing companies. Traditionally, companies have seen warranty costs driven primarily by product quality and secondarily by repair network efficiency. However, there is another factor to be taken into account: As with many other fields of life, if there is a lot of money involved and an opportunity to get a part of that through fraudulent behavior, there will always be a small number of people or companies trying to take advantage of that. In our own client experience and in the news, we have seen the whole spectrum of warranty fraud, starting from a bit of sloppy procedures and occasional overcharging and ending with organized criminal activities in companies whose main business logic includes generating revenues through warranty fraud in addition to doing some real repair service activities.

Various parties can be involved with conducting warranty fraud: customers, sales channel, extended warranty or insurance policy brokers, service agents, warranty administrators, and even the manufacturer or warranty provider themselves.

The fraud done by the service network varies from opportunistic small-scale overbilling to fraud done by organized crime in industrial scale. Sources estimate that 3 to 15 percent of warranty billing is fraudulent (Arnum, 2015, AGMA and CompTIA, 2013, AGMA and PWC, 2009). Consequently, the overall amount of warranty fraud can be estimated to be at least US$1 billion in the United States alone.

During the past 20 years, we have seen a lot of investment in warranty control with improved validation and analytics capabilities—with some companies. However, it looks like the overall picture hasn't changed that much. Although some companies recognize the problem and have taken prompt actions, many company representatives we talked with either have said they think it is a problem but they don't really know for sure or think that this is not an issue in their companies. And every now and then we read about well-known companies (e.g., Apple, Cisco, HP, IBM, Jaguar, Nissan, Nortel, and Nokia) engaging in lawsuits against companies or individuals for warranty fraud.

The devil is often in the details—at the higher levels, everything seems to be in place: validation rules, claim process, statistical data analysis, consumer entitlement—you name it. However, when you dig a bit deeper, you notice big holes that some individuals or companies are ruthlessly taking advantage of.

In this book, we will focus on the different elements of warranty fraud and the fraud detection and prevention mechanisms that have worked with our clients. Where do you need rules-based claim validation? What is the role of statistical data analysis? What are the hurdles we have seen and the ways to overcome them?

WARRANTIES

We often talk quite loosely about warranty without defining which type of warranty is in question. Is a certain product still under warranty? Does the warranty cover a certain type of service activity?

From the customer's perspective, warranty provides assurance and protection against early product failures—I am investing in buying this product and I haven't lost my investment, even if it breaks down shortly after the acquisition. For customers, the warranty promise sets certain expectations of what they are getting if they ever need to fix or return the products.

From the manufacturer's perspective, it can be a market tool to signal reliability and quality—the customer can be confident with our products performing as designed and not breaking prematurely. In the 1980s, Lee Iacocca and the Chrysler Corporation started their recovery largely through improved quality and stating that Chrysler had the best warranty in the industry, with the famous slogan, "If you can find a better car, buy it." In a similar way, currently many automotive manufacturers are increasing the mileage coverage of their warranties. For instance, GM is advertising "a new level of confidence" and "all warranties are not equal" with its 100,000-mile warranty advertisement. However, especially with established producers, warranty is not a strong signal of quality. Many companies are offering different lengths of warranties for products with similar quality attributes to attract different customers with different risk profiles, where the more risk-averse customers may be ready to pay a premium for the longer warranty coverage (Chu and Chintagunta, 2009).

Oxford Dictionary defines *warranty* as: "A written guarantee, issued to the purchaser of an article by its manufacturer, promising to repair or replace it if necessary within a specified period of time." Product warranty is a contractual agreement between the provider and the customer. Thus, the idea is to protect both parties. Customers know that if there are problems with the product, they can turn to the provider for support. Providers spell out what they cover under warranty and also the limitations—that is, what is not covered.

There are several types and classifications of warranties, with different types of obligations for the warranty provider and rights for the warranty holder. The main types are the limited manufacturer warranty (base warranty), extended warranty, and maintenance service contract. The base warranty is usually provided by the manufacturer and is an inherent part of the product—that is, it can't be purchased separately and the product can't be purchased without it. Typically, the price of the base warranty can't be separated from the price of the product. Extended warranties and maintenance service contracts are optional and are always purchased separately from the manufacturer, retailer, maintenance service provider, or other third party.

All of these warranty types require service. The different types of warranty determine both if a certain service event is covered by warranty and who should ultimately carry the cost of the event. A solid warranty management system needs to be able to handle all of the different warranty and service contract types.

From the societal perspective, product liability laws and consumer protection laws have a significant impact on warranty providers. The minimum coverage for consumer products may be longer than, equal to, or in some cases shorter than the base warranty provided by the manufacturer. Statutory warranty and consumer protection legislation is mainly focusing on compliance, while limited manufacturer's warranty is an opportunity to differentiate if the warranty service is managed and delivered properly.

In general, warranty periods have become longer. For instance, in the automotive sector the base warranty was 90 days in the 1930s, whereas nowadays 3 years/100,000 kilometers is very common and we see warranties up to 7 or 10 years coverage.

WARRANTY SERVICING

When a customer has an issue with a product under warranty, the warranty provider needs to restore the product to a working condition, replace the product with a working one, or provide a refund. In addition to rectifying the failures, warranty servicing may include preventive maintenance activities.

These activities involve several players carrying out different tasks, including service agents, customer service, part manufacturers, sales channel, and warranty administrators. Some of the players are internal to the warranty provider and others external.

Depending on the product and the selected servicing approach, warranty servicing can be executed through several channels and in several locations, potentially including reverse logistics for the defective products and parts and forward logistics for the repaired/replacement items. The main warranty servicing channels are:

- On-device diagnostics and customer self-service
- Remote service
- On-site service
- Return to a physical service front-end location[1]
- Return to a physical service back-end location

WARRANTY COSTS

Providing warranty coverage doesn't come free for the manufacturer. Offering warranty always implies additional costs associated with warranty service, typically ranging between 1 and 2 percent of product sales for manufacturing companies.

So how big is the warranty cost? It is impossible to say exactly how big, but the scale can be estimated. In the United States, the Securities and Exchange Commission (SEC) requires listed manufacturers to report their warranty costs and the reserves they have made for the future costs. However, these reported figures are not entirely comparable, since different companies calculate their warranty cost in different ways. What share of contact center, training, spare parts, online support, and so on is allocated to the warranty cost may vary across companies. In other countries outside the United States, companies don't necessarily need to report their warranty costs, so we haven't seen any global statistics. According to the SEC, US companies spent US$29 billion on warranty claims in 2014. The worldwide warranty industry is approximately three times the US figure, about US$90 billion (Arnum 2015).

Some companies take warranty as a cost of doing business and unavoidable. Others are managing their warranty costs to the detail and diligently working through every opportunity for warranty cost reduction.

WARRANTY FRAUD

We don't believe that people in the warranty context would be any more honest or dishonest than other people in general. Unfortunately, this does mean that there are different parties in the field of warranty who are taking advantage of the loopholes in the practices and controls others have. They see the financial benefits to be gained and weigh that against the likelihood and consequences of getting caught. Both in our own client experience and in the discussions with industry experts we have had, we have seen the whole range of fraud and overbilling, starting from sloppy procedures and occasional, opportunistic small-scale overbilling to fraud done by organized crime on an industrial scale.

Warranty fraud can involve one or more fraudulent actors (fraudsters or perpetrators) and one or more victims. The main potential actors and victims are shown in Figure 1.1. The link between the two is shown by an arrow pointing in the direction of the victim.

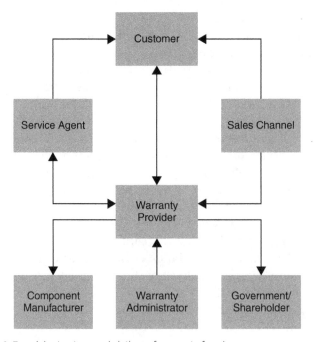

Figure 1.1 Fraudulent actors and victims of warranty fraud

The actors involved in warranty fraud have different motivations and reasons:

- Service agents may conduct fraud to stay profitable if warranty compensation is too low, terms and conditions are too tight, or requirements and preinvestments from service agents are too high. Fraud may also be opportunistic: earning of extra revenues if control mechanisms are perceived to be loose.

- Customers conduct fraud to get a free-of-charge repair and save money or grasp an opportunity to get replacement parts or products for free, which they can then use or sell further and get additional income.

- Sales channel may also be looking for extra revenue and improved profitability. It may also want to improve customer satisfaction at warranty provider's expense.

- Warranty administrators and warranty provider employees may conduct fraud to earn additional income.

- Warranty providers may see their warranty costs as excessive and try to limit warranty coverage or reclaim costs from their vendors to save costs resulting from warranty servicing. This can be the case especially when a major product issue is about to cause significant unexpected costs.

Customer Fraud

Customer fraud may vary from an individual case to systematic generation of a large amount of cases. In the individual case, the customer typically doesn't want to make money, but rather wants to get out-of-warranty service to be done free of charge. Service may be needed as a result of an accident (the customer has dropped a mobile device on the floor or in water) or intentional actions (the customer is hacking the software parameters to get more horsepower in his/her car, resulting in physical problems and then restoring the factory settings once the problems occur). The customer may not even consider himself or herself as doing anything fraudulent, just trying to get the product fixed and avoid paying for it. In some more systematic cases, the customer may try to upgrade the product to a newer model by having so many warranty repairs that the product is ultimately replaced with a new one. At the other end of the spectrum there are cases where the customer issues a large number of claims for replacement spare parts to be delivered as warranty service. The customer then sells them to others. These cases are not directed to getting anything fixed, but purely a mechanism for additional income, where the actors are typically fully aware of being engaged in criminal activities.

Sales Channel and Service Agent Fraud

Sales channel and service agents can cheat the customer by selling unnecessary or uncovered extended warranties, or refreshing own inventory by giving used products or products of old model as replacement for unrepairable products and getting products of new model from the manufacturer.

Sales channel (when also acting as a service agent) and service agents may do goodwill service and additional product refurbishment to their own customers, and charge the cost of the service back to the manufacturer as warranty service. Again, in this case, the sales channel may think they are just providing good customer service, and don't see themselves doing anything wrong.

Service agents can also add cost elements to existing warranty service claims or invent totally new warranty service events, which actually never took place. In this category we have seen systematic, large-scale ruthless actions with a clear intent to generate as much unjustified billings as possible.

Warranty Provider Fraud

In some extended warranty schemes, the customers are very aggressively sold extended warranty contracts, where the coverage of the manufacturer base warranty is already covering essentially the same that the extended warranty covers. So the customer pays for something already included in the product purchase. The majority of the potential problems are covered by the manufacturer's warranty service, so the extended warranty provider has revenues, but only limited additional costs.

Producers of Fake/Fraudulent Products or Parts

Typically, the manufacturer warranty covers the products sold by the manufacturer and the parts used in warranty repair. The customer may have bought a fake product or spare part and may then be hit twice:

- The fake product typically has lower quality and breaks earlier.
- Once it breaks, it may come as a surprise that the genuine product manufacturer's warranty is not valid for that product. The seller and the manufacturer of the counterfeit product do still have their warranty obligations, but getting the related service may in practice turn out to be really difficult for the customer.

In some cases, the customer might intentionally claim warranty service from the manufacturer. Especially for noncritical parts, the customer may purchase counterfeit parts and then try to get them replaced or fixed under warranty when they fail.

IMPACT OF WARRANTY FRAUD

What is the impact of warranty fraud to the industry? By its nature, fraud is hidden and only unsuccessful fraud is uncovered. We don't know what we don't know, and it is difficult to give exact figures of the impact of warranty fraud. Certainly in some industries there are more opportunities in the warranty chain (typically when sales volumes are high, service network is distributed and/or outsourced, end-customers interact with the external parties, there is limited traceability of products) than in others (when sales volumes are low, service is done in-house, there is high traceability). Thus, the impact of warranty fraud varies. It is estimated that 3 to 15 percent of the warranty costs are fraudulent (Arnum, 2015, AGMA and CompTIA, 2013, AGMA and PWC, 2009). With individual companies we have seen much higher figures. The total scale of warranty fraud is significant (billions of dollars) and is clearly having a direct negative consequence on the bottom line of the impacted companies.

WARRANTY FRAUD MANAGEMENT

As there are many potential actors with many potential motivations and many potential fraudulent schemes, a one-size-fits-all warranty fraud control and avoidance mechanism doesn't exist. The warranty provider needs a combination of approaches, tools, and methods to detect and prevent fraud. We call this combination the warranty control framework. It includes four categories:

1. *Contracts* set the rights and duties between the warranty provider and the customer, the service agent, and other parties in the warranty chain. They form the basis for customer warranty claim entitlement and service agents' warranty service claim validation.

2. *Transaction controls* include the process and controls from the customer issue through servicing and financial settlement of the claim, the main elements being customer warranty entitlement, service agent claim validation, and material returns (part returns) control for defective materials.

3. *Analytics* identify customer warranty claims and warranty service claims with high likelihood of being incorrect, whether through fraud, abuse, or sloppy processes and identify service agents or customers with high deviations from expected performance.

4. *Service network* management supports fraud avoidance, sets the right network structure to minimize fraud opportunities, incentivizes service agents to right behavior, sets the rules of operation, drives performance, empowers the right people, audits service agents, and provides clear procedures in terms of what happens when a service agent gets caught.

STUDY OF WARRANTY

There is a wide spectrum of angles toward warranty and a vast number of books and articles written on warranty-related topics:

- Legislation, legal issue, liability, and consumer protection
- Warranty cost management
- Warranty, quality, and reliability
- Warranty and marketing, influence on buying decisions

- Engineering
- Operations improvement

Some often-cited references worth mentioning include the following:

- Warranty overall: (Blischke and Murthy, 1996), (Brennan, 1994), (Murthy and Blischke, 2005)
- Warranty cost management: (Blischke and Murthy, 1994) and (Thomas and Rao 1999)
- Warranty, quality, and reliability (Thomas, 2006) and (Sahin and Polatogu, 1998)
- Extended warranties and maintenance service contracts: (Murthy and Jack, 2014)
- Warranty data and analysis: (Blischke et al., 2011), (Rai and Singh, 2009)
- Review and survey articles: (Djamaludin et al., 1996), (Thomas and Rao, 1999), and (Murthy and Djamaludin, 2003)

However, there are a very limited amount of publications on warranty fraud—a few articles primarily from industry consortia, consulting companies, warranty software providers, and academia. As the subject is very sensitive, the articles in the newspapers and magazines are mainly about cases settled in court or cases that are big enough to force publicly listed companies to disclose them.

Some studies on warranty fraud include the following:

- "IT Industry Warranty and Service Abuse: Stealing Profitability! Core Issues, New Solutions and Emerging Threats" (AGMA and CompTia, 2013)
- "Service Blues: Effectively Managing the Multibillion-Dollar Threat from Product Warranty and Support Abuse" (AGMA and PWC, 2009)

Research papers on analyzing specific methods of warranty fraud include:

- "A Data Warehouse Design for the Detection of Fraud in the Supply Chain Using the Benford's Law" (Kraus and Valverde, 2014)
- "Spare Parts Dispatch Fraud Detection Analysis" (Verma and Rajendran, 2015)

GOALS OF THE BOOK

This book has three primary goals:

1. Increase the awareness and understanding of warranty fraud.
2. Provide concrete and practical methods for warranty fraud management.
3. Describe a holistic approach for how to improve or implement methods for warranty fraud management.

We want to increase the general awareness of the different actors executing warranty fraud, their motivations, and fraud schemes. We also want to raise awareness of the scale and impact of fraud.

Warranty fraud is not a mandatory cost of doing business, but something worth taking determined action to avoid, detect, and manage. In the interviews for this book and in our discussions with companies we have heard too often:

- "There may be something peculiar happening, but we really don't know what it is."
- "This is not an issue for us. We trust our partners, and they would never cheat us."

For those who have the awareness, we want to provide concrete examples and ways to identify, to avoid, and to deal with warranty fraud. Although we try to cover all main fraudulent parties and all main victims of fraud, our main focus is on the manufacturers/warranty providers as victims and on the ways they can manage the situation.

This book is primarily targeted for warranty practitioners. Since there is a total whitespace in the literature on this topic, we hope it will be of relevance in the academic world and bridge the gap between industry and academia.

STRUCTURE OF THE BOOK

The chapters can be divided into two groups:

- Chapters 2–5 introduce the basic concepts of warranty and warranty management, providing the foundation for the rest of the book.
- Chapters 6–13 deal with warranty fraud, the main focus of the book.

Chapter 2 discusses products and warranty as concepts. The correlations between product performance, failures, and reliability are discussed, followed by the role of warranty, and different types and classification of warranties.

The products under warranty need servicing. Chapter 3 describes the warranty servicing process, as well as channels and parties in a warranty service network. Contracts are an important element of and enabler for effective warranty management and also discussed here.

Warranty servicing incurs costs for the warranty provider. Chapter 4 discusses the underlying factors of warranty costs, warranty cost metrics, and warranty cost forecasting and management.

Chapter 5 looks at warranty management from the product life-cycle perspective: What are the key decisions to be made at different stages of product life cycle, and from the service life-cycle perspective, how to manage the warranty process from the issue with the customer product to providing warranty service, managing the claims process, and related invoicing and payments.

Chapter 6 introduces the different methods to conduct warranty fraud and classifies fraud methods by actors, victims, and motivation.

Chapter 7 introduces a generic framework for a manufacturing company to manage warranty fraud.

Chapter 8 deals with specific methods that warranty providers can use for avoidance, detection, and management of fraud by customers.

Chapter 9 deals with specific methods that warranty providers can use for avoidance, detection, and management of fraud by service agents.

Chapter 10 deals with specific methods that warranty providers can use for avoidance, detection, and management of fraud by other parties (sales channel, warranty administrator, warranty provider internal fraud).

Chapter 11 takes a holistic view of the customer service process and service organization and looks at warranty provider strategies to influence warranty management in general and warranty fraud management in particular.

Chapter 12 outlines an initiative to improve warranty fraud management capabilities. It describes the key considerations from understanding the as-is situation through defining warranty policies and rules, building the capability, and implementing the changes needed.

Chapter 13 is an epilogue that concludes the book and looks at various issues such as new approaches, potential impact of new technologies, and ideas for future research.

NOTE

1. Service front-end refers to service locations, which are in direct contact with the customer (field-service onsite at the customer location, a service center, where the customer can return the product for service), online or remote service. Service back-end refers to service locations, which are typically only in contact with the service front end, not with the customer.

CHAPTER **2**

Products and Product Warranty

When investing to buy a product, the customer needs some assurance of the product performing satisfactorily and meeting customer expectations over the designed life of the product. Product warranty (we will call this *base warranty* to differentiate it from other types of warranties) is one way for the manufacturer to provide this assurance. It is a part of the product value proposition (different, but often following the legislation and consumer protection directives—which could vary from country to country). The manufacturer rectifies any problems (technical and aesthetic—for example, brakes functioning properly and the paint not flaking) when the item is still under warranty. Once the base warranty expires, the customer needs to either carry out any rectifications at own cost or buy an *extended warranty* or *maintenance service contract*. The price of extended warranty and maintenance service contract depends on the terms of the coverage. We use the term *warranty* to include the base warranty (BW), extended warranty (EW), and maintenance service contract (MSC). Manufacturers and the associated value chain and sales channel often think about base warranty as a cost item, a mandatory cost of doing business, and potentially as a way to increase sales. Extended warranties and maintenance service contracts are considered as a way to earn additional revenue and improve profitability.

This chapter briefly introduces products and product warranties and looks at various issues that will form the basis for discussions in later chapters. The three first sections are product related and focus on performance, failure, and reliability. The remaining sections deal with warranty-related issues.

PRODUCTS

Oxford Dictionary defines *product* as "An article or substance that is manufactured or refined for sale" (*Oxford Dictionary*, 2015). For the purpose of this book, we define *products* as tangible physical objects, designed and built for a specific purpose. Products can be fairly simple (e.g., an electric kettle) or very complex (e.g., an aircraft).

Product Classification

Products can be classified in several ways in terms of customer segmentation or business logic, product technology, manufacturing technology, and volume.[1] In the academic literature, the classification that has been used in the context of warranties is based on the final end customer (Murthy et al., 2008). Table 2.1 shows the classification along with some illustrative examples of the products.

Practitioners commonly divide products into two categories: (i) business-to-consumer (B2C) products; and (ii) business-to-business (B2B) products, based on the customer being an individual or a business entity. B2C products (e.g., mobile devices, televisions sets, appliances, automobiles, and PCs) are consumed by the society at large. They are characterized by relatively high volumes and a large number of individuals using the products. The complexity of a product can vary considerably. The typical consumer is often not sufficiently well informed to evaluate product performance. B2B products (e.g., large-scale computers, CNC machines, pumps, X-ray machines, and airplanes) are characterized by a relatively small number of customers and manufacturers. The technical complexity of such products and the mode of usage can vary considerably. Products can either be complete units (e.g., cars, trucks, pumps), sold to the final customer, or subunits (e.g., batteries, drill bits, electronic modules, turbines blades, etc.) of a complete unit, sold to another company in the value chain.

Table 2.1 Product Classification

Customers	Products	Some Illustrative Examples
Individuals	Consumer products	Cell phone, watch, etc.
Households	Consumer products	Kitchen appliances, washing machine, dryer, etc.
Service-oriented businesses	Commercial products	Buses, locomotives, trucks, entertainment products, airplanes, etc.
Processing/manufacturing oriented businesses	Industrial products	Lathes, excavators, pumps, etc.
Government	Defense products	Planes, ships, tanks, etc.

Another often-used classification is based on the uniqueness of the product leading to the following three groupings:

Standard products

All units are manufactured to a set specification. They can be manufactured to stock, based on the anticipated demand (make-to-stock), or after receiving the customer order, based on the actual demand (make-to-order/assemble-to-order).

Engineer-to-order/configure-to-order products

These are manufactured using standard subunits, to a final configuration specified by the customer directly or engineered to meet the customer requirements.

One-of-a-kind products

These are complex, engineered systems (ships, industrial sites, airplanes), designed and manufactured to customer requirement and often involving considerable innovation and state-of-the art technologies.

The last two are also often referred to as custom-built products.

Consumer products can be divided further based on the lifetime of the product into consumer durables and nondurables. Nondurables get depleted when used (food and beverages, deodorant, toothpaste), in contrast to durables, which are used several times (such as household appliances). Most consumer durables (with price greater than some minimum amount) are sold with warranty, whereas nondurables are not.[2] In a similar way B2B products can be divided into two categories: (i) processed materials (such as metal, wood, plastic, etc.) used as input in making other products, and (ii) engineered objects (such as equipment, tools, etc.). The former are often referred to as consumables and sold without warranty, whereas engineered objects can have very complex warranties.

In many industries the offered products or their components are divided into hardware, software, and services, which may be sold as a combination or separately. In this book, we think about a product as a tangible entity, comprised of hardware and software, which has a warranty. Pure software products or services typically have a different logic and are not a major focus in this book.

Product Decomposition

Products can be simple (with a few parts) or complex (with millions of parts as in the case of an airplane). The structure can be broken down to several levels. The number of levels appropriate depends on the complexity of the product. Blischke and Murthy (2000) view a product as a system (collection of several interacting elements) and propose an eight-level decomposition:

Level	Characterization
0	System
1	Subsystem
2	Major assembly
3	Assembly
4	Subassembly
5	Component
6	Part
7	Material

In this book we use the term *product* for level 0 and can refer to an individual unit or a class (collection of units). The term *item* is used to denote a product, part, or component. We don't separate levels 5 and 6, and use the terms *part* and *component* interchangeably.

PRODUCT PERFORMANCE, FAILURE, AND RELIABILITY

Product performance, failure, and reliability are related concepts and important in the context of product warranty.

Product Performance

Every product deteriorates with age and usage and its performance degrades. A failure occurs when the product is no longer able to perform as specified. In B2C the specification is typically decided by the manufacturer, whereas in B2B the specification can be decided either by the manufacturer (for standard products) or by the customer and the manufacturer (in the case of custom-built products). The specification includes the performance expectations for the product as well as the expected operating conditions. For instance, an airplane is expected to fly at high altitudes and in very cold environments, where a smart phone might not be expected to function at all.

Product Failure

Product failure is the product's inability to perform in the manner as specified in the product requirement specification (e.g., in a car it could be stopping time for the car traveling at 60 km/hour to be less than 10 seconds).[3] A product failure is due to failure of one or more of the components of the product.

A fault (product or component) is a description of the cause of failure.

There are three types of failures:

Total failure
The failed item is nonoperational and can only be made operational through repair action (e.g., failure of all four engines in a four-engine plane).

Partial failure
The failed item is operational but not able to perform as required (e.g., a four-engine plane can operate with one failed engine but the load it can carry needs to be reduced for it to take off).

Intermittent failure
An intermittent failure is the loss of functionality for a limited period of time and the subsequent recovery of the functionality. Intermittent failures are typical in electronics products with software. Typically, the first remedy for an issue with a PC or mobile phone is to turn it off and restart. Should the failure occur too often, the product is returned for repair.

In addition to the normal break-fix situation, there are specific failure cases, which may have their own handling process:

Dead on arrival (DOA) means a product failure at the point of sale or customer goods receipt (e.g., a consumer buys a new laptop and notices before leaving the retail shop that there is no sound or the display doesn't work).

Dead after purchase (DAP) means a product failure shortly after being purchased. In many jurisdictions, consumer protection laws regulate these cases and also many manufacturers have specific procedures for DAP.

Buyer's remorse means the customer's sense of regret after purchasing the product. It is not a product failure as such, but may lead to product returns anyway. If the product is too complex to use, the customer may get frustrated and return the product. With many consumer products, the quantity of buyer's remorse returns has increased significantly with online sales—the customer is expecting a different type of a product based on the pictures and dimensions in the web-shop and doesn't like the physical look and feel when receiving the product.

No fault found (NFF) means that the product failure cannot be repeated and cause of failure cannot be identified. These are very costly for manufacturers and some companies are setting handling fees for customers for NFF claims, even if the product is under warranty. Typically, NFF claims happen because of (i) intermittent failures, which don't appear during testing to repeat the failure, (ii) lacking fault and symptom descriptions, and (iii) customer not having the knowledge and expertise to use the product, getting frustrated, and claiming the product to be faulty.

Product Reliability

Product reliability is an indicator of the ability of the product to operate without failure over a specified period of time. It is defined as the probability that the product will not fail as a function of time in operation. Product reliability has a direct relationship with warranty costs. Lack of reliability will result in higher field failure rates, which in turn result in increased warranty costs.[4]

Product reliability decreases with age and usage (due to wear and tear of components). Figure 2.1 shows the reliability curves for three products with different reliabilities where t denotes time since put into operation (age). The bottom curve corresponds to least reliable and the top to most reliable. As can be seen, for each the reliability decreases with age.

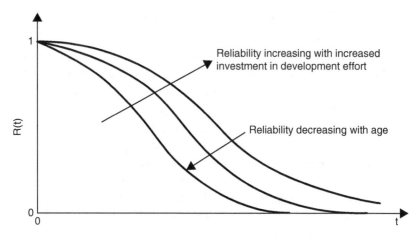

Figure 2.1 Product reliability (Blischke et al., 2011)

Product reliability can be improved with a number of actions resulting in the reliability function shifting toward the upper right-hand corner. The actions include:

- Improving product design
- Using more reliable components
- Improving quality in manufacturing, distribution, and installation processes
- Giving better user instructions to customers (e.g., battery usage, recharge guidelines for electronics devices)

There are several different notions of reliability. When a new product is designed, company reliability standards and customer expectations define the *design reliability*—how the product design supports product reliability. *Inherent reliability* is the reliability of products produced and differs from the design reliability due to the influence of quality variation in sourced materials, component nonconformance, assembly operations, and so on. Further on, distribution and storage have an impact leading to *reliability at sale* being inferior to inherent reliability. Finally, installation, operating environment, and usage mode and intensity result in the *field reliability* differing from the reliability at sale. Harsher environment and higher usage intensity negatively affect product reliability. Figure 2.2 illustrates the different notions of reliability over the product life cycle, the connections

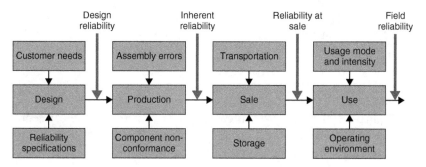

Figure 2.2 Notions of product reliability and the affecting factors (Blischke et al., 2011)

between them, and the various factors influencing the final field reliability, which in turn has an impact on the warranty costs.

Product Failure Rate

Product failure rate characterizes the probability that a functioning item will fail within a small time interval as a function of age (time in operation). As such, it is a function of time and is related to the reliability function $R(t)$.

The shape of the function for most products is either (i) monotonically increasing (due to aging effect) or (ii) bathtub with three phases—decreasing (high likelihood of early failure due to teething problem, which decreases with age), flat (age having no impact), and increasing (due to aging effect).[5] Figure 2.3 shows the failure rate functions for two products with the two described shapes, where t denotes time in operation (age).

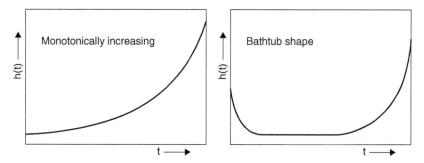

Figure 2.3 Failure rate functions

The failure rate forms the basis for an analytical method to detect certain kinds of service agent fraud and is discussed in Chapter 9.

PRODUCT MAINTENANCE

The purpose of product maintenance is to control the rate of degradation (wear and tear) of a product (referred to as preventive maintenance) and to restore a failed unit to an operational state (corrective maintenance). Calibration and optimization activities may be a part of the maintenance operations, to ensure that the equipment maintained operates optimally (e.g., in terms of fuel consumption, power generated, and quality of output).

Product maintenance can be a significant cost item to the customer and to the manufacturer. For products used in sectors like mining, processing, manufacturing, and transport, the annual costs to owners can vary from 5 to 40 percent of the product purchase price for certain products. For manufacturers the warranty costs vary from 1 to 5 percent of sale price depending on the type of product, length of warranty, and the manufacturer. Ensuring the planned product reliability over the product life cycle requires a certain amount of preventive maintenance activities carried out at regular intervals.

Preventive Maintenance

The logic behind preventive maintenance is that for many products, the actions to reduce the likelihood of failure are often more cost-effective (both in terms of repair cost and the operational impact of the failure to the customer) as opposed to not doing anything until the failure occurs, after which rectification action is initiated.

Preventive maintenance activities are planned and typically include actions like inspection, calibration, adjustment, replacement of worn components, and replacement of degraded material (such as lubrication oil). Preventive maintenance actions depend on the age or usage of the product. For instance, in the automotive industry the typical recommendation is maintenance service every 12 months or 15,000 kilometers, whichever comes first. Engine oil and filter would be replaced in every maintenance session, whereas fuel lines and fuel filter would be checked for leakage and damage every third or fourth maintenance session.

Preventive maintenance is commonly used for products where

- The safety impact of malfunction is high (airplanes, ships, elevators).
- The cost of downtime is high (commercial vehicles, production equipment).
- The product has wearable components (automotive, industrial machines).

For short-life-cycle products, like mobile devices, preventive maintenance makes limited sense.

The right timing is of the essence in preventive maintenance. Carrying it out too early increases parts and material costs and delaying it too late increases the risk of product failure. Condition-based maintenance (where the condition of components is assessed either through continuous monitoring or monitoring periodically) is now being used extensively as opposed to age- or usage-based preventive maintenance.

Optimized preventive maintenance can simultaneously reduce the total maintenance (preventive + corrective) cost and ensure high availability (the time the product is in operational state). Analytics based on historical failure profiles, sensor-based information on the state of the product at any given point of time, and consumption and usage history data are increasingly used to optimize preventive maintenance.

Corrective Maintenance

The purpose of corrective maintenance (often called break-fix) is to restore a failed unit to an operational state. Different approaches to corrective maintenance include the following:

- Minimal repair—restore the item back to the condition before the failure.
- Better than old but not as good as new—replace failed and worn-out components.
- As good as new—replace the failed product by new or a refurbished product.

Corrective maintenance includes by definition the rectification actions taken after a failure. Typically, these actions are unplanned as failures occur in an uncertain manner. However, the correction of partial and intermittent failures can be delayed to take place during a planned preventive maintenance session.

PRODUCT WARRANTY

Customers have an expectation of product performance over its design (useful) life. The purpose of warranty (BW, EW, and MSC) is to provide the customers an assurance that these expectations will be met or the warranty provider will take the corrective actions and fix the potential issues with the product, for the time period specified.

A warranty is a contract between the manufacturer or some other warranty provider and the customer, "A written guarantee, issued to the purchaser of an article by its manufacturer, promising to repair or replace it if necessary within a specified period of time" (*Oxford Dictionary*, 2015).

There are several types of warranties with different types of obligations for the warranty provider and rights for the warranty holder. The three main warranty types are manufacturer base warranty, extended warranty, and maintenance service contract:

1. *Limited manufacturer warranty* (also called manufacturer base warranty or base warranty) is provided by the manufacturer producing the product to the customer buying and using the product. The minimum time period for the manufacturer warranty is often heavily influenced by the consumer protection laws, but not always. For example, whether you bought the goods in a shop or online, under European Union (EU) rules you always have the right to a minimum two-year guarantee period at no cost, but still some manufacturers only have one-year limited manufacturer warranty. Some of these cases have been taken to court and the manufacturers have been forced to change their policies.

2. *Extended warranty* can be given as an extension to the manufacturer warranty, either free-of-charge or more typically sold as an extended service package. It can include an extension in the time period the warranty is valid or provide an additional coverage on issues the base warranty doesn't cover. In other cases, the customer can receive additional services (technical support, on-site service, extended call center support, etc.) not available without the extended service package. Extended warranties are

typically purchased either with the product or shortly before the base warranty expires.

3. In business-to-business context, companies are offering *maintenance service contracts* complementing or replacing the base warranty. Maintenance service contracts can typically start at any point of time agreed and can include a variety of services and related targets and service level agreements (SLAs).

In addition to these main categories, classifications commonly used by practitioners include the following categories:

- *Insurance policies*—Especially in the consumer electronics industry companies have related offerings, which are actually insurance policies. The customer has a chance to get free-of-charge service from the existing service channel either extending the warranty period or also including coverage for out-of-warranty issues like mishandling, accidental damage, liquid damage,[6] or lost/stolen product. For theft and loss there needs to be an insurance product filing process and a licensed insurance underwriter to offer the insurance product. The rules vary from country to country.

- *Supplier warranty* is provided by the component supplier or contract manufacturer to the final manufacturer of the product (often referred to as original equipment manufacturer, or OEM). Based on the supplier warranty the manufacturer can recharge defined parts of its warranty costs to the supplier who has delivered the failed component or subassembly.

- *Repair warranty* can be provided by the manufacturer to the end-customer for the parts and/or labor after a service event or by the external service agent to the manufacturer (a form of supplier warranty). Repair warranty can be a part of base warranty or extended warranty or be given to an out-of-warranty repair paid by the customer.

- *Sales channel warranty* can be given as an extension to the manufacturer warranty, either free-of-charge or more typically sold as an extended service package. It can include an extension to the time period of the warranty and/or provide additional coverage on issues the base warranty doesn't cover.

- *Goodwill service* is service that is not covered by warranty, but is still provided free-of-charge for the customer. Goodwill service can include the actual repair of the defective product (e.g., for failure within a very short period after the warranty has expired) and/or additional refurbishment done together with the warranty repair.

 Lifetime Repair Warranty

CASE STUDY

Volvo Cars announced that it is offering a Volvo Lifetime Replacement Parts and Labor Warranty for all replacement parts purchased and installed at an authorized Volvo retailer (United States and Canada). The warranty is not transferrable and doesn't cover accessories, wear items, consumables, or parts needing replacement for any outside influence (Volvo 2015).

The warranty provider for the base warranty is the manufacturer. For extended warranties and maintenance service contracts it can also be the sales channel or a third-party provider.

Providing a warranty results in additional costs, which need to be covered either by factoring the costs into the sales price of the product for base warranty or by the price of the extended warranty or maintenance service contract. If an extended warranty or goodwill service is offered free of charge to the customer, the extra cost should be covered by the respective sales or marketing budget.[7]

Role of Warranty

The role of warranty depends on the perspective—manufacturer, customer, and societal. Base warranty is integral to the sale of the product and the customer is not charged extra. Base warranty most often covers the whole product, hardware, and software that is required for the product to function in a proper way.

Software, services, and applications typically have a different logic. They come with binding specifications on performance and functionality, with no warranty as such, but rather a one-off or ongoing license fee and related version upgrades and downloadable fixes, against user-specific service entitlement and license keys.

Customer Perspective

The customer is entitled to recovery (through either repair, replacement, or refund in full or at a fraction of the sales price) over the warranty period, which is typically at no cost to the customer. However, there are obligations for the customer as well, such as proper handling and use of the product, servicing the product at authorized service centers, and informing the warranty provider about the defect without unnecessary delay.

Manufacturer Perspective

From the manufacturer perspective warranty can be an important marketing tool to signal product reliability and quality—the customer can be confident with the product performing as designed and not failing frequently. The different forms of extended warranties and service contracts can also be a significant source for additional revenues, longer customer relationships (through repeat purchase), and better customer satisfaction. For one Volvo car owned by a logistics company in Finland and driven 2.6 million kilometers according to the company website, the gearbox was replaced after 2 million kilometers under warranty (evidently, a goodwill service from the manufacturer).

Societal Perspective

Civilized societies demand remedy or retribution for damage suffered by their members that is caused by someone or some activity. This has serious implications for manufacturers of products. Product liability laws and warranty legislation are signs of society's desire to ensure fitness of products for their intended use and compensation for failures. In the United States, various legislations have been passed starting with the Uniform Commercial Code (UCC) in 1952. In the context of warranty, the major legislations are the Magnusson-Moss Act and the TREAD Act.

Classification of Warranties

The two main warranty types are implied and express warranties. Implied warranties are unspoken, unwritten promises on the product performance: a merchant's basic promise that the goods sold will do what they are supposed to do, that there is nothing significantly wrong with them, and the product can be used for a particular purpose (Blischke et al., 2011). A statutory warranty is an implied warranty that does not need to be in a contract for it to be in effect.

Express warranties are the warranties specifically expressed by the seller (manufacturer or sales channel):

1. In the sales contract, or

2. Within the warranty policy, or

3. In a statement in the sales materials, or

4. In a sample product (the sold product needs to conform with the sample), to customers buying the product.

There are myriad different express warranty policies offered by manufacturers, sellers, and third parties. A simple classification is shown in Figure 2.4 and involves several levels.[8]

At the first level base warranties can be grouped into two categories—(i) those that do not have reliability performance as part of warranty contract (mostly for standard products) and (ii) those that have reliability performance included so that the manufacturer has to improve the reliability through design changes (mainly for custom-built products)—and are referred to as reliability improvement warranties (RIWs).

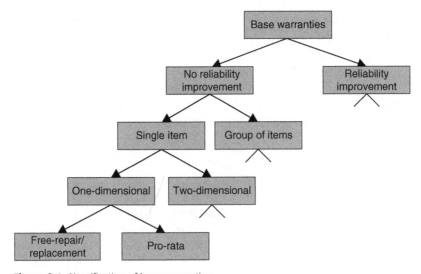

Figure 2.4 Classification of base warranties

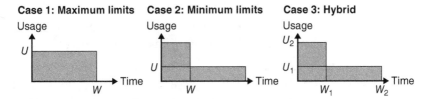

Figure 2.5 Two-dimensional warranty

At the second level the question is whether the warranty is for (i) a single item or (ii) a group of items. The latter is called fleet or group warranties that are used in B2B sales such as a rental business buying a fleet of equipment or a manufacturer buying components in lots.

At the third level the division is based on the dimensions—one or two. In the case of one-dimensional warranty, the warranty interval is usually a time interval (e.g., three years in the case of a washing machine) or in some cases usage (e.g., 100,000 copies in the case of a photocopier). In the case of two-dimensional warranty, the warranty is defined by two variables, typically time and usage. The combination of these two dimensions leads to several different cases. Figure 2.5 (from Blischke et al., 2011) shows three of them.

- *Case 1:* The warranty covers product usage until the maximum time (W) or the maximum usage (U) is reached, <u>whichever comes first</u>. This favors the warranty provider, since for a heavy user, the warranty expires before time W because of the usage limit being reached. For a light user, the warranty expires at time W with total usage below U.

- *Case 2:* The warranty covers product usage until the minimum time (W) and the minimum usage (U) is reached, <u>whichever comes last</u>. This favors the customer, since a heavy user is covered for a time period W, by which time the usage may have well exceeded the limit U and a light user is covered well beyond time W, as the policy expires only when the total usage reaches U.

- *Case 3:* This is a compromise between the above two cases. The warranty covers product usage until the maximum time (W_2) or the maximum usage (U_2) is reached, <u>whichever comes first,</u> <u>or until both minimum time (W_1) and minimum usage (U_1)</u> <u>are reached</u>. This results in fairer policy that takes into account the interests of both parties. The buyer is provided warranty coverage for a minimum time period and usage. At the same time, the manufacturer is obliged to cover the item for a maximum time period and usage, whichever comes first.

At the fourth level, there are many different policies. The two most common ones are: (i) free repair/replacement warranty (FRW) and (ii) pro-rata warranty (PRW) with different terms. Three illustrative examples follow:

FRW policy

The manufacturer agrees to rectify (either through repair or replacement) any failures as long as the item is under warranty.

PRW policy

The manufacturer refunds or provides replacement at a reduced cost leading to renewing or nonrenewing policies:

- *Nonrenewing.* The manufacturer refunds a fraction of the sales price should the failure occur under warranty. The refund is a decreasing function of age and/or usage and reaches zero when the warranty expires.

- *Renewing.* The manufacturer provides a new item (with a new warranty policy) at a reduced price should the failure occur under warranty. The discounted price depends on the age and/or usage at failure. Note that in this case the total warranty coverage (from the instant of initial sale) increases with each such replacement and ceases only when the last replacement does not fail under warranty.

Reliability improvement warranty policy

The basic idea of a reliability improvement warranty is that the manufacturer/contractor includes guarantees on the long-term reliability of the product and not just on its immediate or short-term performance (Blischke et al., 2011). Thus, the manufacturer's commitment is more than to repair or replace the product as failures occur. These are mostly seen with complex, repairable equipment with a long lifetime. These often include targets for MTBF (mean time between failures) and the obligation to provide, at no cost, to the customer:

- Engineering analysis to determine the cause of failure to meet the mean time between failures (MTBF) target.

- Engineering change proposals
- Modification of all existing products in accordance with approved engineering changes
- Consignment spares for the customer use until such time as it is shown that the MTBF target has been reached

Terms and Conditions of Warranty Policy

The terms and conditions for base warranty are typically standard and defined by the OEM for consumer products. When buying a product with warranty, the consumer receives a warranty certificate/proof of purchase, including a reference to the OEM's warranty terms. When buying applications or installing them online, the consumer usually needs to accept the OEM's base warranty terms to proceed with the download.

The terms define the length of the warranty, actions taken in different scenarios (e.g., repair, replace), and where and how the customer can get warranty service. It also defines the customer obligations and the consequences of not following the contract. These consequences can limit the validity of the warranty, increase the customer share of the warranty cost, or make the whole warranty void. The warranty contracts have a reference to dispute resolution—how and where the potential disagreements will be solved in case there is a dispute between the warranty provider and the customer in terms of the liability. In case there is a conflict between the warranty contract terms and legal requirements, the law typically takes precedence. This is often explicitly stated in the manufacturer warranty terms.

 Apple Warranty Terms Referring to the Law

CASE STUDY

"THIS WARRANTY GIVES YOU SPECIFIC LEGAL RIGHTS, AND YOU MAY HAVE OTHER RIGHTS THAT VARY FROM STATE TO STATE (OR BY COUNTRY OR PROVINCE). OTHER THAN AS PERMITTED BY LAW, APPLE DOES NOT EXCLUDE, LIMIT OR SUSPEND OTHER RIGHTS YOU MAY HAVE, INCLUDING THOSE THAT MAY ARISE FROM THE NONCONFORMITY OF A SALES CONTRACT. FOR A FULL UNDERSTANDING OF YOUR RIGHTS YOU SHOULD CONSULT THE LAWS OF YOUR COUNTRY, PROVINCE OR STATE." (Apple 2016)

In business-to-business operations—for example, heavy industrial products, process automation, and defense contracting—the warranty terms are agreed case by case. These can include:

- *Performance guarantees.* The manufacturer guarantees that there will be a certain improvement in process efficiency after installing their product.

- *Reliability improvement.* The warranty provider works over a fixed period of time to achieve set reliability improvement targets and may then receive additional incentives.

- *Threshold limits.* It is acceptable to have a certain amount of malfunctions and the warranty is triggered only after a certain number of failures have occurred.

Warranty Activation

It is important for both parties to understand when the warranty period starts and when it ends. When a consumer purchases a product, the warranty period normally starts immediately. The consumer should get a proof-of-purchase, which is required to get warranty service, when a problem occurs. When using retailers, distributors, and other intermediaries, the manufacturers may have limited visibility to the actual purchase data. In consumer electronics the warranty period is frequently calculated by adding a standard channel lead-time (e.g., three months) to the product manufacturing date. With this calculation warranty service may be accepted, even if the customer is unable to provide the proof-of-purchase. Some manufacturers expect a separate registration to take place to activate the warranty. This can be a recommendation for the consumer or a mandatory part of the setup process, where the product cannot be taken into use without the activation sent to the manufacturer.

In business-to-business cases, the warranty activation can take place in a similar way—either at the time of purchase or after the customer has accepted the product and the related installation services.

Post Base Warranty Options

Once the base warranty expires, the customer has four main options:

1. Take responsibility for repair and maintenance of the product.

2. Use the product until it fails and then buy a new one to replace it.

3. Seek assistance from the manufacturer or an external service agent and pay for each service event separately.

4. Maintain by getting assistance from the manufacturer or an external service agent through extended warranty or maintenance service contract.

Extended Warranties

Extended warranties are offered to the customers by many parties, including OEM, dealers, retailers, and other third parties (insurance companies and dedicated extended warranty service companies). In these cases, the customer pays extra to extend the base warranty (hence the name extended warranty) in terms of time, services included, and/or entitlement coverage. So the terms can vary and extended warranty providers often have several different extended warranty packages in their portfolio.

Extended warranties are frequently offered for a wide range of products, including:

- Automotive
- Consumer electronics
- Appliances
- IT

Compared with the base warranty, extended warranties can include additional elements such as:

- Extended length of the warranty period (e.g., from 2 years to 5 years and/or from 2,000 usage hours to 5,000 usage hours)
- Extended service hours (e.g., contact center support from 5×8 service window to 24×7)
- On-site service
- Free advanced technical support
- Access to additional online services
- Guaranteed availability of service parts or service technician
- Protection for user-caused damages and/or normal wear and tear

For the warranty provider, the extended warranty offering can be very profitable if executed and priced right. However, we have seen cases where the additional cost-to-serve is higher than the fee for the extended warranty and every sale turns out to be unprofitable. Many companies have chosen not to report extended warranty sales and profits in detail. Showing very high profits in one single item could also draw negative attention, which is one reason to report them as a part of the "other" financial revenue category. In some cases, the extended warranty may be a part of a sales campaign and free-of-charge for the customer.

In the electronics and telecommunication sectors, retailers and telecommunications operators are building significant additional revenues through extended warranties. When Best Buy acquired Geek Squad (Trefis Team, 2012) in 2002, the company had 65 service technicians, growing into a workforce of 20,000 technicians by 2015, offering a range of installation, protection, and support services. Initially, the service was targeted to support Best Buy customers, but currently also offered through other channels and as an independent service.

CASE STUDY

Geek Squad Protect & Support for PCs

Geek Squad offers a range of extended warranty and premium technology service packages. The Protect & Support package covers hardware failures after the manufacturer's base warranty has expired (although it might be that the same entity is providing that warranty service on behalf of the manufacturer), technical support, product replacement at the third failure (so called no-lemon benefit), and technical support, also covering accidental damages to some extent (Best Buy 2015).

MAINTENANCE SERVICE CONTRACTS

Maintenance service contracts are similar to extended warranties. They are typically found in B2B environments. For the customer, it can be viewed as outsourcing of maintenance. For the provider, the motivation is to get growth and stability through continuous service revenues and also drive differentiation and new equipment sales. Unfortunately, there is no universally accepted terminology. Companies talk about service agreements, equipment protection plans, operations and maintenance support, lifecycle services, and so on. The research literature also suffers from this. Similar to extended warranties, maintenance service contracts provide services to complement and extend the base warranty, and the customers pay for them.

Manufacturers and third-party multivendor service companies offer maintenance service contracts. Many manufacturers are also seeing multivendor service both as a source for additional revenues and as a route to sell their own equipment, having better visibility to upgrade and replacement plans of the customers.

Maintenance service contracts include corrective maintenance/break-fix and preventive maintenance services as well as other value-added consultative services. The scope for a maintenance service contract can be an individual item or several items (e.g., a plant or a fleet of aircrafts or other vehicles). In these cases, the service agents may form a network with different participants in different roles to ensure the availability of all skills and manpower required to support such complex maintenance activities.

CASE STUDY

Caterpillar Base Warranty, Extended Warranties, and Maintenance Service Contracts

Caterpillar standard base warranty is typically 6 to 12 months. On top of that, it offers extended warranties called Equipment Protection Plans (EPP), backed by Cat Financial Insurance Services, and a range of maintenance service contracts called Customer Support Agreements. Extended warranties have three options with different levels of coverage (Powertrain, Powertrain + Hydraulic, and the most comprehensive, Premier), whereas the maintenance service contracts are tailored for each customer, ranging from simple Preventive Maintenance Kits to sophisticated Total Cost Performance Guarantees (Caterpillar, 2015).

INSURANCES

Extended warranties may be close to insurance policies or include an insurance policy as a part of the offering. The main difference is as follows. A warranty is a result of product sale and the warranty provider's obligation is to ensure that the product performs satisfactorily and meets the required (often statutory) quality standard. In contrast, an insurance policy does not necessarily involve product sale. It is a means through which the customer can get protection against unforeseen events not covered by warranty (e.g., user damage, mishandling, theft, lost products) and/or additional coverage. For instance, in white goods (appliance like refrigerators), the insurance can cover the transport to the service center, whereas under base warranty customers need to return the product for warranty service (and get it back). Base (and most extended) warranties exclude any consequential damages, which an insurance policy may cover. The customer has to pay an insurance premium to get the additional coverage or protection.

For accidental damage or user-caused defect, the warranty provider can offer the additional coverage as a part of extended warranty. For theft and loss coverage, the provider needs to be authorized as an insurance company. So when manufacturers or retailers sell product insurance policies or extended warranties with an insurance component, they need to partner with insurance companies to be the true undertaker of those parts of the contract. Insurance companies are third parties that typically offer further protection to fund out-of-warranty service, but seldom offer the actual service themselves.

Insurance policies do not cover malicious damage. If the customer intentionally damages the product, then it is not covered by warranties or insurance.

NOTES

1. Our list is not exhaustive. Other classifications include, for example, (i) United Nations Central Product Classification (http://unstats.un.org/unsd/cr/registry/cpc-2.asp), (ii) dominant material used (metal, wood, glass, etc.), (iii) degree of innovativeness, and (iv) applications (different industry sectors—manufacturing, mining, etc.).

2. Various other forms of legislation (such as safety) offer customer protection in the case of nondurables.

3. Other specifications (such as paint work on the car not fading in the first three years) are not product failures but important in the context of warranties.

4. Field failure information is an important element in understanding and improving product reliability of existing or new products.

5. For more on this, see Chapter 3 of Blischke et al. (2011).

6. Liquid damage means that the product has suffered from contact with water or other liquids. Most electronics companies state that liquid damage is not covered by warranty.

7. Normally, extended warranty products are highly profitable, and the warranty servicing cost should be calculated against that revenue, not as a part of the base warranty cost.

8. A more comprehensive classification and details of many warranty policies can be found in Blischke and Murthy (1994).

CHAPTER **3**

Warranty
Servicing

When a warranty provider (manufacturer or third party) offers warranty for a product, it needs a service network with internal and/or external parties to deliver the service. These parties then provide the warranty service based on the process defined by the warranty provider and contracts between the warranty provider and the parties involved.

This chapter introduces the parties in the service network, the different steps of warranty service process, and the contracts a warranty provider needs with each of the main parties in the service network.

PARTIES IN THE WARRANTY SERVICE NETWORK

The main parties involved in the service network are shown in Figure 3.1 and are discussed in this section.

Warranty Provider

The warranty provider is responsible for putting together a network of parties that jointly provide an effective warranty service. Each party has a specific role and discharges specific tasks. Some of the parties can be internal to the warranty provider while others are external independent agents carrying out tasks that are outsourced by the warranty provider. The two extreme cases are all the parties being either internal or external to the warranty provider. This is seldom the case.

Customers

In this book, *customer* is defined as the owner of a product sold with warranty (base warranty, extended warranty, and/or maintenance service contract). Often, but not always, the customer is also the user of the product, raises the warranty claim, and is the recipient of warranty service. Furthermore, the term *customer* embraces a large number of different parties, including individuals, households, small and large businesses, and government. Customers purchase the product either directly from the manufacturer or through the sales channel. Distributors and retailers are not called customers in this book. Instead,

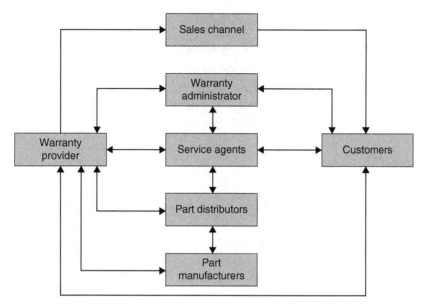

Figure 3.1 Key parties in the warranty service network

they are referred to as sales or distribution channel and discussed later in the section.

Service Agents

Service agents carry out the actions to rectify customer problems by repairing or replacing the defective products. Service agents can be internal to the warranty provider or external. If an external service agent conducts the warranty servicing, the warranty provider compensates the service agent based on an agreed compensation model. Typically, the warranty provider has a process to approve, certify, and recertify service agents and their employees as a prerequisite before allowing them to conduct repairs. The certification can be product or repair-type specific.

Service agents receive products to be repaired either directly from the customers or through intermediaries, namely sales and distribution channel, other service agents, manufacturer, or other warranty provider.

Single versus Multibrand Service Agents

Service agents can be classified based on the products they service:

- Single brand or exclusive service agents only do service for a particular manufacturer and/or brand.
- Multibrand or multivendor service agents serve products manufactured by several manufacturers.

Level of Specialization

Service agents may or may not differ in terms of their level of specialization and may be working in a multiechelon (i.e., tiered) model:

Varying level of specialization organized using tiers

A tiered structure service network has two or more tiers, each dealing with different service activity. This model is used, for example, in the electronics industry:

- Service agents acting on the first tier can act as the contact points for the customers, conduct basic repairs, and do product and module replacements. These can also be a part of retail shops.
- Service agents on higher tiers can be specialized and conduct complex repairs, often requiring major investments in service equipment. If certain types of defects cannot be fixed on the lower tiers or it is more economical to fix such defects centrally, the product can be delivered to the next tier to be repaired. Often, there is only a small number of specialized service agents within a region operating in high-volume repair factory mode.

Varying level of specialization without interconnections

Alternatively, the network can be organized in such a way that service agents have different levels of competence, but do not deliver products to each other. For example, some of the service agents repairing automobiles have competence and are authorized to do mechanical repairs while software updates and electronics-related repairs are done by specialized service agents with the right service equipment.

No specialization

Service agents are not specialized, and each of them conducts all service activities.

Number of Service Agents and Level of Centralization

Depending on the level of centralization and the scale and nature of business, a global manufacturing company may have a few, hundreds, or even thousands of service agent locations within its network providing services in different geographical regions. From the perspective of physical locations, there are alternative ways to set up the network:

Distributed network

There is a large number of low-volume workshops providing wide geographical service coverage and easy access for customers.

Centralized network

The service network can be highly centralized. In this case, there are one or few service agents within a country, region, or globally. All products are shipped to a central location to be repaired. This model works best with relatively small products with limited shipping costs. It allows economies of scale to be obtained and services to be conducted in low-cost countries.

This categorization also applies to field service, where the pool of technicians can be highly centralized or geographically distributed. A distributed network reduces response time in case of customer issue as customer sites can be reached quicker, but is likely to reduce technician utilization and increase cost of service.

Relationship with Warranty Provider

The relationship between the warranty provider and service agents in the network also varies:

- Each service agent has a direct relationship with the warranty provider.
- Larger service agents do the repairs themselves; take the responsibility of managing the next layer of smaller service agents; and act as the interface with the warranty provider. In this model, the warranty provider may or may not have a contractual relationship with the smaller service agents.
- Sales and distribution channel gets sellable products at a discount, and in return takes the responsibility of arranging service and managing the network of service agents.

Part Manufacturers

Part (or component) manufacturers produce the parts and other materials needed in warranty servicing. They sell the parts either directly or through a distributor. Parts can be delivered to a service agent either directly, through another service agent, through a third party responsible for parts distribution, or via the manufacturer.

Warranty providers often maintain a list of authorized parts and part manufacturers. Genuine and certified third-party parts can be purchased while gray-market parts are not allowed. Depending on the contract, a part manufacturer may provide warranty for the parts it sells to the manufacturer.

Part Distributors

Part distributors deliver spare parts manufactured by a large number of part manufacturers but do not manufacture the parts themselves. Warranty providers may define authorized part distributors to reduce the risk of counterfeit parts entering their supply chain and to leverage centrally negotiated terms of purchase.

Sales and Distribution Channel

Sales and distribution channel relates to the modes in which products get delivered to customers. It can be either direct or indirect. In the latter case, there can be either one (retailer) or two parties (distributor and retailer) responsible for sales and distribution of the products. The promotion can be done by one or more parties in the sales channel. Sales channel is one of the interfaces through which a customer can get warranty service, acting as a collection point or often also as a service agent.

Part distributors, sales and distribution channel, service agents, or other parties can maintain swap stocks with products or modules. This stock is then used to supply parties conducting replacements with new replacement products while returned products are repaired, refurbished, and returned to swap pool where possible—or scrapped and recycled.

Customer Service

Customer service is often the first contact point for customers seeking warranty service. It can also provide support and give authorizations for service agents. Customer service responsibilities in the warranty context include:

- Entitlement to verify customers' eligibility for warranty repair within the return material or return merchandise authorization (RMA) process
- Minimization of the number of no-fault-found products entering the servicing process through customer dialogue
- Instructing customers on how to proceed in the warranty servicing process (e.g., where to deliver the defective product)
- Authorizing service agents to conduct out-of-warranty service for goodwill reasons
- Authorizing service agents to conduct predefined high-cost repairs

Customer service typically operates as a contact center or through an online channel

Warranty Administrators

Warranty provider has various administrative activities directly related to controlling warranty costs:

- Administering service agent master data within warranty provider's systems
- Validating warranty service claims submitted by service agents to warranty provider
- Analyzing claim data for product quality improvement and cost-control purposes
- Processing payments to service agents
- Verifying that materials to be returned by customers, service agents, and sales and distribution channel are received, and diagnosing their condition (This can also be done by another party, such as reverse logistics partner.)

Other Parties

In addition to the main parties just discussed, other parties play an important role, depending on the warranty and the monitoring process:

- *Leasing companies lease products for use by customers when their failed products are under services.*[1]

- *Inspectors act on behalf of the warranty provider.* An inspector can, for example, verify the cause of a defect and determine if it is covered by warranty.

- *Logistics companies transport products.* They pick up failed products from customers, deliver replacement or repaired products back to the customers, deliver products between different service agents, and manage the logistics of material replenishment and material returns and recycling.

- *Reverse logistic providers repair, remanufacture, refurbish, and or recycle returned products and parts.* This, for example allows returned products to be reused as refurbished products, as parts dismantled from returned products or as a recycled material.

- *Underwriters and insurers back up extended warranty operations.* For example, an extended warranty provided by a retailer, dealer, manufacturer, or other party can be backed up by an underwriter or an insurance company, who cover the costs in case the warranty provider goes bankrupt. A manufacturer can also buy a coverage for base warranty costs from an insurance company.

WARRANTY SERVICE PROCESS

Warranty service process involves several elements. Service channels are the contact points through which a customer can initiate the service process. Return channels are used to physically deliver a product to service or to obtain service on site. The service process itself involves several activities that need to be executed sequentially. There are variations in the service process, depending on the service channel. As a result of the service process, the customer product may be repaired, replaced, or the customer given a refund. In this section, we discuss all of these topics.

Service Channels

To obtain warranty service, the customer needs to follow the channel(s) set up by the warranty provider. Warranty service can be provided through multiple channels, as shown in Figure 3.2.

A brief description of each is as follows:

- Service center technicians conduct repairs or replace products at a service center.

- Point of sale replaces a defective product, gives a refund, or acts as a return channel forwarding products to service agents.

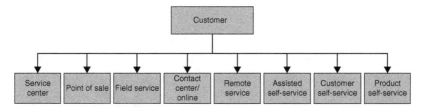

Figure 3.2 Service channels in case of product issue

- Field service technicians conduct repairs at customer site.

- Contact centers and online channels provide access to personnel providing remote service or assisted self-service. They can also be the gatekeepers for service by field service or service center personnel.

- In remote service, technicians solve issues remotely. Activities that can be conducted remotely include, for example, diagnostics, software updates, calibration, tuning, and changes in settings.

- Assisted self-service is a model where the service organization assists the customer to solve the issue (e.g., a module change by the customer). In this case, the customer can be anything between a layman and a trained technician in customer organization.

- Customer self-service allows customer to solve issues without raising a warranty claim. This can be done, for example, using the instructions provided by the warranty provider or instructions available from other sources like discussion boards and YouTube. On-device applications (e.g., in PCs, TVs, and smartphones) allow customers to run diagnostics, run troubleshooting, and trigger software updates.

- Product self-service relates to cases where the product itself conducts self-diagnostics and fixes issues, such as by an automated software update. If product self-service solves the issue, no customer warranty claim is created and customer may not even notice the issue. Product self-diagnostics can also be a trigger for physical service activities when a product reports about an issue in it.

These options are not provided by every warranty provider, nor are they applicable for every product.

Return Channels

When a product needs to be physically delivered to service center or a technician is needed to carry out the service on site, there are several return options, shown in Figure 3.3:

- The customer can mail or ship the product to a service center.
- The warranty provider can organize the product to be picked up from the customer location.
- The customer can bring the defective product to a point of sale, which then forwards it to a service center (if the product is repaired).
- The customer can directly deliver the product to a service center.
- The customer can deliver the product to an alternative collection or drop-off point (e.g., kiosks or logistics service provider locations). From there, the product is delivered to a service center.
- Field service can physically visit the customer site and conduct the service.

However, not all of these are available in every company.

Whether the unit is repaired at a service center, on site, or remotely depends on the product. The best approach is determined by several factors:

- Physical size of the product
- Cost of shipping the unit to service versus cost of one or more site visits

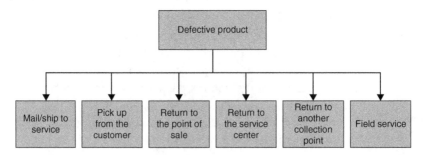

Figure 3.3 Options to get the defective product to service

- Technical experience required to detach the defective product from a larger system
- Level of specialization required in service
- Diagnostics, repair equipment, and parts required in service
- Criticality of the product and minimization of disruptions
- Type of product and fault
- Technical capabilities to service the product remotely

Many household products (such as white goods, air-conditioners, etc.) are repaired on site, whereas others (such as computers, mobile phones, watches etc.) are repaired at service centers. The same is true for industrial and commercial products. Smart connected products (from computers to ventilation machines) can, in some cases, be serviced remotely.

Activities within the Warranty Service Process

Warranty service process involves a chain (commonly referred to as the *service chain*) of activities that are largely the same, independent of the service channel used by the customer. This process comprises the phases shown in Figure 3.4.

RMA and Entitlement

The way the service process starts depends on the warranty provider policies. The customer can do either of the following:

- Directly contact the service channel.
- Be required to obtain authorization (i.e., RMA) from the warranty provider. Authorization can be obtained through warranty provider's contact center or through an online channel. Only after obtaining RMA, the failed product can be taken to a point of sale, to a service center, or to another return channel or service provided remotely. Not all warranty providers require preauthorization. In such cases, customer can directly approach available service channels.

When the customer contacts a service channel, entitlement check is conducted. This is done by the warranty-handling personnel in the service channel or an online application. The purpose of entitlement is to distinguish in-warranty and out-of-warranty claims and

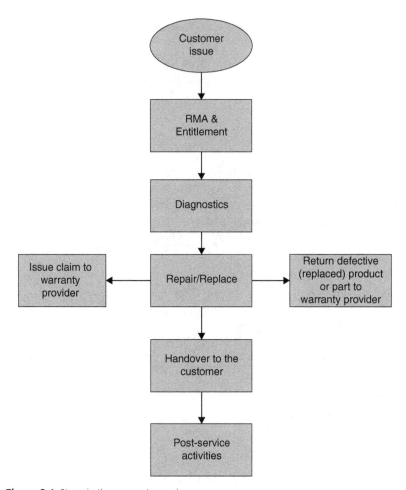

Figure 3.4 Steps in the warranty service process

allow in-warranty claims to be processed partly or fully at warranty provider's cost.[2]

Warranty provider's obligations cease:

1. Once the warranty expires, or

2. There is a failure due to misuse of product (e.g., using metallic objects in microwave ovens not designed for it), or

3. The customer is negligent (e.g., not ensuring adequate oil in automobile engine).

In some cases even if the claim is not valid (e.g., failure caused due to customer negligence) the manufacturer might carry out the repair at no cost to the customer for a variety of reasons such as goodwill, epidemic failure, or negative impact of rejecting the claim.

The purpose of entitlement is also to reduce the number of no-fault-found products entering the service chain. Although full diagnostics cannot be done in this phase, there can be a dialogue with the customer during which customer can be given support. The issue can also be repeated with the customer if the customer is physically present with the product, or warranty-handling personnel can contact the customer by phone or e-mail or remotely access the product.

As a result of this, the outcome can be one of the following:

- Customer product is accepted to be (partly or fully) serviced under warranty.
- The customer is given or delivered a replacement product.
- The customer is given a refund.
- The process ends due to no fault found.
- Customer's warranty claim is rejected due to not being under warranty unless service is granted to avoid disputes and bad will.

Diagnostics and Repair

If a defective product is accepted to be serviced under warranty, the repair process can start. Also, if the customer has been given a replacement product, the defective product can be delivered to be repaired and be used to replenish the pool of replacement units.

The repair process can include one or more of the following steps:

- Repeating the issue reported by the customer
- Locating the source of the issue
- Full check for customer damage
- Diagnostics for further problems
- Software update and verification of settings before any physical repair is done to exclude software-driven issues
- Replacement or repair of failed parts or modules

- Other product-specific service activities like cleaning of parts, change of lubricants, or tuning the product
- Testing the device after repair
- Filling in repair data to service system
- Storage or return of defective parts

The repair process is conducted following the procedures defined in the service manuals and using the diagnostics tools and other equipment available for repair.

Issuing of Warranty Service Claim

After the repair has been completed, administrative personnel may conduct additional steps to verify and finalize the warranty service claim and submit the claim to the warranty provider individually or as a batch. Once the warranty provider has reviewed the claims, the service agent may invoice the warranty provider and be paid.

Return of Defective Parts and Products

If a faulty part is replaced by a new one, then the failed part is either discarded or sent back to the manufacturer. The latter action can be taken for a number of reasons, such as:

1. To reduce possibilities of fraud done by the service agent
2. For more detailed analysis of the failed part
3. For possible refurbishment, resale, or other type of reuse

Hand over to Customer

In the end of the repair process, the product can be returned to the customer. If the customer has been given a replacement product earlier, the repaired product can be used to replenish a pool of replacement products (i.e., swap stock).

Post-Service Activities

After the service event, customer can be contacted to obtain feedback and to measure customer satisfaction.

Variations in Service Process Depending on the Service Channel

The process just described primarily relates to service done in service centers. When other service channels are used, some variations in the process occur.

Field Service

In field service model, technician travels to customer site to conduct the repair. Otherwise, the steps of the repair process are similar to the work done at a service center. Often, on-site repair consists of module replacements, where the defective module is later repaired at service center. Multiple site visits may be required to complete the service. This is the case, for example, if additional spare parts need to be ordered after the initial diagnostics.

Remote Service

Remote service includes similar steps as service in a service center. However, as the product cannot be physically repaired, the scope of possible activities is limited.

Assisted Self-Service

As assisted self-service is done in cooperation between the warranty provider technician and the customer, some of the easier issues requiring physical access to the product can be solved. Some organizations, like factories and hospitals, have their own technicians, who can conduct more complex activities independently or with the support of the warranty provider's specialist.

Replacements and Refunds

As an alternative to repair, the customer can be given a refund or the defective product can be replaced. The replacement product can be identical or similar to the product customer originally had. If the product is not identical, it typically is a slightly better or newer model, but it can also be the latest model. This allows the number of different models in the swap stock to be reduced.

The replacement product can be given to the customer at the point of sale or at the service center, it can be shipped to the customer, or a field service technician can deliver it to the customer. Typically, the defective product needs to be returned in exchange to the warranty provider. Warranty provider's requirement can be to have the product returned either in advance, at the same time, or after a replacement product is delivered or given to the customer. After that, returned defective products can be discarded and recycled or repaired, refurbished, and used to replenish a pool of replacement products, thus providing some value for the warranty provider.

Replacement rather than repair is used when:

- Cost of repair exceeds cost of replacement.

- Repair turnaround time is critical.

- Replacement allows optimization of the repair network (e.g., centralized repairs with economies of scale or repairs in cost-competitive countries).

- The repair is complex and requires special skills/tools.

- Replacement (with a newer model) allows ramp-down of repair capability for products no longer sold.

- Spare parts are no longer available.

- Products are not personalized in such a way that replacement would not be possible (e.g., watches with engravings).

- Defective products can be repaired and reused as replacement products (this is not possible with hygiene products like shavers).

Service Data Collection

In each phase of the service process, data are collected. This is needed for effective warranty management. This topic is discussed in detail in Chapter 5.

OUTSOURCING OF WARRANTY SERVICE

Some or all of the tasks in warranty servicing can be outsourced as discussed earlier. Typical activities outsourced to a service provider include repair services, warranty administration, customer service, reverse logistics, inspection, and spare parts management. When warranty servicing is outsourced, the service provider charges a fee and in exchange the warranty provider is provided with the service at a guaranteed quality or service level.

Quite a few companies have chosen to outsource warranty servicing, based on one or more of the following arguments:

- Outsourcing allows the warranty provider to focus its resources on the core competencies of the company.
- Companies specialized on warranty servicing may have economies of scale and higher utilization of resources achieved through providing services to several warranty providers as well as other customers.
- The warranty provider may not have the competences and skills required to provide warranty servicing.
- The warranty provider may not have the resources to establish a service network with required geographical reach or the network could not be set up within a reasonable time frame.

Many companies have also chosen to keep warranty servicing in-house, typically with the following arguments:

- Feeling of having better control on service operations
- Keeping product knowledge in-house
- Ensuring reliability of and access to product defect and diagnostics data needed for product quality improvement
- Keeping the customer interface in-house
- Difficulty of finding technical skills for proprietary technologies from external companies
- Fear of fraud

There are also issues that need to be addressed before deciding on outsourcing:

- What are the alternative outsourcing scenarios?
- Which parts of the warranty servicing process should be kept in-house?
- How should the service providers be selected?
- What terms should be set in the contract?
- What is a feasible compensation level in different countries?
- What incentives and/or penalties should be defined in the contract?
- How should the service providers be monitored?

- What information systems are needed to support outsourced warranty service tasks?
- What in-house competences are required for service management?
- What risks are involved with outsourcing?

CONTRACTS

Contracts are needed between the warranty provider and the parties involved in the warranty servicing chain to define their rights and duties. This section discusses contracts with the key players (i.e., customers, service agents, part distributors and manufacturers, sales and distribution channel, customer service providers and warranty administrators).

Contracts with Customers

Chapter 2 described different warranties and categorized them into base warranties, extended warranties, and maintenance service contracts. From contractual point of view, the relationship between a manufacturer and its customers can be divided into two categories:

1. *Customer has no role*. Warranty is a part of the guarantee made to a customer as a part of product sales. Here the customer has no direct role, as the warranty terms and conditions defined by the manufacturer are applied together with local legislation. Typically, this is the case when a consumer purchases a product with a base warranty.

2. *Customer plays a role*. This is the case for certain extended warranties and maintenance service contracts for products where the customer has some negotiation power (e.g., buying an expensive product or a fleet of products with a lower price). The terms are jointly negotiated. In the case of very expensive products (such as defense products), the customer is the dominant partner and can dictate the terms to the warranty provider.

Warranty contracts define the terms and conditions under which the customer is entitled for repair, replacement, or other predefined services within a specified period of time. Key warranty-related terms in the contract include:

- The warranty period and maximum usage covered under warranty
- Costs covered under warranty
- Regional limitations for warranty coverage
- Defects not covered under warranty (e.g. customer damage, alterations, cosmetic issues, wear and tear, consumable parts and defects caused by unauthorized service)
- Requirement on original parts usage
- Preapproval required from warranty provider for specific service activities
- Included services and related service levels
- Repair and replace options
- Ownership of replaced, defective items

These and more specific terms are discussed in detail in Chapter 8.

Contracts with Service Agents

The contract between a warranty provider and a service agent, later called the service agent contract, defines the rights and duties of both parties in relation to warranty repair and possible other services. In the following, key terms of service agent contracts are introduced.

Pricing Models

Pricing model is a key element of service agent contracts. Pricing models can be divided into six categories:

1. Fixed price
2. Cost/resource based pricing
3. Hourly charge
4. Transactional pricing
5. Value-based pricing
6. Hybrid model

A brief description of the different models is as follows.

Fixed Price

Under a fixed price (or warranty buyout) model, the responsibility for warranty services is purchased from a service agent who assumes full responsibility for warranty service for a fixed payment. The service agent takes all the risks. If costs exceed the compensation agreed with the warranty provider, the service agent incurs a loss.

A manufacturer can, for example, sell the products to a distributor without warranty at a reduced price. The distributor then becomes liable for arranging warranty services and carrying the costs of service.

Cost- or Resource-Based Pricing

Cost- and resource-based pricing models refer to various models where the service agent charges the warranty provider based on costs incurred or reserved headcount or capacity. In these models, warranty provider takes all the risks related to volume and cost variations.

The open-book pricing model is a cost-based model where the service agent and warranty provider agree on the costs that are remunerable and the service agent charges the warranty provider based on the actual costs plus a margin on top of the realized costs.

The full-time equivalent (FTE) model is a resource-based model where the service agent charges the warranty provider based on the number of employees reserved for carrying out warranty service. This model typically covers labor only, whereas spare parts, travel, and other cost components are charged separately.

An alternative to the FTE model is one where the service agent charges the warranty provider based on the reserve capacity to conduct a specified amount of repairs within a specified time period.

Hourly Charge

When hourly charge is applied, the warranty provider is charged based on the number of hours spent for warranty service activities. Hourly charge normally covers labor only while other variable costs are charged separately. Also in this pricing model, the warranty provider carries all the risks. However, low volume implies less revenue for the service agent and too-high volume implies that demand may exceed capacity.

Transactional Pricing

In a transactional pricing model, service activities are defined and a fixed price is agreed for each service activity. Transactional price may or may not include spare parts and other cost components. In this pricing model, the service agent carries the risk related to variations in effort of individual service transactions while the warranty provider carries the risk of volume variations although the revenue and capacity impact is the same as in the hourly pricing.

Value-Based Pricing

In value-based models, service agent compensation depends on the outcome of the service. The outcome can, for example, be measured in terms of product availability (i.e., the percentage of time it is operable), thus providing incentives for the service agent to maximize uptime. In this model, the service agents are compensated based on the outcome of the service and carry the risks.

Hybrid Models

Hybrid models combine elements from different pricing models. For example, a service agent's labor compensation can be transactional, compensation for spare parts based on cost-plus model and additional services paid by hour.

Hybrid models allow the risk to be shared by including pricing elements from different pricing models. Transactional compensation with outcome-based incentives is one example.

Other Terms

Key items to be defined in the service agent contracts include the following:

- Products and services in the scope of the agreement
- Procedures to follow regarding customer service, entitlement, repair, and replacement
- Service locations, appearance, and business hours
- Service agent and technician resources, competence requirements, certifications, and recertifications
- Acceptable repairs to be repaired at warranty provider's cost
- Repair authorizations required from warranty provider
- Quality of premises, safety, and security
- Service equipment to be used and responsibility on investment costs
- Spare parts to be used and authorized sources for parts

- Stocking of parts—inventory levels and storage requirements
- Ownership, storage, return, and/or recycling of defective parts and products
- Requirements for documentation, data collection, and reporting
- Claim reporting process and tools
- Invoicing and payment process and terms
- Service agent compensation model (affects risk) and rules for price changes
- Service levels, bonuses/incentives, and penalties
- Warranty provider's right to audit
- Dealing with customers when warranty terms are breached by the customer
- Termination clauses

Additionally, the contract needs to include standard terms and definitions as in any outsourced services agreement like governance model, escalation process,[3] confidentiality and nondisclosure rules, and liability for damages. Chapter 9 continues the discussion on the content of these rules from warranty fraud detection and prevention point of view.

Contracts with Part Manufacturers and Distributors

The contract between the warranty provider and part manufacturers defines the terms for supply of parts (e.g., the parts supplied under the contract, price, volume discounts, payment terms, and rules for price changes). In addition to general terms in the contract, there are specific terms that are relevant from warranty management point of view:

- Part specifications, including quality requirements
- Inspection and acceptance of parts
- Return policies
- Sources of supply, delivery destinations
- Time from order to delivery—regular and emergency shipments
- Parts availability

▪ Warranty granted for the parts, the scope of warranty cost coverage (e.g., full repair cost or part costs only), and procedures to be followed in case of defects

If a supply contract is made with a part distributor, the contract follows a similar structure as the contract with part manufacturers.

Contracts with Sales and Distribution Channel

Many of the key terms in the contract a manufacturer has with part manufacturers can also be found in the contract a manufacturer has with the sales and distribution channel. However, in this case, the manufacturer acts in the role of a seller instead of a buyer. There can be additional rules that are not highly relevant in part distributor contracts or from warranty perspective, like rules on the use of trademark, promotion of products, and exclusivity.

From warranty point of view, key rules include procedures to be followed when a customer returns a defective product to the sales channel or sales channel to the distribution channel:

▪ Requirements for entitlement

▪ Possible return authorization that needs to be obtained from the manufacturer

▪ Requirements for defects-related documentation, data collection, and reporting

▪ Guidelines on refund, product replacement and return of defective materials to manufacturer when defective products are replaced

▪ Supply of replacement units to sales and distribution channel

▪ Guidelines on sending the products to repair (when the product in question is a product that is repaired)

▪ Manufacturer's responsibility on covering costs incurred to sales channel from warranty handling

Very often, warranty obligations are transferred to a distributor (or another party) in particular geographical areas (e.g., distributor will get 5 percent additional stock to cover all warranty claims in a particular country and will cover the full risk of failures, except epidemic failures). If this is the case, the rules already mentioned are not needed.

Contracts with Customer Service Providers and Warranty Administrators

Customer service and warranty administration activities may vary because the content of the contract may also vary. Key items to be defined in the customer service provider and warranty administrator contracts include the following:

- Services in the scope of the agreement
- Description of the customer and administrative services provided and related service processes
- Required resources and their competence requirements (e.g., in IT, language and/or analytics skills)
- Requirements for documentation, data collection, and reporting
- Compensation, rules for price changes, and payment terms
- Service levels, bonuses, and penalties (e.g., performance targets for cost control)
- Warranty provider's right to audit
- Security requirements
- Termination clauses

Contracts with Other Parties

Additional contracts may be needed with inspectors, logistics companies, leasing companies providing loaners, underwriters and insurers, and reverse logistics providers.

NOTES

1. For example, when the warranty involves providing a loaner until the failed product is fixed.
2. In some industries, customer orders repair from warranty handling personnel, after which repair or other service activities are conducted. Entitlement is only conducted in the end of the process to determine who should pay for the service. This is the case in many of the heavy industries, where defective parts and equipment usage patterns may need to be analyzed before the responsibility can be determined.
3. Escalation process ensures that unresolved issues are promptly addressed. It includes the triggers and responsibilities for assigned managers higher in the organization to whom issues can be escalated if they cannot be solved by lower-level management.

CHAPTER **4**

Warranty Costs

arranty costs are the costs that a warranty provider incurs in servicing claims under warranty. These costs can be significant. In the United States, where accounting regulations force the publicly listed manufacturers to disclose their warranty cost figures, companies spent US$29 billion on warranty claims in 2014 (Arnum, 2015). Global warranty expenditures cannot be calculated with the same accuracy, as reporting them is not universally required. Arnum estimates that the global warranty costs are approximately three times the US costs, US$90 billion. This figure is solely for servicing base warranties. Expenditure on extended warranties and maintenance service contracts comes on top of this figure.

In the United States, warranty costs are on average in the range of 1.5 to 2 percent of product sales in the manufacturing sector. For individual companies, the costs can be significantly higher. However, comparing different companies is difficult, as there are differences in the accounting practices. Call center and training costs, for example, may or may not be included in warranty costs (Arnum, 2015).

Based on *Warranty Week* (2012), industries with above-average warranty expenditure included computer and automotive OEMs. In 2011, they accrued roughly 2 to 2.5 percent of their product sales as warranty costs. During the same period, computer peripherals, data storage, medical imaging systems, network equipment, and mobile phones had warranty accruals between 1 and 2 percent. The accrued costs for furniture, building material, medical equipment, auto, and aerospace parts warranty were below 1 percent.

In fiscal year 2015, Apple spent US$4.401 billion on product warranty and accrued[1] US$5.022 billion (Apple Inc., 2015). Ford spent US$2.850 billion in warranty costs in calendar year 2014 (Rowley, 2015) while HP's expenditure for the fiscal year of 2014 totaled US$1.927 billion (HP, 2015).[2]

Costs of base warranty are factored into the product price, resulting in higher sales price or lower margin. They are also the basis for pricing of extended warranties. Future warranty costs related to product sales need to be estimated and accrued in financial accounting.

Warranty costs are uncertain and they vary over time due to several different factors. Underestimation of warranty costs can have significant impact on company's performance.[3] Whether the costs are completely borne by the warranty provider or shared with other parties in the warranty service chain depends on the contracts between the warranty provider and other parties.

This chapter discusses the following topics related to warranty costs:

- Warranty costs from the perspectives of the various parties involved in the service chain
- Factors affecting the volume of customer warranty claims, their occurrence over time, and servicing-related costs
- Metrics used to measure warranty costs
- Warranty accruals and reserves
- Controlling of warranty costs

DIFFERENT PERSPECTIVES

Warranty provider and other parties involved in the warranty service chain have different, often conflicting objectives for warranty cost management. The perspectives of different parties are discussed briefly in this section.

Warranty Provider Perspective

Warranty is an important cost element impacting warranty provider's bottom line. For manufacturing companies, it is also an important element of new product development and product profitability estimation.

Warranty providers need to fulfill statutory warranty requirements and decide on the terms of base or extended warranties. At the same time, warranty providers' interests are to minimize the costs of warranty service within the legal and contractual limits while ensuring that customer satisfaction remains on or above the desired level. To minimize costs, warranty providers may want to maximize warranty cost recovery from their vendors. However, this is not always possible, as many sourcing contracts with suppliers exclude warranty obligations unless there is an epidemic failure. When warranty is excluded, parts can be purchased at a lower price.

Warranty cost forecasting and accruals management is also a part of any warranty provider's financial management.

Warranty can also be a source for revenue. Extended warranty and maintenance service contracts can be highly profitable, but the cost to serve needs to be understood and managed. It is not uncommon that extended warranties are a major source of losses for companies that have incorrectly estimated their costs.

Part Manufacturer, Subcontractor, and Contract Manufacturer Perspective

Part manufacturers sell parts to manufacturers, and manufacturers have several vendors. Manufacturing work can be partially or fully outsourced to contract manufacturers. Complete products that are part of a larger system can be purchased from subcontractors. Depending on the contract, these vendors may grant warranty with varying coverage for the supplied products and receive warranty claims from the manufacturers.

Manufacturers recover warranty costs from their vendors within the contractual boundaries. Vendors' options are to control the incoming claims where possible while focusing on quality improvement. In a similar way to the manufacturers managing the claims process with customers and service agents, the vendors need to get timely reclaims with adequate transparency and details to be able to make the correct, fact-based analysis and decisions on the validity of the reclaim and execute corresponding root-cause analysis and corrective/preventive actions on product quality issues when applicable.

As a long-term solution, vendors can manage their warranty costs by negotiating better contracts with the manufacturers.

CASE STUDY

▼ Challenges in Controlling Recovered Warranty Costs

There is only one margin in the value chain that is shared by the sales & distribution channel, manufacturer, and its vendors. Manufacturer's recovery of warranty costs from vendors affects the distribution of this margin. Vendors often lack visibility on customer interface and what has actually happened, which limits their possibilities to challenge what is being charged back. From a solid warranty-control perspective this may be problematic, since the OEM can be satisfied with accepting all warranty claims it receives from service agents without proper control and then pass the cost to the next level.

As one PC contract manufacturer stated, they are largely passive recipients of OEM's warranty claims with limited ability to reject claims.

Service Agent Perspective

Service agents earn revenue from the warranty provider through providing warranty service to the customers of the warranty provider. The service agent perspective is to be able to fulfill the obligations to the warranty provider and manage the warranty servicing costs in a way that enables a profitable business for the service agent. Chapter 3 discussed alternative pricing models warranty providers use to compensate service agents. Service agent perspective depends on the pricing model:

1. *Fixed price (warranty buyout) and outcome-based contracts:* Both the volume and the effort-related risk are borne by service agents. As a result, service agents focus on cost control and transaction volume minimization.

2. *Open book/cost-plus compensation:* In this model, service agents are protected from both the variations in volume and the variations in service effort related to individual claims. Service agents can maximize their absolute margin by maximizing their service volumes. There is negative incentive for cost minimization, as this would reduce service agent's revenue and absolute margin.

3. *Transactional or hourly compensation:* In these models, service agents are to some extent protected from variability in total claims volume as an increase in claims volume also increases compensation. Service agents have an incentive to maximize their profitability by maximizing their service volumes. Additionally, when transactional pricing is used and the price of an individual service activity is fixed, the service agents have an incentive to minimize their costs.

When service agents have a warranty on repairs in their contracts, additional costs are incurred. This provides an incentive for repair quality improvement.

Sales and Distribution Channel Perspective

Typically, the main goal for the sales channel is to keep the customer satisfied and minimize the time spent (and related cost) with warranty issues. Depending on the contract, sales & distribution channel may be compensated for acting as a return channel for customers looking for warranty repair, product replacement, or refund. If this is the case, their interest can be to maximally off-load their cost of front-end customer handling to the warranty provider when working with warranty claims. Sales & distribution channel can also use their product buying power to force the manufacturers toward commitments on what to pay for warranty claim handling.

FACTORS UNDERLYING WARRANTY COSTS

Two elements determine the warranty costs: (i) the number of warranty claims and (ii) the cost of servicing each claim. We discuss these briefly.

Warranty Claims

As shown in Figure 4.1, warranty claim volume depends on four factors—sales volume, product usage (which depends on the customer), product reliability (which depends on the design and manufacturing decisions made by the manufacturer), and the warranty policy.[4] The number of products sold and the related warranty policies determine the warranty population. Product usage and product reliability determine the field failure rate of products. These two, warranty population and product reliability, in combination determine the amount of warranty incidents. There is a fifth element—warranty fraud—that affects warranty claims, and this is discussed in more detail from Chapter 6 onward.

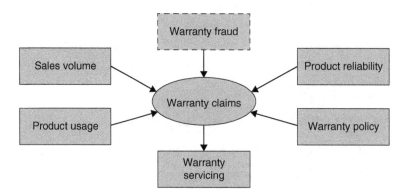

Figure 4.1 Factors affecting warranty claims and servicing

Failure of a product still under warranty does not necessarily lead to warranty execution, for several reasons. In some cases, the customer is simply not aware of the possibility of warranty service. In other cases, the effort involved in exercising the warranty claim may not be worthwhile in relation to the benefits achieved. The customer may develop dissatisfaction for the product and switch to a competitor's product instead of filing a warranty claim. The customer may have lost the receipt or other proof-of-purchase. The product may be sold before the warranty expires and the warranty is not transferable.

In the following subsections, we first look at a typical pattern of failures and claims received from a single customer and then from multiple customers.

Single Customer

A single customer may raise zero, one, or more warranty claims over the warranty period. White goods (i.e., refrigerators, ovens, and other large household appliances), consumer electronics, and watches, for example, typically have no or a limited number of warranty repairs during their warranty period. More complex products like cars or large industrial installations will have a higher number of warranty claims over the warranty period.

Customer warranty claims occur in an uncertain manner over time. The cumulative count of claims follows a stochastic (unpredictable) counting process over time, as illustrated in Figure 4.2.

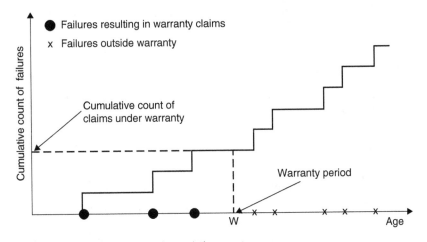

Figure 4.2 Failure instances and cumulative count

This allows us to see the number of claims as a function of product's age starting from the point when the product is taken into use. In the figure, the *x*-axis indicates the point of time when a warranty claim occurs and the *y*-axis indicates the cumulative count of warranty claims, over time.

The modeling of this and of the cost of each service allows one to predict warranty cost per unit sold. This can be used as a cost component (cost of base warranty) when pricing the products and when pricing extended warranties.

Multiple Customers

The same logic can be used when examining the occurrence of warranty claims within the overall product population. Sales occur over time, and each generates a claim pattern similar to that shown in Figure 4.2. The pooling of all the counts from all of the customers over the product life cycle (discussed later in the chapter) yields the total number of claims.

The modeling of this and the cost of each claim allows one to predict total warranty costs. This is useful for making decisions at the front-end stage of product life cycle and is discussed further in Chapter 5. However, one needs to acknowledge quality improvement measures and other factors that cause differences in claim rates between products manufactured at different points of time. This is the case especially with products that have ongoing engineering, updates, and upgrades. For example, the field failure rate for mobile phones normally drops during the first 90 days after product launch and then stabilizes.

Cost of Servicing a Claim

Costs of servicing a claim under warranty can be grouped into two categories: (i) direct and (ii) indirect.

Direct Costs

Typical direct cost components of warranty servicing are:

1. Labor costs for repair or replacement and related handling of the item
2. Costs of replacement units, spare parts, and other materials

3. Travel costs in the case of field service

4. Packaging and shipping costs if products need to be shipped between different parties and locations (e.g., picked up from customers, shipped back to customers, shipped between different service agents or service agent and the warranty provider)

5. Taxes and duties paid on top of these costs

Additionally, there are administrative costs that can be directly linked with warranty servicing:

1. Costs of customer service including RMA and authorizations

2. Inspection costs

3. Claim validation costs

4. Handling costs in the sales and distribution channel

Indirect Costs

Besides the costs directly related to an individual product, there are indirect service center costs. These include—for example— management overhead, costs of spare parts ordering, inventory holding costs, costs of obsolescence, return and recycling of defective materials, repair tools and equipment, licensing costs for diagnosis applications, online tools and other systems, service center information systems, data and telephony, rent, and facility services. If the warranty servicing is outsourced, these costs are either included in the service costs or charged separately (open-book contracts), depending on the contract.

There are further indirect costs within warranty provider's service operations. These include general management of service operations, selection and management of service agents and vendors, technician training and certification, development of repair tools and equipment, costs of spare parts, and swap stock inventories and information systems—for example, for claim validation, analytics, and spare parts management. The indirect cost assigned to each service depends on the accounting principles used in cost allocation.

Total Cost of Servicing a Claim

The total cost of an individual service is a sum of all the cost elements. This cost varies from claim to claim as it depends, for example, on the part(s) that have failed and repair/replace decisions.

The cost elements included in warranty costs vary between companies. Also, there are different practices in allocating these costs to cost of goods sold (COGS)[5] (typically under other costs) or under operating expenses (typically indirect addressable costs, like service IT systems, call center costs, management etc.).

WARRANTY COST METRICS

Different metrics are used in warranty cost measurement. Key metrics used by the manufacturers include the following:[6]

- Cost per claim
- Cost per unit sold
- Warranty cost rate
- Product life-cycle warranty costs
- Warranty cost as a percentage of product sales

We discuss each of these briefly.

Cost per Claim

Cost per claim is a key warranty cost metric. It is also called the cost of claim resolution. Cost of repair is a similar metric, but more narrow in scope as it for example excludes replacement costs and the claim handling related costs that are not directly related to a repair. Cost per claim includes all of the cost elements listed in the previous section that can be directly allocated for an individual claim.

Figure 4.3 illustrates the occurrence of claims and associated costs over time for a customer with multiple claims over the warranty period. Note that there is variation in the cost per claim, and this is

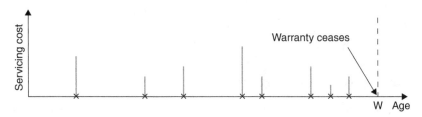

Figure 4.3 Cost per claim—when customer has multiple claims during the warranty period

due to the activities and material/spares needed that depend on the failure mode.

The average cost per claim, obtained using models or estimated using data collected during warranty servicing, is used to:

- Monitor and improve cost efficiency in service operations.

- Benchmark service agents in terms of average costs and costs related to servicing individual claims.

Cost per Unit Sold

Cost per unit sold is the cumulative cost of all claims related to an individual product over the warranty period. Figure 4.4 shows the cumulative cost impact of the claims and is obtained by summing the individual claim costs shown in Figure 4.3.

Warranty cost per unit sold varies across the customer population. Different customers have different costs over the product lifetime, as shown in Figure 4.5. This can be explained by a variety of factors, such as usage mode and intensity, operating environment, and the customer's likelihood of warranty execution, as discussed in the previous section.

The variability in the warranty cost per unit can be large for reasons discussed earlier. As the number of customers (K) increases, the

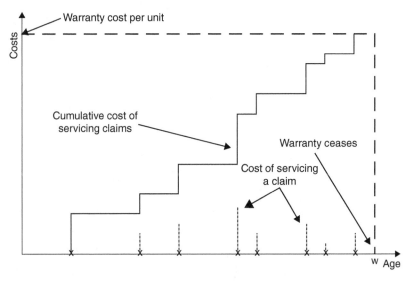

Figure 4.4 Warranty cost per unit sold

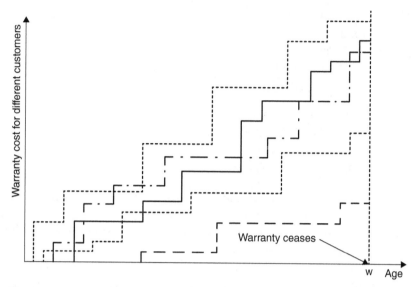

Figure 4.5 Cost variations across customer products

variability in the cost per unit decreases due to the principle of large numbers—units with high warranty costs being averaged out with units having low warranty costs. Figure 4.6 shows this graphically and is a graph of the density function of costs per unit with single and multiple customers.

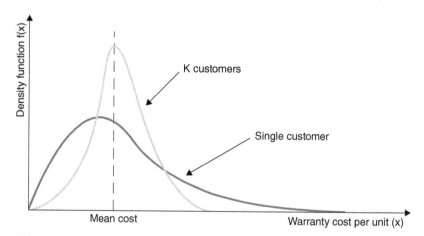

Figure 4.6 Variations in cost per claim—for a single customer with multiple claims (and product items) and for overall customer population

The density function (y-axis) in the figure is an indicator of the likelihood of that cost being incurred. The higher the value, the greater is the likelihood. For a single customer, the cost has a high variability (the range of values that the warranty cost per unit can assume is wide and can deviate from the mean value significantly), whereas when the number of customers increases, the variability comes down (the warranty cost per unit is more likely to be close to the mean).

Understanding of the variations of warranty costs is needed (i) for risk management—especially in the pricing of extended warranties—and (ii) in identifying anomalies across customers (discussed further in Chapter 8).

The average or expected value of the cost per unit, either obtained using models or estimated using data collected during warranty servicing, is used, for example:

- As one component in cost of goods sold (COGS) calculation
- In new product development for similar products
- As a component in calculation of the sales price (based on cost per unit for base warranties)
- In the pricing of extended warranties

Warranty Cost Rate

The warranty cost rate is a measure of warranty costs over time. It is also called the cost per unit time. It depends on the servicing costs (cost per claim) and warranty claims rate (with sales rate an important factor, as shown in Figure 4.1), as indicated in Figure 4.7.

Figure 4.8 shows the typical shape of sales rate and warranty cost rate over the product life cycle. In Figure 4.8, the life cycle is marked with L. Warranty cost rate follows the sales volume with delay and reaches its peak after sales has peaked. Warranty reserves are needed to cover the warranty costs over $L + W$ where W is the warranty period. The warranty cost rate is important in deciding on warranty reserves.

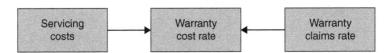

Figure 4.7 Factors affecting warranty cost rate

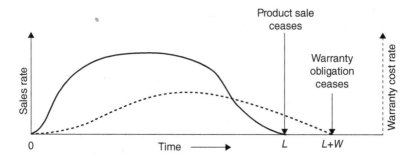

Figure 4.8 Typical sales and warranty cost rates

Product Life Cycle Warranty Cost

Product life cycle warranty cost is the total cost of servicing all warranty claims over the life cycle of the product—from the launch of the product on the market until the warranty for the last unit sold expires. It is obtained by integrating the warranty cost rate over $L + W$ and is given by the area under the cost rate curve in Figure 4.8.

The product life cycle warranty cost is important in the context of new product development (NPD) process.

Warranty Cost as a Percentage of Product Sales

Warranty cost as a percentage of product sales is a ratio of warranty costs and product sales revenues over a given time interval (usually one year). It is another metric used by companies.

This metric allows comparing different companies in an industry for benchmarking purposes and for improvement in warranty cost management using best practices (practices followed by company with small values for the ratio). The same metric can also be used to compare costs in different countries for a multinational company for internal benchmarking.

The metric is a lagging indicator as warranty costs over an interval are due to product sales over the warranty period prior to the start of the interval (whereas the sales revenue is from sales over the interval). In cases where the sales are growing, this metric gives overly positive results. Conversely, if the sales are decreasing, the metric may suggest that there is a serious quality problem when there is none.

To get a true picture of warranty cost as a percentage of revenue, one should calculate the warranty cost for each product instance as a percentage of the unit sales price at date of sales. In most cases companies take actual warranty cost percentage of actual revenue, which does not give the true picture.

High Growth Provides Optimistic Warranty Cost per Sales

A consumer products manufacturer was experiencing double-digit growth with high profitability over several consecutive years. Comparing its warranty cost per sales with the peer companies (which were not growing), the company thought that its warranty processes were leading practice. Taking a closer look, however, revealed serious gaps, which could then be turned into major additional savings over the subsequent years.

WARRANTY RESERVES AND ACCRUALS

Warranty costs materialize over time until warranty expires. In order to show all the costs related to product sales in the financial statements, companies should make accruals for the expected warranty costs—assuming that they can reasonably estimate such costs. The warranty accruals accumulated over time, but not yet spent, constitute the warranty reserve. This reserve is used to cover the costs of servicing when warranty claims materialize.

Warranty reserves for a few big US companies are shown in Table 4.1.[7] As mentioned earlier, these are for servicing base warranties.

Sales of extended warranties are not directly connected to product sales. Consequently, different rules apply. Accounting guidance for FASB (1990, p. 4) suggests that "revenue from separately priced extended warranty and product maintenance contracts should be

Table 4.1 Warranty Reserves and Reserves as a Percentage of Annual Warranty Costs

Company	Warranty Reserves, USD Billion	Reserves as a % of Annual Warranty	Period
Apple	4.780	109%	Fiscal year 2015
HP	1.956	102%	Calendar year 2014
Ford	4.785	168%	Fiscal year 2014

deferred and recognized in income on a straight-line basis over the contract period except in those circumstances in which sufficient historical evidence indicates that the costs of performing services under the contract are incurred on other than a straight-line basis. In those circumstances, revenue should be recognized over the contract period in proportion to the costs expected to be incurred in performing services under the contract." International Financial Reporting Standards (IFRS) originating from the European Union set similar requirements for extended warranty related revenue recognition.

Historical information about claim rates and average cost of service and prediction on future reliability is used to estimate future warranty costs and determine the value of accruals at the time of product sales. This figure can then be periodically reviewed and adjusted. If no reasonable estimate of historical costs is available, the manufacturer may use figures from other companies in the industry as a reference.

WARRANTY COST CONTROL

Different components of warranty costs were discussed earlier in this chapter. Cost accounting that accurately allocates costs to different cost components and provides transparency to the cost baseline is the starting point for warranty cost control. Tracking of costs by product, customer, service agent, and part distributor/manufacturer provides additional means to control costs also for parties outside of finance department. Variations in cost level provide an opportunity to analyze reasons for variations and identify improvement opportunities. Warranty cost data are used for many different purposes:

- Product managers can track warranty costs related to their products until the end of product life cycle and evaluate the impact on products' profitability. They can also compare deviations across different geographical areas and environments (e.g., due to humidity, dust, and temperature differences), and provide this as an input for product design.

- Account managers can use warranty costs to track individual customers' profitability with warranty costs included. Differences in warranty costs across different customers can be evaluated and actions taken in case of excessive deviations.

- Sourcing managers can evaluate warranty costs of different vendors and parts, and use them as a part of vendor recovery or quality improvement activities.

- Service managers can compare cost levels of different service agents and act in case of deviations.

To reduce warranty costs, cost targets need to be set, improvement activities planned and executed, and cost savings measured. This needs to be monitored and additional actions need to be taken, when necessary. Chapter 5 discusses different methods to reduce warranty costs.

NOTES

1. Accruals refer to the expense posted in accounting as an estimate of the future warranty liabilities related to current accounting period's product sale, including a change in costs estimated earlier.
2. The length of warranty period varies and has a significant impact on warranty costs. The warranty period for consumer electronics is typically 1 to 2 years, depending on the market, while automotive warranties are typically 2 to 5 years and sometimes even 10 years in duration.
3. A factor underlying Chrysler's bankruptcy in the 1970s was the increase in warranty costs when the warranty period was increased from two years to five years.
4. For example, what is the duration of warranty for a product? This depends on whether the warranty is renewing or nonrenewing and whether it is one- or two-dimensional.
5. Cost of goods sold includes total of all direct costs needed to create a product or service.
6. Blischke and Murthy (1994) deal with models based on product reliability and replace/repair options to estimate warranty costs for several different types of base warranties.
7. Higher warranty reserves to warranty expenditure ratio at Ford reflects the differences in warranty period (Apple Inc., 2015; HP, 2015; Rowley, 2015).

CHAPTER **5**

Warranty
Management

hapter 2 described products, failures, reliability, and warranty concepts. Chapter 3 looked at warranty servicing, and Chapter 4 at the costs incurred. This chapter describes warranty management as a whole and how it has evolved over the last 50 years. Warranty fraud management is an elementary part of warranty management, so this chapter sets the context for Chapters 6 to 11, where we discuss warranty fraud and warranty fraud management.

The outline of the chapter is as follows. We start with a discussion of the three stages of warranty management and highlight the salient features of each stage. Stage 1 focuses mainly on warranty administration. Stage 2 is based on managing the servicing of customer incidents under warranty (we call this the *service life-cycle perspective*). Stage 3 views warranty as a strategic element of new product development, addressed from the very first stage of product life cycle (we call this the *product life-cycle perspective*). These are discussed in the subsequent sections of the chapter. Then we look at the organizational structures required for effective warranty management. Data play a critical role in warranty management, and we discuss systems to manage the data. We conclude the chapter by looking at two available models for companies to assess the maturity of their warranty management capability.

EVOLUTION OF WARRANTY MANAGEMENT

Murthy et al. (2007) have defined three stages in warranty management:

- Stage 1—Administrative approach
- Stage 2—Operational improvement
- Stage 3—Strategic warranty management

Most companies are still at Stage 1 or Stage 2, whereas some pioneering companies are increasingly moving to Stage 3.

Stage 1—Administrative Approach

This stage started in the early part of last century and gained more impetus around 1960. Many companies are still in Stage 1 with warranty viewed as an unavoidable cost of doing business. The overall approach is reactive as the focus is on claim administration for effective servicing of customer warranty claims and processing of warranty service claims to keep warranty costs under control. The process focuses on:

- Receiving claims from the customers
- Verifying entitlement of claims through simple schemes
- Receiving warranty service claims from service agents
- Arranging for reimbursement for the service agents
- Managing the service parts inventory replenishment for own repair and for service agents

Only warranty cost data are collected during the process and used for accounting purposes.

Stage 2—Operational Improvement

The second stage started around 1980 and was influenced by the total quality management (TQM) movement. Here, the focus is moving to the relationship between product reliability and warranty costs and understanding the underlying causes behind the warranty claims. Warranty is still an afterthought—addressed mainly as a part of marketing and product support, with the main focus on the servicing aspects of warranty. However, there is an increasing focus on service response logistics, the process of coordinating nonmaterial activities necessary for the fulfillment of the service in an effective way (Davis and Mandrodt, 1996).

Service response logistics has a different focus from supply chain logistics. This difference is effectively illustrated in Figure 5.1.

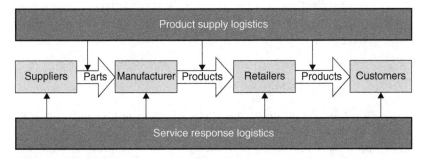

Figure 5.1 Product supply and service response logistics

Simply put, one can say that supply chain logistics focuses on physical supply and distribution of products, while service response logistics (also referred to as service chain logistics) emphasizes building responsive organizations, which can respond to different customer requests. Often, the contributing parties in a service network can be different from the product supply chain. In the latter case, the manufacturer sells to distributors, who in turn sell to retailers who finally sell to the customers, whereas in the former case there are totally different touchpoints.

At this stage information technology starts to have an increasing role in data collection, storage, and transfer. The perspective on warranty management is purely focused on the service life cycle, starting from the customer issue and ending with the closed warranty service case. Data analytics is mainly based on warranty claims data to have a more transparent picture of the overall warranty position. In a similar way, process improvements mainly focus on the warranty servicing process.

Stage 3—Strategic Warranty Management

The third stage started around 2000 with some pioneering companies viewing warranty as part of the new product development and addressed from the initial concept creation to the end of the product life cycle. The basic underlying principle is that decisions with regard to warranty must begin at a very early phase in the product life cycle and not as an afterthought just prior to the launch. Various stakeholders are involved and their interests are taken into account. The focus is on both product and product support services and these issues are addressed during the new product development process.

These strategic decisions are based on warranty claims data and a much wider collection of supplementary warranty data obtained from different sources (as discussed in the later section, Product Life-Cycle Perspective).

SERVICE LIFE-CYCLE PERSPECTIVE

In addition to the amount and type of warranty claims, the warranty provider's ability to provide warranty service depends on the geographic location of the customers, the type of product (can it be returned for repair or does it require on-site service, can it be serviced remotely, etc.), and the customer requirements for the warranty service lead-times. Typically, warranty service is provided through a network of service centers, where spare parts are stored, the warranty servicing is executed, or field-service technicians are stationed and dispatched to do on-site servicing. The service life-cycle perspective is looking at warranty management across the entire service life cycle. The main elements of the service life-cycle perspective are shown in Figure 5.2.

The strategic and tactical issues related to warranty management across the service life cycle are the following:

- Warranty and service offerings
- Service network management
- Servicing approach
- Warranty cost management

Strategic and Tactical Elements

Warranty and Service Offerings

- Warranty/service offering definition
- Warranty entitlement rules definition
- Service agent rules and policies

Servicing Approach

- Return avoidance approach
- Repair and servicing approach
- Supplier recovery approach

Service Network Management

- Service network structure
- Service agent management

Warranty Cost Management

- Warranty cost forecasting
- Warranty provisions/reserves accounting
- Warranty cost management principles

Operational Elements

Service Sales and Execution

- Service configuration and purchase
- Registration/activation
- Customer claim entitlement
- Service execution
- Returns processing

Service Claims Process

- Claims submittal
- Claim validation
- Claim payments
- Supplier recovery

Figure 5.2 Service life-cycle perspective

The operational issues related to warranty management across the service life cycle are the following:

- Service sales and execution
- Service claims process

We discuss each of these in more detail in this section.

Warranty and Service Offerings

Warranty and service offerings deal with the overall direction for the warranty offerings the company wants and integrates them with the other service offerings the company may have. Traditionally, all service offering development has been executed with less structure and system support than new product development. As manufacturing companies are shifting their focus from products to services and moving to set up service businesses, leading companies are moving to similar structures with service development and service product management, as with product development and product management, including clear phases and stage gates between them:

- Service ideation/market needs analysis
- Service concept creation
- Service generation and filtering (addressing any open issues and checking external limitations)
- Service portfolio planning (new services evaluated in the context of customer needs, desired customer experience, existing services, and product portfolio)
- Service capability planning
- Service go-to-market

The key warranty-related questions to be answered in this phase cover the warranty offerings and the associated contracts and contractual terms and conditions, which are then translated into customer claim entitlement and service agent claim validation rules:

- What is the overall approach to warranty? Is the focus on warranty cost minimization or customer service and customer experience?
- What should be the base warranty?

- What are the extended warranty and maintenance service contract offerings on top of the base warranty?
- What are the customer value-adding elements and what is the business logic[1] of the extended warranty/maintenance service contract offering?
- What are the rules and approach for customer claim entitlement?
- What are the rules and approach for service claim validation?
- How and to what extent are these communicated to customers and service agents?

Service Network Management

The different parties and service channels in the service network were introduced in Chapter 3. Service network management includes strategic decisions of the network structure and tactical activities to recruit and manage service agents. Although there are other channels involved with warranty servicing, the main focus in this section is on the physical repair channel and managing the (outsourced) service agent network.

The strategic questions related to the service network structure are:

- What service lead times does the network need to support (influenced by customer service approach, customer requirements, contracts etc.)?
- What tiers should the service network have?
- How many service centers or service locations are needed to support the defined warranty offerings and related obligations?
- Which types of centers—walk-in centers, drop-off collection points, repair factories—to have?
- Which are the most cost-effective service locations?
- Do they have the required competences?
- What is the capacity and role of each center?
- What are the competence requirements for the technicians?
- Are they operated in-house or outsourced?
- What are the channels and customer touchpoints? What are the customer-facing parts of the service network (also called

the service front end)? What are the non–customer-facing parts (also called the service back end) of the service network, needed to support the service front end?

▪ How is the return logistics handled between the customer and the service center?

The key activities related to service agent management are:

▪ Service agent selection, contracting, training, and induction

▪ Service agent certification

▪ Service agent performance management, incentivization, auditing, and support

▪ Service engineer training, certification, and recertification

Servicing Approach

Servicing approach includes the overall approach to execute warranty servicing. It is comprised of two phases.

In the first phase, the main question is how to reduce unnecessary (e.g., non-product-failure-related, no-fault-found, or out-of-warranty) cases. How can customer returns be minimized through remote diagnostics and no-fault-found filtering? How can on-boarding, installation, and proactive user support reduce customer returns?

The next phase (dealing with valid cases) is to guide the customer to the service, through on-product or online service agent finder or connection to the contact center for RMA handling.

The main question is to decide on issues relating to service execution:

▪ Should the servicing approach be online/self-service, remote service, on-site service, or return to service center?

▪ In which cases should a failed product be repaired or replaced?

▪ In which cases should a module be repaired or replaced?

▪ Who manages/owns the swap stock for modules and products?

▪ How much refurbishment can be done with a warranty servicing case?

▪ Does it depend on the customer?

- Are only new parts used, or are defective parts repaired and reused as spare parts?
  - Are they priced differently?
  - What is the warranty for the service parts?

And finally the approach for supplier recovery needs to be defined and included in the supplier contracts and supplier management framework and internal responsibilities defined. The importance of that is illustrated by the following.

 Organizing for Supplier Recovery

CASE STUDY

A heavy industrial equipment manufacturer had sourcing managers assigned with the responsibility for supplier recovery. At that point of time, the supplier reclaims process worked very fluently. As a part of a larger procurement improvement initiative, the sourcing manager roles were changed and they only participated in procurement activities. "For a while, we missed the tight collaboration and the supplier reclaims process got missing entirely for a few years. Now we have vendor claim handlers in the after-sales service organization in collaboration with the sourcing managers and have the situation back under control."

 Organizing for Supplier Recovery

CASE STUDY

A heavy industrial equipment manufacturer had negotiated back-to-back warranty agreements with its main part suppliers. Due to gaps in the process, and roles and responsibilities, the information of potential recovery cases never reached the supplier management organization and no supplier reclaiming was done.

Possible approaches include reclaiming everything, reclaiming epidemic cases only, and no reclaiming by excluding warranty cost from component prices. However, at the end of the day there is only one margin in the end-to-end value chain. Purely passing on costs to other players in the chain does not reduce the total cost as such. To have the best focus on total cost reduction, some companies are following the principle that the party best able to prevent the cost from occurring should carry the cost. Whichever strategy is selected, it should support joint reliability improvement, reduce the total cost, and improve the total margin in the end-to-end value chain.

Warranty Cost Management

Chapter 4 discussed warranty costs, factors affecting them, metrics, accruals, and reserves. In this section, we discuss warranty cost management. It includes four elements:

- Warranty cost planning and forecasting
- Warranty accruals and reserves management
- Warranty cost management principles
- Warranty cost reduction

Warranty Cost Planning and Forecasting

Warranty cost planning and forecasting is needed at the new product development phase in relation to the individual product and as a part of the annual planning and budgeting across all products.

Both of these elements are based on estimating the amount and nature of future warranty claims. This can be tricky for a number of reasons (Borgia et al., 2012):

- There is variation in the usage conditions.
- The product reliability may change over time—often the reliability may be lower at the product launch, improve as the product matures, and then be lower again due to degradation of the item.
- The manufacturer often doesn't know the true warranty population in service, due to unknown sales volume and lack of acceptance or activation information.
- Field data often do not differentiate product failures from other returns not related to product quality.

Many companies are using simple heuristics to estimate future warranty claims, like using the historical claims rates and repair costs of the product, product family, or similar products. Others are using sophisticated models to understand the impact of product and process design on product reliability and further on to future warranty costs.

Warranty Accruals and Reserves Management

Warranty accruals and reserves management is related to the financial statements and understanding the warranty provider's warranty position:

- What are the changes in the warranty population? New products sold to the customers under warranty increase the warranty population and older products, where the warranty has expired, reduce the warranty population.
- When the warranty population changes, what is the estimated warranty cost of that change?
- What has been the actual cost of warranty service?
- Are there any product design changes impacting number of claims or cost of servicing a claim and further on the expected warranty cost per unit item sold (e.g., changes impacting reliability or serviceability)?
- Are there any changes in the overall service network or servicing approach?

Effective accruals and reserves management requires cross-functional and cross-regional cooperation. The warranty population information comes from sales and delivery data, material cost rates from procurement, and warranty claims rate estimates from product development. The local labor cost rates and the realized warranty costs come from the local country organizations.

Warranty Cost Management Principles

Warranty cost management principles set the rules and guidelines for warranty cost management. This requires addressing the following questions:

- Which organizational unit is responsible for warranty cost? In some cases there can be several organizational units responsible for the cost—for example, the product line can have the responsibility for the first year, the country organizations for anything above that.
- What are all the cost elements that are reported under warranty?

■ Allocating warranty servicing costs:

　■ Who is taking the cost of goodwill service and extended warranty coverage given or sold?

　■ How strongly are base warranty and extended warranty servicing costs separated?

Typically, either the product line or the service organization is *the unit responsible for warranty cost*. When the service organization has the responsibility, they may suspect that manufacturing has lower interest in producing high quality. When the product line carries the warranty cost, they may feel that services are charging them too much.

In most companies, all direct cost components of warranty servicing are *reported under warranty costs*. With administrative costs and indirect costs, there is more variation in reporting practices as the cost elements vary and they can be allocated between warranty costs and potential other costs. For example, contact center costs can include many other activities than warranty and RMA handling.

In many cases, the sales organization in a country may give an extension to the warranty period as a part of a quote or sell an extended warranty with the product or provide goodwill service to an important customer. Then it depends on the company policy and the ability to monitor and *allocate the warranty servicing costs* that determine which organizational unit is to be charged. For example, if a servicing event includes several repairs, some of which are covered by base warranty, some by extended warranty, some are charged to the customer, and on top of everything the customer is given a goodwill refurbishment, the correct allocation of costs to different parties can be very complex.

Warranty Cost Reduction

Traditionally, the methods for warranty cost reduction include:

1. Claims rate reduction

　■ Product quality improvement—in design, sourcing, manufacturing, transportation, installation, and commissioning (see the case on distorted quality metrics)

　■ Customer training and instructions

　■ No-fault-found filtering

2. Repair cost reduction

　■ Design for service

　■ Optimization of the repair network structure

- Sourcing and repair pricing
- Repair efficiency improvement
- Improved claims resolution management[2]
- Spare part inventory optimization

3. Claims management and control

- Definition and adjustment of customer warranty terms and conditions
- Warranty entitlement
- Warranty service claims control
- Vendor recovery

4. Administration costs

- Efficiency improvement in administrative processes
- Sourcing and pricing of outsourced administration

Warranty fraud reduction is an additional major opportunity for cost reduction. The methods of controlling warranty fraud originating from different sources and avoiding fraud are discussed in detail in Chapters 7 to 11.

 Distorted Quality Metrics

CASE STUDY

In a quality improvement initiative, an industrial equipment manufacturer set a focus on production quality as a specific KPI. The work seemed to pay off and the KPI improved year-on-year for three consecutive years. The downside was that the warranty cost increased dramatically during the same time period, since the effort spent on manufacturing testing was reduced to be able to show fewer quality issues during production.

Service Sales and Execution

Warranty servicing was described in Chapter 3. In this section, we describe the management of warranty service sales and execution, starting from warranty activation, through a customer warranty issue, servicing claims, and related transactions.

The base warranty typically comes with the product, but the extended warranty programs may be configured from a diverse set of options, with different coverage, service-level commitments, services included, and price. Warranty service configuration and purchase can occur at the time of product purchase, but in many cases warranty is sold separately at a later date and covers either an individual product or a number of products for the same customer.

The warranty provider needs to define clearly how the start of the warranty period is determined. In some cases, there is a separate registration/activation of starting to use the product and initiating the warranty period. In B2B environments, this is often triggered by the final acceptance of the delivery or installation of the product or a larger system. In B2C, especially, when the product is sold through the sales channel, the warranty provider does not necessarily know when the warranty period starts. An increasing number of companies are including self-activation in the product or require a separate registration from the consumer as a part of the product start-up activities. The other option is that the warranty provider does not know when the product is sold or taken into use, but uses different types of rules of thumb (e.g., counting two to three months for the channel lead time after the manufacturing date) or relies purely on retailers' registers, the purchase receipt, and/or warranty certificate.

Once the customer has a warranty issue, the customer claim entitlement—is the product under warranty and is it a valid case—can be verified directly by the service agent or through the RMA process in the contact center or in an online service using the contract, sales, and activation information just discussed.

Initial diagnostics and no-fault-found filtering can be done through product self-diagnostics, online self-service, contact center agents, remote service support, service agents, or points of sale.

As discussed in Chapter 3, service execution can be provided through several channels, remotely, on-site by a field-engineer, in a service center, or via assisted self-service or customer self-service.

The operational service execution management includes spare parts management, service center job planning and scheduling, field service planning, scheduling, dispatch, and route optimization and service case tracking and completion management. For products with connectivity, remote diagnostics and maintenance support capacity and response times also need to be managed.

Technical analysis can support the customer warranty entitlement or impact the earlier entitlement decision (is the product used in a proper way, is there a physical damage etc.). It is also an important element in root-cause analysis (what is the root-cause for the failure) and product quality feedback (is there an emerging issue or is it a one-off incident).

Service Claims Process

Service claims process starts after service has been executed and claims are received from the service agent. The claims are checked and validated to ensure correctness (accurate, complete, and timely) and to decide on the right compensation for the claim.

The payment transactions are executed to the service agents, potentially subtracting open payments from any open service part orders. In case of in-house warranty servicing, the internal cost allocations are determined and managed.

If the part supplier contracts allow it and there is evidence of the warranty claim being directly related to a component issue, a reclaim is presented to the part supplier. The case is verified and its validity is agreed upon. The case is closed with the supplier recovery payment transaction.

Issues with Supplier Reclaiming

CASE STUDY

The issues with supplier reclaiming were highlighted in a survey by BearingPoint on warranty management practices in the automotive and truck OEMs and suppliers (BearingPoint, 2008). No fault found and customer abuse were significant contributors for suppliers, whereas for OEMs they were low to average issues.

"The returned allegedly failed parts often arrive damaged and/or incomplete. Accompanying descriptions of symptoms and failures are extremely rare, leading to no fault found and absence of meaningful information to perform root-cause analysis. In our view, it is critical that the principal goal of warranty defect analysis be continuous improvement, rather than justification for cost recovery," stated one of the survey participants.

PRODUCT LIFE-CYCLE PERSPECTIVE

The product life-cycle perspective deals with strategic warranty-related decisions across the product life cycle. There is a high correlation between product reliability and the volume of warranty claims.

Similarly, there is a strong link between warranty repair cost and product serviceability. As a result, product reliability, serviceability, and warranty-related issues need to be addressed in the different phases of the product life cycle, noting that the decisions made in the earlier phases have an impact on the decisions in the later phases.

Figure 5.3 describes the typical product life cycle phases. In the front-end phase, the initial decision is made to start new product development, the customer needs are analyzed, and the goals for the new product are defined. In design and development phases the customer requirements and desired product attributes are turned into technical specifications and prototypes. Production converts raw materials and components into final products, which are then marketed and sold to the customers. Post-sale phase includes warranty servicing, other customer support, and the management of the product end-of-life. The end-to-end warranty approach is targeted to support brand loyalty and customer purchase-to-repurchase cycle.

We discuss the issues that need to be addressed in the different phases of the product life cycle as part of effective warranty management.

Phase 1: Front End

In the front end phase, the overall business objectives for the new product are defined. Is it a totally new product or a new generation or a replacement of an existing product? What are the key customer requirements the new product needs to fulfill? What are the primary new value propositions? What are the targets for sales, market share, and position? What is the investment required (product development investment, manufacturing technology investment, target cost for production)? What are the revenue and profit targets?

The key warranty-related decisions to achieve the business objectives above include the overall warranty approach—is the target cost minimization, customer satisfaction, or revenue generation? What is

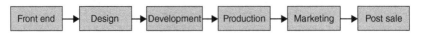

Figure 5.3 Product life cycle

the customer satisfaction target in terms of reliability and failures over time (e.g., not more than 5 in 1,000 should have a failure in year 1, not more than 100 should fail in years 1 to 3, etc.)? What are the overall warranty offerings and warranty terms linked with the product? What level of warranty cost does this all lead to and what is the impact on product pricing and profitability?

Phases 2 and 3: Design and Development

In design and development phases, the customer requirements and desired product attributes are turned into technical specifications and prototypes. This is the phase where the production and delivery cost and warranty costs are largely determined. The reliability and service-ability strategies should have a direct impact on product design decisions, ensuring that the customer satisfaction and warranty cost targets can be achieved subject to investment constraints (time and money). High reliability requires greater investment in R&D, better quality of sourced materials and components, and proper control of manufacturing process. The benefit is lower warranty costs. Correspondingly, lower investments in R&D, inferior sourced materials and components, and poor control of manufacturing process result in lower reliability and higher warranty costs. High serviceability may imply higher investment in R&D (the impact on manufacturing cost may be increasing, decreasing, or neutral), and result in lower warranty servicing costs and the other way around. The trade-offs between reliability, service-ability, and warranty control investments and benefits are highlighted in Figure 5.4.

At this phase, many decisions that are made have a major impact on the product warranty cost and potential extended warranty and maintenance service offerings. How is the product design supporting effective repair and maintenance operations? How is the product design supporting warranty control? How can the fault diagnosis, part identification, and exchange be done in the most productive way? What sensors are included and how are the sensor data captured, stored, and analyzed? What are the new service offerings enabled by the captured data?

The component and raw material suppliers are selected and the terms and conditions for the supply agreed.

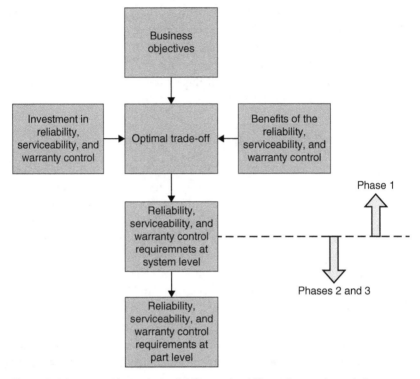

Figure 5.4 Investment in product reliability, serviceability, and warranty control

---

▼ **Design for Service Ignored**

CASE STUDY

A consumer electronics manufacturer had the connectors for software updates outside the cover of the products, so that the field engineers could easily do software updates during the home visit. In a new product generation, the connectors were inside a fixed cover, so that the products had to be returned to a regional repair factory even for simple software updates.

Phase 4: Production

In production phase the components and raw materials are converted into final products. The strategic questions are related to the network structure (number, location, and role of the production and distribution facilities), operating model issues with diverse variations in terms of the triggering signal to start production (make to stock, make to order, assemble to order, configure to order, engineer to order) and make-or-buy decisions, and which parts of the operations to own and operate and which parts to outsource.

The quality approach selected to ensure minimum noncon-formance has a profound impact on warranty at the operational level. This should include quality control in manufacturing and testing, what traceability data to be collected in manufacturing and distribution, product quality feedback from previous similar products and the production/supplier-related root-causes, as well as ensuring that part manufacturers and distributors supply the parts in accor-dance with manufacturer-defined technical specifications and quality requirements.

Phase 5: Sales and Marketing

In this phase the key sales and marketing messages are decided—what are the unique selling points of the product and what are the most important financial and commercial elements of the total sales pack-age. The warranty-related questions to be answered in this phase are the role of warranty as a part of the sales and marketing strategy and what are the commercial aspects of each warranty offering on top of the base warranty (e.g., content and pricing of the extended warranty and maintenance service contract offerings). Warranty terms offered can form a strong and straightforward marketing message on prod-uct quality: The higher the quality, the less there are product failures and the longer the warranty period the manufacturer can offer. As a principle, this is not always correct. New entrants or companies with a lower quality brand may use extensive warranty coverage as a vehicle to increase market share and make other companies to follow, whereas established players with a strong quality brand may choose to stick with a shorter warranty.

 Warranty as a Part of Marketing Message

CASE STUDY

In 1982, Chrysler claimed that it had improved quality so significantly that it could offer the best warranty in the industry. Ford and GM moved quite quickly to match the warranty terms offered by Chrysler, whereas Toyota extended its warranty length seven years later.

Across the industry, there was a negative correlation between product quality and warranty length for a period of 10 years, returning back to the expected positive correlation in the early 1990s.

(Continued)

> **(Continued)**
>
> However, changes in warranty coverage appear to have a clear impact on market share. In 2001 Kia had seen a 65 percent increase in the market share in the United States as a result of extending powertrain warranty to 10 years/100,000 miles, whereas one year later Volkswagen reduced powertrain warranty from 10 years/100,000 miles to 5 years/60,000 miles and saw a 30 percent sales drop in market share over the subsequent three years (Etzion and Pe'er, 2013).
>
> In 2007, Kia introduced a seven-year warranty in the United Kingdom and saw its market share almost triple from 1.2 percent in 2007 to 3.2 percent in 2013 (Foxall, 2015).

Phase 6: Post Sale

Naturally, post sale is the phase, where most warranty-related activities take place. Warranty-servicing management includes strategic elements related to the service network structure and service delivery approach, and operational aspects related to service parts and service engineer planning, contact center, and online support. Warranty servicing was discussed in Chapter 3.

ORGANIZATIONAL STRUCTURE

The organizational structure for warranty management depends on several factors:

- The size of the company
- Business strategy
- Geographical reach
- Product and service portfolio and strategic differentiators in both
- Customer structures and priorities
- In-house versus outsourced warranty management

In some companies warranty management is a part of sales and marketing, in others a part of operations or after-sales service. In many others, some elements of warranty management are split between other organizational units. There is no one-size-fits-all organizational structure for warranty management, but it always needs to be integrated into the overall product development, supply chain, and customer service processes. Since warranty, extended warranty, and maintenance service offerings may be a part of a wider service offerings portfolio and require the same delivery capabilities, they are often managed in the same unit. However, there are common activities that need an owner within the organization and considerations to be taken into account, when formulating the organizational structure for effective warranty management:

- Service development
- Service network management
- Customer support operations management
- Back-office support
- Warranty administration and control

Service Development

Service development is typically a part of the services organization. It has three main responsibilities:

Service product management

This includes service portfolio management, product-related and product independent service offering development, costing and pricing guidelines, service delivery, and sales documentation.

Service engineering

This is the link between R&D and the warranty service operations, also responsible for product quality feedback from the field.

Service implementation

This is responsible for taking warranty service for new products and new service offerings to market.

Service Network Management

Service network management function is responsible for setting the right network structure and to manage the nodes in the service network. In case of outsourced service, service agent management includes selecting and recruiting service agents, ongoing service agent performance management, and continuous renewal of the service agent base and adjustment of the network, depending on changes in the product portfolio and customer base.

Customer Support Operations Management

Customer support operations management includes contact center management, field service management, online support platforms and tools, and knowledge management to support all parties and warranty service channels.

Back-Office Support

Back-office support includes the diverse functions not involved in the actual service delivery or development. Quality management should cover both the product quality aspects and warranty process quality aspects. Finance and business control is responsible for warranty cost planning and reporting, as well as the warranty reserves and accruals. Other functions in back-office support are human resources, compliance, legal, environment, and sustainability.

Warranty Administration and Control

Warranty administration and control includes the management of the customer warranty claims process and the warranty service claim validation process, warranty data analysis, and warranty-related service agent audits. The case at the end of this section illustrates the long-term perspective of improving warranty control.

In many companies, warranty administration and control is executed in a distributed setup "close to the customers and the service agents." Although there are clear advantages, like knowing the local circumstances and shorter travel distances, this may be problematic for the following three reasons:

1. Focus and consistency of the work
2. Lack of global benchmarks
3. Segregation of duties

Focus and Consistency of the Work

In a distributed setup, warranty administration often is an additional effort for someone whose main responsibilities and incentives are elsewhere. When the main focus is on other activities, warranty administration is done only occasionally and in a hurry. People don't get really good at the activities they do only once a week or once every second week.

Unless there is very strong global governance and process ownership, the distributed model also leads to locally developed tools and processes, with local interpretations and guidelines. We have often seen cases where some countries are then managing warranty very effectively, with rigorous processes and high discipline, and other countries are not.

Lack of Benchmarks

The incompatibility between locally collected data makes global or regional benchmarking very difficult, reducing overall transparency and control.

If the entire warranty administration is distributed, it may be that each local organization is concentrating on their own figures, with missing focus on global trends and benchmarking between the areas.

Segregation of Duties

Since the day-to-day communications and relationship building with customers and service agents is typically a local activity, having the warranty administration activities handled outside of the local organization reduces the risk of both erroneous and inappropriate actions. Over the years, the local organization may have built (and rightly so) tight connections with the local business community. As a result, local organization may have difficulties in taking corrective actions against their long-term partners when such actions are needed.

 Organizing for Warranty Control

CASE STUDY

A global heavy industrial equipment manufacturer started a determined journey to improve warranty control in 2005. It was operating in close to 100 local country organizations, each of them with their own way of working. The equipment has long product life cycles with reasonably low volumes. Quality issues could surface after a long usage period, meaning that the same issue could have existed for several years before being detected. The effectiveness of product recalls was very important.

(Continued)

(Continued)

There was a small central team arranging parts and field service support to resolve the cases escalated from the local level. At that point of time, there was no transparency or control of the total warranty situation at the global level. "We had absolutely no clue of how many claims we had totally. Using data for analyzing was out of the question. We had no clear picture of the real lead time and the understanding on warranty costs was blurry. There was clearly lack of trust with the businesses, since it was very hard to explain how things really were. There was a central fund to cover the warranty costs but gold plating fraud was hard to spot."

A global SAP system implementation was ongoing, so gradually the claims were recorded in one global system. The improvement journey over the past 10 years included the following main steps:

1. Get organized around warranty.
2. Establish proactive issue resolution.
3. Establish a warranty analytics capability.
4. Expand the role of warranty services.

The content of each step was the following:

(1) *Get organized around warranty.* In 2005 a central warranty management organization was established, reporting directly to the global head of the Service Business. "During the first year we had real challenges to become a part of the business as the culture had to change in how we as a company approach the people behind the claims."

(2) *Establish proactive issue resolution.* A new strategy was created to become more proactive with warranty issues. "Our focus was on product engineering to get the product improvement cycles faster and on professional product/component recall management. The target was to be able to solve the problems before they reached the customer. This was, however, very challenging the first years as the business was doing well."

(3) *Establish a warranty analytics capability.* "In 2009 we decided that our unit will become the nonconformity data analyzing provider inside the company. This was also a very important step to reach to the long-term target of proactive warranty management.

"The first years we were trying to cope with this important task with limited resources. Over time we managed to build the supporting systems and a very skilled analytics team. They are very effective in getting the data, doing the necessary drill-downs and slicing and dicing, and making the right conclusions as a result."

(4) *Expand the role of warranty services.* The focus has been on building additional flexibility on warranty offerings for solutions including several products or business lines. A portfolio of warranty service offerings from the central warranty unit to the business lines is being launched. "We are building a differentiated model taking into account diverse customer needs and fitting into different organization models."

An online solution for warranty claims and spare parts orders has been launched. It will increase transparency, speed, and accuracy for the company and for the people behind the claims. "Digitalization will offer us further opportunities in enhancing the services. Need to proceed step-by-step with relatively conservative customers."

Results Achieved

The efforts over the past 10 years have paid off.

"The most important achievement has been the improvement with customer satisfaction. Currently over 80 percent of our customers rate us to be better than our competition.

"We have also seen a significant improvement in product quality, although the cycles are very long and it took us almost 8 years to get there.

"At the same time, we have been able to integrate a number of acquired companies into the same global structure with the same global systems and processes, showing a unified brand and warranty service experience to our customers, across our business units.

"The key internal development was to build an organization dedicated to warranty-related matters and developing warranty professionals for the future. This change ensured a constant development of the warranty expertise with us. We have warranty professionals that know human behavior and can deal with difficult cases. We also have professional recall project managers, who can deal fast with possible cases in the field and thereby we minimize the exposure for the company."

WARRANTY MANAGEMENT SYSTEMS

The number of warranty service transactions and the amount of warranty-related data vary from company to company. In many industries, the volumes are so high that sophisticated automation is needed to support the warranty processes. For instance, according to the Center of Automotive Research (2005), the automotive industry handled more than 100 million warranty claims per year in 2005.

Since then, this number has increased further. The same is true in other industries such as electronics, home appliances, and other consumer durables. Warranty management information system is needed to handle this complexity, both through the product life cycle and through the service life cycle. It can be used (i) for formulating warranty strategy for new products, (ii) for continuous improvements to reduce warranty costs for products on the market, and (iii) for managing the transactional complexity across the service life cycle. The system manages the data flows through the warranty process and needs data to support effective warranty-related decision making.

As manufacturing companies are increasingly moving from products to services and integrating services into their core product offerings, they are increasingly investing in holistic solutions covering their entire service business. Warranty management system is a critical part of the company service management system.

New technologies such as cloud, mobile connectivity, big data, and predictive analytics provide a range of new opportunities for building effective warranty management systems.

This section deals with the following three topics:

1. Elements of a warranty management system
2. Integration with other systems
3. Warranty data

Elements of a Warranty Management System

The main elements of a warranty management information system can be broadly divided into three areas: (i) warranty transaction support; (ii) warranty analytics; and (iii) warranty and service contract management, as shown in Figure 5.5. Each element deals with specific issues or aspects of warranty, and the different types of data (discussed in more detail later in this chapter) needed to address the issues.

Warranty Transactions

Warranty transaction software supports the entire process from customer claim for service to entitlement, from service execution and warranty service claim validation to financial transactions and closing of the warranty service claim to supplier recovery. The system covers the process for base warranty transactions as well as for transactions related to extended warranties and maintenance service contracts.

Warranty Management System		

Warranty Transactions	Warranty Analytics	
• Warranty claims • Material returns • Supplier recovery • Retrofit and recall campaigns	**Product life cycle** • New product development • End-of-life decisions • Warranty cost forecasting	**Service life cycle** • Product quality and early warnings • Claims and fraud • Warranty accruals and reserves

Warranty and Service Contracts

Figure 5.5 Elements of a warranty management system

The main functionalities of warranty claims management include registration and entitlement of customer warranty claims, RMA handling, and service agent claims management. In modern systems there is a multichannel support for claim entry through web, mobile applications, system-to-system integration, and file upload for diverse user groups, like contact center personnel, service center or field engineers, and warranty provider personnel. Effective claims approvals and rejections require access to the warranty contract data that determine product's warranty coverage and the validation rules.

Parts returns functionality supports the workflow from the initial request to return the defective material to the receipt of material. Automatic determination of parts to be returned and linking the returned parts to the customer or service agent claims supports tracking and verification that all defective parts and products are covered for.

Supplier recovery functionality supports the workflow to create supplier reclaims, material returns to suppliers, and the tracking of supplier settlements against the reclaims.

Retrofits and recall campaigns functionality supports organizing the retrofits and recalls, related service bulletins, and exception codes to approve campaign-related claims.

Warranty Analytics

Davenport et al. (2010) define analytics as using data, analysis, and systematic reasoning to make decisions. Taking an analytical approach means converting data to information and further to insight, answering specific questions, as highlighted in Table 5.1.

Table 5.1 Key Questions Addressed by Analytics (Davenport et al., 2010)

	Past	Present	Future
Information	What happened? (Reporting)	What is happening now? (Alerts)	What will happen? (Extrapolation)
Insight	How and why did it happen? (Modeling, experimental design)	What's the next best action? (Recommendation)	What is the best/worst thing that can happen? (Prediction, optimization, simulation)

The purpose of warranty analytics is to use data, analysis, and systematic reasoning to support the strategic, tactical, and operational decisions across the product and service life cycles. Analytics requires the right data, the right tools, and the right contextual understanding. The following simple example shows how totally different conclusions can be drawn from the same claims data for one product, when combined with other data. Each graph is showing claims for the same products collected over a 2.5-year period. The data consisted of the following:

- D1: Claims count on a monthly basis
- D2: Number of products under warranty at the start of each month (population at risk)
- D3: Claims count on production month basis (based on claims and production month data)
- D4: Number of products produced (based on production month data)

Figure 5.6 shows a graph of the number of claims on a monthly basis (D1). It looks like there is an escalating problem. Figure 5.7 shows a graph of the claims rate based on population at risk (D1/D2). It looks like a problem, but the metric seems to have reached a steady state. Figure 5.8 shows a graph of the claims rate based on production month (D3/D4). It indicates that there was a quality issue for some months. It seems to be resolved and there is no need for any action. This highlights the point that analysis should be done properly to get the right information and to make right interpretations for decision making.

Product Life Cycle
New product development is supported by warranty data analysis (as discussed in the section on Product Life-Cycle Perspective).

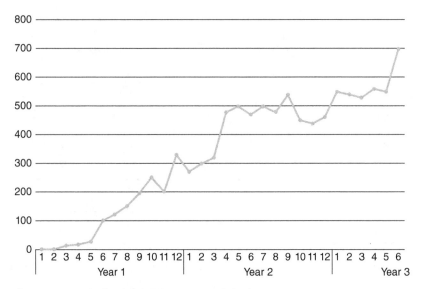

Figure 5.6 Graph of monthly claims—an escalating issue?

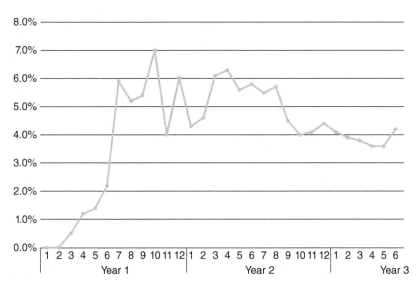

Figure 5.7 Claims rate based on population at risk—a stabilizing issue?

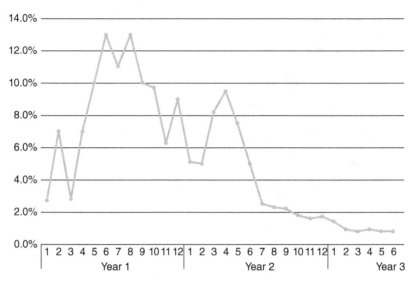

Figure 5.8 Claims rate based on production month—issue solved?

The basic reporting provides the big picture of the warranty cost profile of similar products. That information is turned into insight on the root-causes of the failures and further to recommendations on design, material selection, and supply chain issues to avoid similar failures. Predictive models are used to create scenario and sensitivity analysis on what could be the warranty cost profile of the new product.

Product end-of-life decisions are made largely based on the product sales forecasts, profitability estimates, and the plans on new product launches, where warranty analytics mainly supports the profitability estimates.

Warranty data analysis allows warranty cost forecasts and product reliability and serviceability trade-off decisions to be made during product development.

Service Life Cycle

The functionalities related to service life cycle include warranty fraud analytics (discussed in Chapters 7 to 10), warranty accruals and reserves accounting, and product quality feedback analytics.

Warranty accruals and reserves calculation uses similar analytics methods as new product development–related warranty cost estimation, but now the focus is not on one single product but on the entire portfolio of products under warranty.

Product quality feedback analytics aims to support the entire feedback process from issue detection to correction and preventive actions cycle. It includes (i) the identification and validation of potential emerging issues, (ii) supporting the root-cause analysis, and (iii) corrective and preventive actions.

The commonly used methods of root-cause analysis and corrective and preventive actions include statistical process control (SPC), the 8-D method, failure mode effects analysis (FMEA), and the define, measure, analyze, improve, and control (DMAIC) cycle of continuous improvement (Blank, 2014).

Issues with Product Quality Feedback Data

CASE STUDY

A global manufacturer had a good process for product quality feedback on paper. Taking a closer look there were a number of issues in timeliness and accuracy of the data. The claims were collected from the service agents on a monthly basis, creating an average of 15 days' delay. Then the data were consolidated and aggregated across a number of databases, all these through nightly batch runs, causing a further 10 days of delay. Finally, there were different opinions on who is responsible for the product quality feedback analysis. Product development felt they get unreliable and late recommendations in an industry with short product life cycles.

Warranty and Service Agent Contract Management

Warranty and service contract management covers both customer and service agent contracts, including the templates for different types of contracts. It supports creation of customer and/or service agent–specific contracts utilizing the templates. The contractual terms stored in the system are then used within the entitlement, claim validation, and material returns processes as well as in analytics.

Integration with Other Systems

The end-to-end warranty management process involves multiple parties. In a similar way a warranty management system needs to integrate with the information systems of a number of units—some internal to the organization (such as engineering, production, marketing systems, etc.), and others external to the organization (such as parts distributor

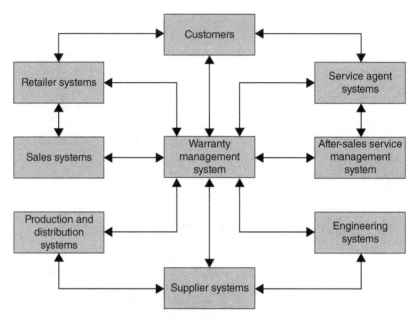

Figure 5.9 A warranty management system needs to integrate with several internal and external systems

or manufacturer, service agent, retailer, and customer systems). Each unit, both within the organization and external to it, can have different information systems. Effective warranty management requires that the manufacturer has a warranty management system that can utilize relevant data from all the other systems indicated in Figure 5.9.

We discuss briefly some data that the warranty management system needs from these other systems:

- *Engineering systems*: Static information related to product design (product configuration, as-designed bill-of-materials, suitable spare parts).

- *Production and distribution systems:* Product serial or batch number, manufacturing date and time, quality control records, materials and processes used in the production phase, as well as the delivery and installation related data, as-produced bill-of-materials, batch or serial numbers of different parts, and product and part version information. This may include similar information from the part supplier systems or that can come directly from the suppliers.

- *Sales system:* Customer data (i.e., sales channel data if products are not directly sold to end-customers), warranty contract data, and potentially information on products, as-sold bill-of-materials, and sales or activation date per customer.

- *After-sales service systems:* Customer interaction, claim and service history of the customer and the product, as-maintained bill-of-materials, and customer-claim-related data from the RMA process.

- *Retailer systems:* Customer warranty claims and potentially customer- and sales-related information. In many cases the lack of visibility to the retailer systems prevents the manufacturing companies from getting relevant data, which is an issue for them.

- *Service agent systems:* Customer warranty claim data as well as service agent claim data (including warranty servicing data and certification data for specific products or levels of repair).

The data are used (i) to support warranty entitlement, claim validation, and analytics, (ii) for formulating warranty strategy for new products, (iii) for continuous improvements to reduce warranty costs, and (iv) for managing the transactional complexity across the warranty servicing process.

Warranty Data

Effective warranty management requires proper data collection and a system to manage the collected data. The data needed can be broadly divided into two categories: (i) warranty claims data (discussed in this section) and (ii) warranty supplementary data. The latter one is referring to the great deal of data and information at each phase of the product life cycle that are of relevance for effective warranty management (Blischke et al., 2011).

Warranty data needed to manage warranty from the service life-cycle perspective are shown in Figure 5.10.

Warranty Claims Data

Warranty claims data are the data collected during the processing of claims and servicing of repairs under warranty. These data are collected in multiple phases throughout the servicing process. The phases, their

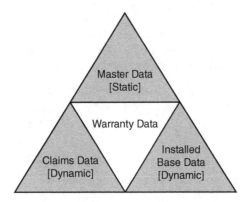

Figure 5.10 Warranty data

sequence, and the collected data vary depending on the servicing pro-cess, product being serviced, and data collection requirements.

The warranty claims data collected during the repair process can be grouped into the following categories: (i) customer-related data, (ii) product-related data, (iii) service-center-related data, and (iv) cost-related data.

Customer-related data

- Customer data
- Entitlement data, potential RMA number

Product-related data

- Product model and serial number
- Customer symptom codes
- Failure/fault codes
- The source of the issue, possible customer damage, possible other problems in the item
- Repair location (in onsite service)
- Service activities conducted
- Parts replaced and parts used
- Identity of the new product (if product replaced)
- Old and new software version (if software updated)
- Diagnostics and test results before and after the repair

Service center data

- Service agent company (if outsourced)
- Service center or service organization
- Technician

Cost-related data

- RMA (return of material authorization) and transactional administration process expenses
- Service center repair/replace/refurbish expenses
- Field services repair/replace/refurbish expenses
- Indirect expenses, including, for example, inventory and end-of-life expenses if separately charged

Claims data should be available on the level of individual claims, serial numbered and available in one place, covering all customers and service agents. In addition to being the basis for service agent compensation, claims data provide insight on product's service history. They should also provide information on exchanged products, where customer product has been replaced by a new one and the replacement product inherits the warranty period of the original product. These data should identify the service technician and a means to verify the certification and qualification for the corresponding service activities for the product.

The right level of detail in fault and symptom codes and their correct recording is often tricky, and the quality of entered data varies considerably from service agent to service agent:

- If the level of detail is too generic, it is difficult to use warranty claims as a source of product quality feedback data. If the level of detail is too detailed, the likelihood of unintentional coding-errors increases and/or the motivation of the service technicians to enter high-quality data decreases, both leading to unreliable data.
- The fact that a component failed might be obvious, but the cause of failure might not be readily apparent.
- The repair technician may need to make rapid decisions (for entry into the service agent's warranty system) because of time and cost constraints.

Increased complexity and lack of experience and motivation on the part of the technician affect the data quality. Often, the technician does not know the purpose of filling the seemingly large number of data fields. Increasing the transparency on why the data fields are important and how they are used improves data quality.

The main usage of warranty claims data is for managing the transaction (customer claim entitlement, service claim validation, service execution, and compensation), warranty cost management, and for analytics and reporting to support new product development and corrective and preventive actions on product quality issues.

▼ **Unreliable Warranty Claims Data**

CASE STUDY

A global heavy industrial equipment manufacturer was using a simple database to store the warranty claims from its service agents and from direct service customers, including claimed and approved amounts. However, a part of the claims were handled outside the claims database. The financial transactions (claim payments to service agents, warranty accruals, and reserves management) were handled in the ERP and some reported in Excel. The company had three different figures for their warranty cost in three different systems (with quite significant deviations) and nobody could tell which figure would be the correct one (actually probably none of them was).

Claim Reporting Methods

Information system support is needed to collect claims data and deliver it to the warranty provider. The three main options for claim reporting are the following:

1. The service agent or customer enters claim data directly to warranty provider's system.

2. The service agent or customer enters claim data to its own system and delivers data through an interface in a standard format allowing data to be uploaded to warranty provider's system.

3. The warranty provider retrieves data directly from service agent's system.

Additionally, manual or semimanual solutions are being used, although these are not ideal. Claims can be, for example, sent on paper or as e-mail attachments. Applications like MS Excel or MS Word can be used for claims data collection and reporting.

Option 1 works best in the situations where a single warranty provider dominates service agent's operations and justifies use of warranty provider's systems.

In a multibrand workshop supporting several manufacturers, where a technician needs to switch between different brands, use of different applications for each different brand becomes cumbersome. In such a situation, the service provider may prefer to use its own system and deliver claims to the manufacturer's system through a systems interface or allow warranty provider to retrieve data from its systems (i.e., use option 2 or 3). Even in this situation, the service agent should be required to provide a standardized data set, and in option 2, build the interface in a standardized, warranty provider–specified format.

Installed Base Data

Installed base data include data about products at the customer site and the configurations of these products. Furthermore, the installed base can include additional data about the products and their components, such as serial numbers, hardware and software versions and service history, and modifications done over the product's life cycle.

Installed base data are the main starting point for any customer warranty entitlement:

- What products has the company sold?
- To which customer?
- Under which type of contract?
- Under which type of warranty?

Access to the original configuration may reveal customer-installed parts, which might not be under the same warranty as the entire product.

Depending on the coverage and level of detail of the data, installed base can support many other functions. Having accurate installed base data related to an individual product (serial number traceability and as-designed/as-sold/as-built/as-installed/as-maintained product life cycle information) enables thorough service event preparation:

- Plan the next service event for a particular product.

- Access the current configuration to ensure right parts when going to the site for a service case.

- Ensure compatibility with the other parts when a product/component is upgraded.

- Find where the faulty product is physically located and where the part to be replaced is located.

- Understand other safety, access, or tool-related information needed for service execution.

- Check the service history of the product instance.

- Check the potential usage history and self-diagnostics information of the product.

- Check the software and operating system versions of the product.

Having accurate installed base data overall enables product planning, sales planning, and service planning:

- *Strategic product portfolio and product development planning:* What type of new development should the manufacturer invest in—entirely replacing the product, a major version upgrade, or just some new features or fixing known defects?

- *Sales planning:* What type of cross- and upselling opportunities are there for a specific customer or region? What service offerings should we propose for this particular customer? When does a maintenance service contract expire? We have a new product generation; when should we start the upgrade discussions with the customers?

- *Marketing planning:* How to launch new products in the market with focus on the right customers? What marketing campaigns are needed to replace obsolete products?

- *Service planning:* How much spare parts and field service capacity do we need? Service engineer is on his way to a site for an issue—what other products could the engineer service during the same visit?

- *Retrofits and recalls:* There is an epidemic failure with this product batch—where are the products located?

Although installed base data may be distributed into several physical databases, different organizational units should have unified access to the same installed base information (with different views and access rights). For instance, the entitlement check should provide the same answer to the customer making an online check, to the contact center providing the RMA, to the service agent making the customer entitlement, or the manufacturer's own warranty department making the entitlement decision. The unified access concept is shown in Figure 5.11.

The industrial Internet, new communications, analytics, and cloud- and sensor-technologies can bring the understanding of the installed base to the next level. Knowing not only what has been

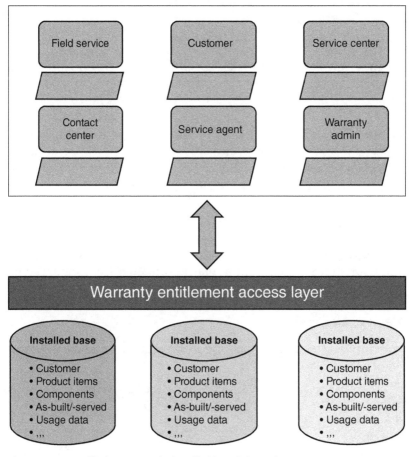

Figure 5.11 A unified access to the installed base information

delivered to whom but how the product is used (time of actual use, weather conditions, rounds per minute, energy consumption, calibration and settings, etc.) creates a number of opportunities for new service offerings and for better warranty control.

Real-time Analytics Revealed Customer Misuse

CASE STUDY

A global heavy industrial equipment manufacturer implemented new analytics to predict component failures for cargo handling equipment. One result of the analytics was that certain drivers were accelerating too fast and doing sudden breaks to stop very rapidly, leading to certain components wearing much faster than designed. In addition to predicting the failures, real-time monitoring and analytics helped the company to train the drivers to handle the equipment differently and actually prevent the failures from happening at all.

Installed base information is often fragmented in different databases and even in paper-based files. Companies who sell through the sales channel may lose track of the actual end-customer and timing of the sale. If the company is not managing the service of individual products, the installed base information for these products is degrading, as service activities are conducted, new parts installed, software versions upgraded, and so on. Acquisitions lead to situations, where installed base information is in different formats in different systems. Understanding the installed base is crucial, when selling extended warranties or maintenance service contracts for larger entities (e.g., maintenance for all servers in a company or all machines of a certain type in a factory), where the installed base defines the scope for the contract. Getting that information from the customer can in some cases be quite tricky.

Warranty Master Data

Warranty master data include the data required to support the warranty processes:

- Warranty service offerings describe the base warranty, extended warranty, and maintenance service contract offerings the company has.

- Service bill-of-material can be used to ensure that servicing activities and parts used are for the right product and to help the field engineer to have the right spare parts taken to the customer site.

- Fault/failure and symptom codes are used in customer warranty entitlement, product quality feedback for new product development and manufacturing process improvement, and early warnings to detect emerging product quality issues.
- Customer claim entitlement rules and service claim validation rules are needed for analytics and automating the claims process.
- Customer master data include:
  - Customer data (name, address, contacts, etc.)
  - Customer products
  - Warranty contracts with the customer
  - Customer price lists, if any
- Service agent master data include information on:
  - Service agent company data (name, address, contacts)
  - Service agent contracts
  - Service agent certifications
  - Service price lists

Warranty Management Software Alternatives

The application of IT tools to manage warranty is highly inconsistent in the industry (Brennan and Barkai, 2011). Some companies are investing in the warranty IT capabilities, whereas quite a few invest just the minimum to survive. The main alternatives for warranty management software include (i) dedicated warranty management packages, (ii) generic software packages with specific warranty management functionality, and (iii) custom-developed systems. Historically, many companies have relied on custom-developed warranty management systems, often with manual interfaces and limited integration with other internal and external systems. There are two approaches for a custom system:

- *Low-cost alternative with just basic support and minimal investment:* This approach typically includes limited automation and manual data-entry, potentially entering the same data several times in different applications.

▨ *High-cost alternative:* In this approach, the rationale is to build a solution matching the exact needs and processes of the company. Often developed over an extensive period, system maintenance becomes more difficult and expensive, but it is difficult to migrate to a commercial solution.

However, companies are more and more turning to commercial software packages and software-as-a-service solutions. There are basically three main alternatives:

▨ Niche packages dedicated to warranty management

▨ Enterprise resource planning (ERP) and customer relationship management (CRM) packages, migrating functionally into warranty management

▨ Product life-cycle management (PLM) packages, migrating into service life cycle and installed base, looking at different views of the product configuration (as-designed, as-manufactured, as-sold, as-installed, as-serviced)

Commercial software solutions are typically selected to enforce more standard processes and to support application consolidation. Replicating all old custom system features into a commercial software solution often turns out to be quite difficult and costly.

Companies have four main alternatives for warranty analytics:

▨ Spreadsheet

▨ Reporting tool

▨ Analytics tool

▨ Analytics as a part of a commercial warranty solution or the warranty module of another software package solution

Over the years, there has also been industry consolidation, with PLM and ERP vendors acquiring the niche players and integrating their functionality into the broader offering. There has been a significant improvement in warranty management software and service agent's housekeeping software and the integration between those two over the past five years (Nagelvoort, 2015).

WARRANTY MANAGEMENT MATURITY MODELS

IDC Manufacturing Insights has together with the Global Warranty & Service Contract Association and Warranty Week developed a five-level Warranty Management Capability Maturity Model.

The more mature levels build on the less mature levels. The levels of maturity (from lowest to highest) are as follows:

- Level 0—Ad hoc
- Level 1—Standardized
- Level 2—Managed
- Level 3—Integrated
- Level 4—Optimized

At the lowest level of maturity, the organization is purely reactive and focused on transactions, processes are not automated, and unsystematic exception management is the norm. When reaching higher levels of maturity, the focus moves to product and process quality. With this transition, the behavior is changing from reactive to the ability to anticipate and take proactive actions. The maturity model includes four key dimensions, which are considered at each maturity level:

1. Organization
2. Governance
3. Measurement
4. Technology

The model is intended for use as an assessment framework: Where are they, and what can they do to reach the higher levels of maturity? (Brennan and Barkai 2011).

Aberdeen Group is using a broad definition of warranty management, which may include any of the following components:

- Warranty creation/structure/pricing
- Warranty sales
- Warranty administration
- Asset recovery
- Claims management
- Supplier recovery
- Customer management

Their competitive framework is looking at company performance in the following dimensions:

- Process
- Organization
- Knowledge management

- ▨ Technology
- ▨ Performance

According to their benchmarks, best-in-class performance is not a result of one factor, but requires a variety of capabilities and automation processes (Pinder and Dutta, 2011).

NOTES

1. The business logic for the new services defines the customer value of the service (why is it valuable or the customer), the service delivery approach, and the revenue logic of the service (what are the billable elements, and how does the service provider make money with the service offering).

2. Resolving claims with lower cost methods, such as software update over the air or module exchange at point of sale instead of centralized repair.

CHAPTER **6**

Warranty Fraud

W arranty fraud affects warranty costs. Controlling this cost requires a proper understanding of the nature of warranty fraud. This chapter deals with this topic. The outline of the chapter is as follows. We start with an introduction to fraud in general and continue with discussion on warranty fraud. The subsequent sections deal with actors (fraudsters) and victims of warranty fraud, classification of warranty fraud, warranty fraud patterns, and consequences and impacts of warranty fraud. The last sections deal with the actor being (i) customer, (ii) service agent, (iii) sales channel, (iv) warranty administrator, and (v) warranty provider, respectively. In each section, we discuss the motivation and the methods/techniques used by actors and the impacts of the warranty fraud on one or more victims.

FRAUD IN GENERAL

Oxford Dictionary (2015) defines *fraud* as "Wrongful or criminal deception intended to result in financial or personal gain." So it is intentional trickery, to get dishonest financial or other advantage over others.

If there are significant financial benefits to be gained and limited risk of getting caught, there are some people and companies who try to take advantage of the opportunity, resulting in fraud. This can occur in the context of individuals and companies. Figure 6.1 shows the key factors that are important in the context of fraud. Naturally, most people and companies have higher integrity and won't take advantage of the opportunity. Additionally, the likelihood and consequences of getting

Figure 6.1 Key factors leading to potential fraud

caught have an impact on the likelihood of fraud taking place. With the current mobile and social media technologies, fraudsters have access to a larger number of potential victims and a statistically better likelihood to find people who will eventually fall into the trap. We have seen the traditional street trick for tourists and Nigerian letters turn into a much wider collection of tricks to watch out for. The UK National Fraud & Cyber Crime Reporting Centre has categorized types of fraud into a list of 150 schemes, starting from the West African Letters to Internet auction fraud and website domain name scams.

During the past year, the first author kept a log of fraudulent e-mails received, and the results are as follows:

- Nine e-mails announced a lottery prize of US$500,000 or more waiting to be collected.

- Fifteen e-mails with a link to get an iPhone with US$1.

- Five e-mails announced the passing of a remote relative and the possibility to collect between US$5,000,000 and US$15,000,000.

- Three e-mails requested the collection of valuable packages from the main railway station in Rome.

- Around 10 e-mails from "our bank" included an urgent message to follow a link to reset password.

- A message announced the winning of a Samsung Galaxy with a link to collect it.

- A very professionally written e-mail came from a courier company stating that a posted package could not be delivered, since no one was home. There was a link to the courier website to check where to pick up the package. However, there was still something that didn't feel right. This trick was so common that the courier customer support number had an automated message saying that "we never inform about non-deliveries with e-mail."

In addition, the author had credit card withdrawals worth US$2,000 during one day in a trip to the United States.[1]

One might expect fraud in other business contexts to be different but, unfortunately, it is not. According to a 2014 survey carried out by the Association of Certified Fraud Examiners, a typical company loses 5 percent of revenues each year to fraud. On a global level, this would translate to a potential projected fraud loss of nearly US$3.7 trillion.

The individual cases were sizeable, the median being US$145,000 and 22 percent of the cases involving losses of at least US$1 million. The estimated annual fraud costs for companies is GBP 66 billion in the United Kingdom (Sadgrove, 2015, pp. 243–245).

In this book, we focus on warranty fraud and other excess costs. There are several scenarios in other business processes where frauds of similar nature occur and include the following:

- End-customer insurance claim fraud

- Overcharging in healthcare or non-warranty equipment service, especially when the incident is covered by insurance

- Using refurbished parts instead of new parts without informing the customer and/or without proper testing and quality control

- Using counterfeit parts not meeting the OEM quality standards

- Part manufacturer employees stealing and selling parts that have not passed the quality checks and should be scrapped

Some of the methods of analysis and controls that are proposed in the book in the context of warranty fraud are also effective in tackling these frauds.

Several interacting elements characterize warranty fraud. In the following sections we discuss the key elements: (i) actors and victims, (ii) classification, (iii) patterns, and (iv) consequences and impacts of warranty fraud.

ACTORS AND VICTIMS OF WARRANTY FRAUD

Applying the definition of fraud introduced in the earlier section, warranty fraud can be defined as any act committed to obtain financial or personal gain from warranty process.

Using a theater analogy, warranty fraud can be viewed as actions of the different "actors" on the "warranty fraud stage." The actors can be any party in the warranty servicing process—end-customers, retailers, distributors, manufacturers, service agents, warranty administrators, part manufacturers and distributors, and possibly others. Actors can act alone or in collusion—leading to different patterns of fraud discussed later in the section. The main victim of warranty fraud is the warranty provider. When warranty provider is responsible for fraud, also other parties such as customers, part manufacturers, and government can be the victims.

This book deals mainly with fraud targeted at warranty providers. After addressing the various classifications, patterns, and consequences of warranty fraud, this chapter focuses on describing the actors who commit such fraud.

CLASSIFICATION OF WARRANTY FRAUD

Warranty fraud can be broadly classified into two categories based on the nature of fraud:

1. *Systemic fraud*: These result from actions of one or more parties in the sales and in the warranty service chain carried out on a regular basis.
2. *Ad hoc fraud*: These result mainly from the actions of customers but can also include other parties in the chain.

Another way of classification is to divide fraud based on the reasons of the actor:

1. Intentional (a criminal activity)
2. Opportunistic—using gaps in the system when they are observed (unethical behavior)
3. Unconscious—behavior due to person being unaware of conducting fraud (due to ignorance)
4. Necessity—caused by other factors (cost pressure and operating to survive)

Fraud can also be classified based on the victims of fraud. The victims include:

- Customers
- Warranty providers (company)
- Part manufacturers
- Sales channel
- Government
- Shareholders

Finally, fraud can be classified based on the actor leading to the following types:

- Customer fraud
- Service agent fraud

- Warranty provider fraud
- Warranty administrator fraud
- Sales channel fraud

In all of these cases, fraud can be done by an individual or by a company. We will be using actor-based classification in this and later chapters.

Fraud can be (i) single-actor fraud and (ii) multiactor fraud where two or more actors collude to defraud the victim. Fraud done by different actors results in different fraud patterns, discussed next.

FRAUD PATTERNS

There are many methods that the actors use to defraud the victims. The same types of methods are used in different countries across the world. Some of the methods are specific to certain industry sectors (goods and services), some are general across industry sectors.

Understanding the different methods of fraud is important as it allows one to design a set of targeted actions to detect and prevent each known method of fraud. However, many of the methods of fraud go undetected and the warranty provider is unaware of them. Also, actors are continuously coming up with new methods for defrauding the victims.

To detect new methods of fraud, one needs to look for anomalies and try to understand why they exist and to decide whether fraudulent behavior is involved, as illustrated by the following case.

 Inventing Claims and Customers

CASE STUDY

A service agent conducting repairs for a consumer goods company had submitted several thousand claims. Declaring customer name and telephone number within each claim was mandatory. When the data were analyzed, there were only about 30 different first names and 30 different last names in the data. All customer names were combinations of these first and last names. Additionally, telephone numbers of dead people were included. In the end, the claims were found to be largely fraudulent.

The previous subsection classified reasons of fraud, actors, and victims. The following examples illustrate fraud that can occur in practice within these categories:

- Service agents may defraud warranty provider to stay profitable if warranty compensation is too low, terms and conditions are too tight, or requirements and preinvestments are too high for service agents. Fraud may also be opportunistic: earnings of extra revenues if control mechanisms are perceived to be loose.

- Customers in most cases conduct fraud to get a free-of-charge repair and save money. They may also be looking for better or extra replacement products or service level improvements utilizing identified gaps in the warranty provider controls and policies.

- Sales channel may also be looking for extra revenue and improved profitability. It may also want to improve customer satisfaction at warranty provider's expense.

- Warranty administrators and warranty provider employees may conduct fraud to earn additional income.

- Warranty providers may see their warranty costs as excessive and try to limit warranty coverage or reclaim costs from their vendors to save costs resulting from warranty servicing. This can be the case, especially when a major product issue is about to cause significant unexpected costs.

It is important to acknowledge that overbilling and other abuse in the warranty process is caused not only by fraudulent intentions but also by other reasons illustrated by the following examples:

- A customer requesting warranty repair may not be aware that her camera is not working because it has suffered from liquid damage caused by condensation.

- Technicians may be inadequately trained and be changing parts that do not need to be changed.

- Sales channel may want to satisfy an unhappy customer whose warranty has just expired.

- Rules for acceptable repairs may be unclear.

- Improperly repaired products may fail again and come back for repair just few weeks after the original repair. The contract between the OEM and the service agent may be loosely defined. This may allow the repair company to conduct extra activities to satisfy the customer while increasing its own revenue.

- Overbilling may also be done by mistake. Service agent's system and processes for handling repair activities may be working poorly, resulting in incorrect claims. A technician's typing error might increase the cost of repairs.

Altogether, the outcomes of fraud and actions done with good intentions a may in the end look the same.

Single-Actor Fraud Patterns

As the name suggests, single-actor fraud is the result of fraudulent actions by an actor acting alone. We discuss the different known patterns of fraud. New ones may evolve over time.

Customer

Customer fraud and misbehavior typically relates to cases where a customer tries to have a repair or replacement done although there is no warranty coverage. This can be the case when the warranty has expired, the customer has damaged the product, or the service action is not covered by a warranty.

Typically, the fraud done by a customer is limited to one or few cases per purchased product, although large-scale fraud also exists. Customers having large installations may try to utilize gaps in manufacturer's entitlement process to get service and support for a large number of products that are no longer covered by warranty or service contract.

Service Agent

From the warranty provider's perspective, the most significant sources of fraudulent claims are often the service agents. There is an inherent conflict of interest between warranty providers and service agents. Although warranty providers aim to minimize warranty costs, service agents' earnings depend on repairs. The more there is to claim, the higher the revenue for the service agent. Additionally, the contracts between the warranty provider and the service agent can be unclear and the training of the technicians insufficient, resulting in increased costs. In addition to ad-hoc fraud, there can be large-scale systematic fraud. Service agents can also charge both the customer and the manufacturer at the same time, although only one party should be invoiced.

The starting point for service agent fraud can be an individual fraudulent claim, a claim that is not covered by warranty, or a claim with inflated costs. If the manufacturer accepts the claim, the service agent learns that the controls are not working. Next time, a few more invalid claims may be submitted. If these claims are again accepted, the service agent may continue increasing the volume and unit cost of the claims. If the perceived probability of being caught is low, the service agent may institutionalize the generation of fraudulent claims. In some cases, warranty fraud may become the primary source of revenue for a service agent. Repair operations are only continued as a façade for criminal activities. In such cases, operations may be run by organized crime. In an extreme case, we have seen a cluster of service agents that have been set up in order to generate claims, with up to 97 percent of the claims being fraudulent.

Sales Channel

Sales channel is one of the interfaces through which a customer can get warranty service. Unless the manufacturer has sold the products to the sales channel without warranty coverage, the manufacturer covers the costs related to servicing the base warranty.

Sales channel may aim to please its customers at the expense of the manufacturer or offset its front-end store cost with warranty handling fees. Sales channel may modify manufacturers' base warranty by offering a better warranty, such as by offering a longer warranty period. The manufacturer might still be charged for servicing outside the original, but within the new warranty. Products may be replaced or passed forward to repair without proper entitlement to save own effort or for goodwill purposes—even when the manufacturer is not ready to pay for the goodwill. Sales channel may also report nonexisting customer replacements to get extra products free of charge. If a company is both selling and repairing products, further possibilities of conducting fraud become available.

Warranty Administrator

As discussed in Chapter 3, warranty administrators authorize repairs and returns and manage claims received by the warranty providers.[2] They approve or reject warranty claims and are in contact with service agents to obtain additional information on pending claims. Their responsibilities may also include management of master data in the warranty provider's warranty management systems.

If warranty administration is handled internally, possible fraud is conducted by a business unit or an individual employee.

If it is external, then there is a contract between administrator and warranty provider, including set procedures to be followed in claim validation and other warranty administration tasks. Fraud can occur due to breaching the terms or due to poor drafting of the contract and related procedures allowing warranty administrator to act in own interest and not that of the warranty provider.

Warranty administrator fraud can for example, result from abusing their power to do entitlement and authorize service or intentionally failing to validate claims as required.

Warranty Provider

Manufacturers and other warranty providers can, for example, aim to avoid costs and deny customers from service that should be covered by warranty or do excessive vendor recovery from their part suppliers. They can also overstate warranty costs to reduce tax payments or understate warranty reserves to increase short-term profits.

Multi-Actor Fraud Patterns

Two or more actors may collude to defraud the warranty provider. Although a multitude of possible combinations exists, the most relevant combinations are the following:

- *Customer and service agent:* For example, out-of-warranty or fictitious repairs at warranty provider's expense
- *Customer and sales channel:* For example, unauthorized product replacement
- *Customer and warranty administrator:* For example, authorizing replacement of nonexistent products

▨ *Two or multiple service agents together:* For example, exchange of claim data to allow generation of fictitious claims or creation of fictitious claims by front-end (tier 1) and back-end (tier 2/3) service agents

▨ *Service agent' and warranty administrator:* For example, failing to reject invalid warranty service claims

▨ *Service agent and warranty provider's employees:* For example, failing to take action when fraud is detected

CONSEQUENCES AND IMPACTS OF WARRANTY FRAUD

Warranty fraud affects the warranty provider, the customers, and other parties in the service network. This section discusses the scale of fraud and its impact on different parties.

Scale of Warranty Fraud in General

Estimates on the scale of fraud should be taken with reservations. The concept of warranty fraud is vague. When looking from outside, there is a thin line between a goodwill repair done to protect manufacturer's image and the use of goodwill as an excuse to pass the cost of out-of-warranty repair to the manufacturer. Repair costs charged using the loopholes in the contract with the manufacturer is another example.

Also, by its nature, fraud is hidden and its exact scale is unknown. If the companies had been able to identify fraudulent claims with precision, those claims would have been rejected and there would be no fraud. When companies become aware of fraud, they are reluctant to talk about it publicly. Based on our own experience, companies find it difficult to believe and admit that fraud exists even in their internal discussions.

Furthermore, global warranty costs are not accurately measured. Reporting requirements exist in the United States, but in many other countries there are no such requirements and companies don't need to report warranty costs. Importantly, service is given not only under base warranty, but also under various types of extended warranty and maintenance service contracts and insurances. Their volume comes on top of base warranty and is not universally reported. Consequently, the exact volume of warranty and service costs, let alone the fraud related to these operations, is not known.

Despite the difficulties to measure the scale of warranty fraud, some estimates exist. Different sources estimate warranty fraud to be in the range of 3 to 15 percent of the total warranty costs. Global warranty costs again are estimated to be US$90 billion per annum (Arnum, 2015). As a result, global warranty fraud could approximately be in the range of US$3 to US$14 billion. Although this figure is not scientifically accurate, we can assume that warranty fraud is a multibillion-dollar problem and highly significant. This figure does not include fraud related to other maintenance and service contracts.

Impact of Warranty Fraud on the Warranty Provider

Warranty fraud can have a significant impact on company's overall profitability. In a company where warranty costs are 2 percent of the overall revenue and 10 percent of the warranty costs are caused by fraud and overbilling, the direct bottom line impact is 0.2 percent. In a company with 5 percent profit margin, this is a significant figure.

For an individual company, the scale of warranty fraud can be much higher than the average. As a result, warranty fraud may significantly erode profitability.

Warranty fraud can impact warranty provider's costs in two ways:

1. *The volume of warranty claims is inflated, resulting in an increase in the field failure rate.* Part of the claims may not be covered by warranty, although service is still provided by the service agent and charged to the warranty provider. Claims can also relate to activities that never happened and where the claim was simply fabricated.

2. *The cost of repair in individual claims can be inflated.* The claim as such may be valid, but it may include too high labor, spare part, or other costs. The excess repair activities may have been done and spare parts used in practice, but the work done may be unnecessary or not covered by warranty. The claim can also contain work that was never done and parts that were not used.

As a result, the total cost increases as the degree (or level) of inflated repair cost and repair volume increases, as shown in Figure 6.2.

In addition to direct costs, warranty fraud has indirect consequences. Repair data received from service agents are an important source of information for research and development. Based on

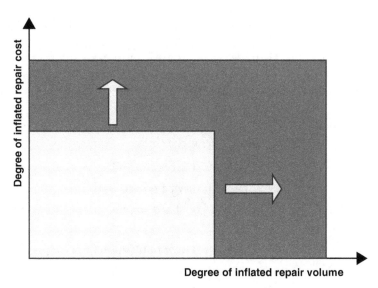

Figure 6.2 Increase in total warranty cost due to inflated figures

the field failure data, product quality issues can be uncovered and corrective actions taken. However, if the repair data include dubious claims, separating real quality problems from fraudulent billing can be difficult, as illustrated by the following case.

 Warranty Fraud Distorting Product Quality

CASE STUDY

A consumer products manufacturer used repair data to identify product quality issues. To focus the attention to high-priority issues, the report made using repair data focused on faults with highest frequency. After having a closer look, it became obvious that 14 out of top 15 quality issues were caused by fraudulent claims and only one was caused by a real problem with product quality.

As a result, unreliable product quality feedback may delay corrective actions. It might also result in unnecessary and highly expensive product recalls and reduce the effectiveness of predictive maintenance. Further on, it can lead to costly engineering changes, additional quality improvement activities with the part suppliers, and in the worst case unfounded decisions regarding product portfolio and terminating profitable products or product families that incorrectly seem to be loss making.

Warranty fraud can also affect the warranty provider's reputation and damage its brand. This is the case, for example, when customers are wrongly denied warranty service or receive poor service due to fraud.

A study by AGMA and CompTIA (2013) identifies several additional consequences of warranty fraud:

- Cost in time, staff, and resources to "police" abuse
- Compromised trust with service providers
- Good channel partners penalized for the actions of a few bad players
- PR challenges/fighting negative perceptions

A report by AGMA and PriceWaterhouseCoopers (2009, p. 8) raises further issues caused by service abuse:

- Loss of revenue due to undercoverage (i.e., customers don't buy a service contract for all products but expect to receive coverage on all purchases).
- Downward price pressure and revenue loss resulting from products obtained through service abuse and sold on the gray market.
- Decreased service levels for valid service claims (service provided to unentitled customers can delay legitimate claims and deplete the inventory of parts on hand at your service depots).

Impact of Warranty Fraud on Other Parties

The impact on part manufacturers and distributors is similar to the impact on the primary warranty provider when the part manufacturer is responsible for warranty costs for the parts used in warranty servicing. Primary warranty provider can pass on unjustified costs to its part suppliers.

Service abuse also has a significant impact in the service network. Warranty fraud can distort competition. Fraudulent companies can win warranty service contracts with the manufacturers as they can afford repair costs that are below their breakeven point. Later on, fraudulent claims are used to make the business profitable. This can make the business unprofitable for honest players and drive the service companies toward overbilling. Service agents can also suffer from customer fraud through inflated claim volume when there is a fixed price service contract between the warranty provider and the service agent.

Customers can be affected by warranty fraud in two ways.

1. *Excess costs:* The customer can be charged for service that should be covered by warranty. Extended warranties with questionable benefits or nonexistent coverage can be sold to the customer.

2. *Inferior service:* Service activities may be intentionally skipped, or service done with delay or done poorly, resulting in product failures and unnecessary service visits.

As manufacturers and other warranty providers add controls to fight back against warranty fraud, the service process becomes more complex for all parties in the chain—the customer, the service agents, and the manufacturer itself. This may reduce customer satisfaction and increase the administrative costs of both the service agents and the manufacturer.

CUSTOMER FRAUD

In the remainder of this chapter, we look at the actors who commit warranty fraud, beginning with customers. Customer fraud may take place during the warranty period or after the warranty has expired. Fraudulent warranty claims may also be associated with products that have never been purchased. Figure 6.3 shows the four categories of customer fraud based on the motivation underlying the fraud. Also shown are the methods that customers use in each case. We discuss each category in more detail.

Refund for or Replacement of Product that Is Not Faulty

Claiming the product to be faulty although there is nothing wrong with the product is one of the methods used by customers to obtain unjustified benefits. This can be done to obtain:

- Refund
- New or refurbished product
- Better product
- Extend product's lifetime

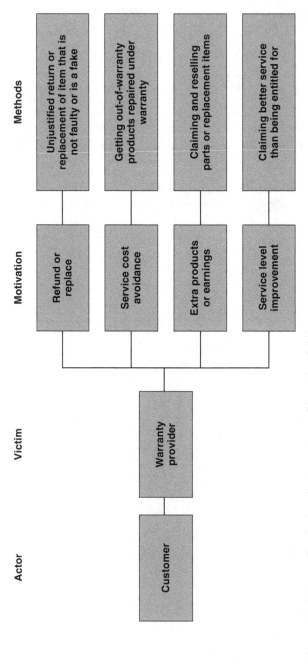

Figure 6.3 Customer fraud categories (warranty provider as the victim)

Refund

Return of purchased products for any reason is acceptable when it happens within the time period defined by retailer policy or consumer rights legislation. During this period, the return period has expired, the customer is entitled to a full refund. Return of goods is explained by buyer's remorse.[3] Customers may also return products they have bought at discounted prices and get undiscounted price as a refund if purchase prices are not tracked. After the return period has expired, the customer may claim a fictitious problem in order to be entitled for a refund. No fault is found in large proportion of products returned by customers. Consumer electronics in particular is prone to this behavior. Also, online sales have high return rates when compared to purchases done in traditional brick-and-mortar shops.

Replacement to Get a New or Refurbished Product

Alternatively, the customer may report a fictitious issue to get a replacement unit. Instead of having the customer product repaired, warranty providers may replace the faulty products. Replacement units may be refurbished second-hand products or new products of the same model as the original one. If the customer's original product has been worn out or is a fake, even a refurbished product may be of more value than the original one.

Replacement to Get a Better Product

In some cases, warranty providers hand out newer versions of the same product or upgrade the product to a better model. This may be done to keep the number of stock-keeping units manageable or for goodwill purposes. Customers may perceive the replacement units to be superior to the original products. This may result in some customers claiming their original products are faulty to get their products upgraded, as illustrated by the following two cases.

 Forging Evidence of Faulty Products

CASE STUDY

A global camera manufacturer had a continuously renewing product portfolio. When its customers faced issues, they were in touch with the manufacturer's contact center. Typically, defective products were replaced. As the portfolio kept changing, a customer often got a newer version of the camera than the one they had originally purchased. In order to get return

(Continued)

(Continued)

material authorization (RMA), the customers were asked to send a picture taken with the defective camera with issues with image quality. When received images were analyzed, it was observed that occasionally, customers had used PhotoShop or a similar application to edit the image to make the camera appear faulty and to qualify for replacement.

 Product Upgrade with Three Repairs

CASE STUDY

A global printer manufacturer applied a policy that the device will not be repaired but replaced if it comes to service for the third time. Many of the customers were aware of the policy and tried to abuse it. The aim was to get a replacement unit that was a newer model than the original one. Calling to a contact center to obtain RMA was required before the product could be sent for repair. Contact center agents had a checklist of questions that needed to be asked before authorization could be granted. Through the questions asked, it was obvious for the contact center agents that some of the customers tried to prove that the printer that had just been repaired for the second time was faulty.

Customers may also try to get fake products replaced by genuine products.

Replacement to Extend Product's Lifetime

Product replacement may also be used as a method to extend product's lifetime. Customer can, for example, claim that there is an intermittent failure in the product. Although the service is not able to repeat the issue, the product may be replaced. If the product in question has an average lifetime of three years and it is replaced with a new one when the product is 18 months old, the customer will enjoy a 4.5-year total expected lifetime.

Service Cost Avoidance

As customers need to pay for out-of-warranty repairs, customers use various methods to get products repaired at warranty provider's expense:

- Getting customer-damaged products repaired under warranty
- Use of goodwill
- Use of extended warranty

- Use of falsified proof of purchase
- Tampering with usage figures
- Use of cross-country differences in warranty policies
- Use of an other product item's warranty

Getting Customer-Damaged Products Repaired under Warranty

A large proportion of product failures is caused by customer damage—often by accident, which is not covered under warranty. Based on a study published by SquareTrade, Sands and Tseng (2009), two-thirds of iPhone failures were caused by customer damage. The damage may be caused by installation. The customer may drop the product or there may be a liquid damage or an electrical fault external to the product. The product may be used improperly—for example, an engine may be allowed to run at a very high speed or for an excessive period without a break. The product—for example, a motorcycle—can also be tuned, resulting in a defect in the product. Sometimes, the damage happens without the customer perceiving it. A liquid damage may be caused by condensation resulting from sudden temperature changes. In most cases, customer damage is not covered by statutory warranty. However, the customer may still try to have the product fixed under warranty, making the manufacturer carry the cost of the damage.

An example included in the AGMA and CompTIA (2013) study highlights the impact of counterfeit parts in the printer industry when unauthorized ink and toner products are used. "To save money, an end user may purchase delusive ink or toner, unaware that the viscosity and chemical composition of the ink can cause the printer to fail. The end user may then make a request for a warranty repair, but if properly diagnosed by the service provider (agent), it would be identified that the counterfeit part compromised the functionality of the printer, and therefore is not an OEM warranty defect in material or workmanship."

Using Goodwill

Once warranty has expired, customers may still try to have the product repaired free of charge. If the warranty has just expired, customer claim for warranty coverage can be justified and is often accepted for goodwill purposes. In such cases, the fault can have appeared already before the warranty expired. As days pass by, the interpretation becomes more controversial and it is harder for the customer to justify free-of-charge repair. If the controls are leaking, customer may get the product repaired long after the expiration of warranty.

▼ Getting Free Out-of-Warranty Service

Various tips for getting free service for out-of-warranty products are available in the Internet. Lifehacker.com website lists several such methods. One of the suggested tricks is the following: "Sometimes, it's all about the particular customer service rep you get. If you go into the store and they won't repair your device, try going again in a few days or going to a different branch down the street. If you try a few times, you might find someone who's a bit more generous and will try to get a repair approved for you. It isn't foolproof (if you call in, they're more likely to have a record of your request), but it can be handy if you get shot down the first time" (Gordon, 2014).

Using Extended Warranty

If the base warranty has expired, a fraudulent customer may purchase an extended warranty when the product breaks down. The repair can then be done free of charge right after the extended warranty comes into effect. This is possible if warranty provider's policy allows selling of extended warranty after the base warranty has expired without a prequalifying inspection.

Using Falsified Proof of Purchase

Customers may try to falsify the proof-of-purchase document to get the warranty period extended. Information in the original proof-of-purchase document may be changed, a fake proof-of-purchase document created from scratch, or one obtained from a sales point working in collusion with the customer as illustrated by the following two cases.

▼ Warranty Card with Open Date

A personal experience of one of the authors relates to the purchase of a Sony digital camera. The retail shop filled in the warranty card, entered model and serial number information, and stamped the card. However, as a customer service, the date-of-purchase field was left empty to allow the buyer to put in whatever date later on.

Proof of Purchase with Open Date

In a project done for a consumer products manufacturer, a pattern was identified. A large number of points of sale systematically gave a proof of purchase to the customers, but left the date field empty. The customers could then fill in a later purchase date if they wished and got the product covered under warranty.

Tampering with Usage Figures

For products sold with usage-based warranties, the usage figures can be reduced to qualify for warranty. Tampering with car odometers, for example, is commonplace, although mainly done to increase the resale value of the product. Another method is to use larger tires in cars. As a result, many of the cars show reduced odometer readings, which somewhat extends warranty coverage.

Using Cross-Country Differences in Warranty Policies

Utilization of cross-country differences is one way to get warranty coverage or warranty period extended. If a product has been bought in a country with no warranty coverage or one-year warranty period, the customer may take it to a country where a two-year warranty period is the norm. The customer can then try to have the product repaired at manufacturer's expense, although the product did not have any warranty or the original warranty has already expired.

Using Another Product Item's Warranty

Having bought multiple similar products at different times (e.g., LED light bulbs or tablets), the customer may try to utilize the warranty of the newest product to have the old one replaced. In a similar way, defective parts in an out-of-warranty product can be changed to an in-warranty product and claimed under warranty. If the equipment or the proof of purchase does not have a serial number or the parts used are not serial number tracked, it is hard to control whether the proof of purchase relates to the faulty product. The same applies to large installations that consist of multiple equipment installed at different times and that contain in-warranty and out-of-warranty products. In this situation, gaps in the warranty provider's entitlement process or data can be used to obtain service also for out-of-warranty products.

Extra Products or Earnings

Loopholes in replacement policies provide opportunities for customers to get parts and/or products for free. This is the case when manufacturers deliver spare parts or replacement units without requiring the original part or product to be returned at all or before the original part or product has been returned. Even when the manufacturer policy requires the original product to be returned afterward, the customer might intentionally forget it, trusting that the manufacturer does not bother to take further actions. Replacement fraud can be divided into:

1. Ad hoc replacement fraud
2. Systemic replacement fraud

Ad hoc replacement fraud is limited to an individual case or a small number of cases. In some cases, fraud can be systemic. Replacement part orders can be generated in large volume for products that never existed, as illustrated by the following case.

 Reselling Parts from Advance Replacement

CASE STUDY

A Massachusetts man defrauded Cisco Systems of more than US$15.4 million between 2003 and 2007. He used a loophole in Cisco's SMARTnet program that provides customers with technical support, including advance hardware replacement. Advance hardware replacement allows customers to obtain replacement equipment from Cisco immediately, without having to first return the broken part. He obtained parts with a list price of US$995 to US$25,000, which he then sold to resellers around the country. He generally did not return any parts to Cisco (Gomez, 2011).

Service-Level Improvement

Customers may also utilize valid warranty or service contracts to obtain faster service than is justified by the contract. Also, the service levels for different products may vary. Still, the customers may try to get products with better service levels than they have paid for, as illustrated by the following case.

CASE STUDY

Unjustified Next-Day Service Requested

Industrial electronics provider had over the years delivered equipment to the customer in diverse projects and with myriad after-sales arrangements, including maintenance service contracts with fully outsourced managed service responsibilities, products with base warranty coverage only, products with an extended warranty coverage, and contracts with a premium spare part management arrangement. In a warranty cost reduction engagement, we noticed that in many cases the customer called and demanded an expedited next day/same day delivery for a most urgent case, according to the highest level maintenance service contract, whereas the actual service level agreement for the particular product was two weeks.

SERVICE AGENT FRAUD

Service agent fraud is a key focus area of this book. Service agent fraud can be divided into two main categories: (i) against warranty provider and (ii) against customer. In each category there are several combinations of motivations and methods.

Service agent fraud can originate from different levels. An individual technician might replace too many parts to avoid diagnosing the root cause of the problem. The technician might also report unnecessary parts to allow him or her to sell those parts. Individual repair team or service center can generate extra claims to reach performance targets. On a company level, management may inflate costs to improve profits. In one case, the top management of a multinational service company organized training for its employees on ways to conduct fraud.

Not only fraud, but also other factors like competence issues result in increased warranty costs.

Warranty Provider as the Victim

Figure 6.4 shows the nine categories of service agent fraud with warranty provider as the victim. The motivation for five of them is to generate extra revenue and for the remaining four it is service cost avoidance. The methods that service agents use in each case are also shown in the figure. We now discuss in detail the methods used by service agents.

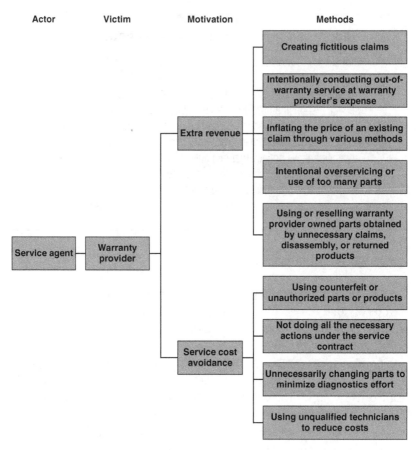

Figure 6.4 Service agent fraud categories (warranty provider as the victim)

Earning Extra Revenue from the Warranty Provider

Service agents can inflate their warranty billing and obtain additional revenue from the warranty provider through several methods, as shown in Figure 6.4. The methods applied by service agents continue to develop over time. This is illustrated by the following quote: "Fraud perpetrators share strategies, meaning weaknesses are further exploited through increasingly sophisticated techniques, exacerbating the problem and implications" (AGMA and PWC, 2009).

Creating Fictitious Claims

Fictitious claiming refers to scenarios where a warranty provider is invoiced for service events that never took place. Additional claims are included among real ones, thus inflating the number of claims. An obstacle for creation of fictitious claims is the warranty provider's requirement to report individual claims, serial number of the product, and data on the service event. There are several methods used by the service agents to create fictitious claims, as indicated in Figure 6.5. The different methods and techniques used are as follows:

1. *Individual claims are not reported.* The easiest case for a fraudster is the situation where only a monthly invoice summarizing the number of repairs done is required by the warranty provider. In other words, no breakdown showing individual service events and their details is required. In this situation, generation of claims is easy and warranty provider's ability to control their validity is close to zero. Surprisingly, some of the warranty providers accept monthly invoicing on summary level.

2. *Claims are not serial numbered.* It is also possible that repairs need to be individually reported, but serial numbers are not reported. This can be the case when:

   ▪ Products are not serial numbered.

   ▪ Reporting serial numbers with the claims is not required.

   Also in this case, creating fictitious claims is relatively easy, as serial numbers are not required.

3. *Validity of serial numbers is not controlled.* Warranty provider may not have registers on valid serial numbers. In this case, only the format of the serial number can be controlled, but there are no means to verify if the product with a given serial number was ever manufactured. This allows claims with whatever serial numbers to be created if they only meet the format requirements.

4. *Serial numbers are from own earlier repairs.* If the validity of the serial numbers is controlled, there are several alternative methods that service agents can use to obtain valid serial numbers.

   Service agents can use their earlier claims to generate new claims. One option is to wait a couple of months after sending the original claim and then resend the claim, as illustrated by the following case. The claims can be sent without any modifications with the original serial number, date, fault, and repair information. This allows the service agent to argue that the claims were sent by mistake. On the other hand, this

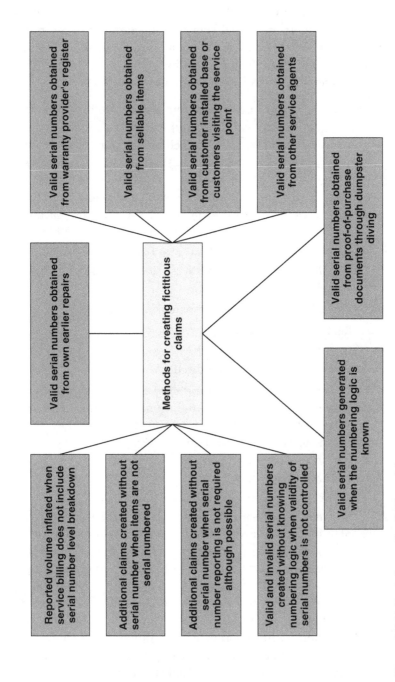

Figure 6.5 Methods for creating fictitious claims

makes detection of duplication relatively easy. Another option is to reuse the serial number but modify the other fields in the claim data.

CASE STUDY

▼ Resubmitting Already-Paid Claims

A service agent serving products of multiple major electronics manufacturers submitted roughly 10 000 repair claims to the same manufacturer three to four months after the original repairs were made and claimed. The service agent had already been compensated about 0.5 million euros for these claims. Later on, wider analysis of the service agent's claims was made and more similar cases were identified. The contract with the service agent was discontinued, the company was sued, and later it discontinued its operations.

5. *Serial numbers are from other service agents.* In addition to using their own claims, service agents can exchange serial numbers with each other. If claims made using these serial numbers are randomly distributed among other claims, the bogus claims can look like any other claims. A shortcoming in using serial numbers from earlier repairs is that the warranty period may come to an end unless the serial number is used relatively soon after the original repair. This again increases the risk of being caught.

6. *Serial numbers are generated when the numbering logic is known.*

Another method is simply to generate new serial numbers. If the service agent knows the serial number format and the logic used when creating serial numbers, new serial numbers can be created with ease. However, the service agents do not typically know the manufacturing volumes or customers and countries to which the products have been shipped. Consequently, it is possible to create out-of-range serial numbers that have never been manufactured or use serial numbers that have been sold to distant geographical locations.

If the service agent does not know the serial number logic, a safe bet is to create a serial number that is close to a known serial number. For example, if the company has repaired a product with serial number ABC00123, the subsequent serial number ABC00124 is probably also valid. The downside is that the serial numbers get clustered close to each other.

If the service agent has access to manufacturer's warranty registers, it can use the register to verify if the serial number exists and that the warranty is valid. This allows the service agent to avoid the use of nonexistent serial numbers.

7. *Serial numbers are from sellable products.* Those service agents who are also resellers of the products can obtain serial numbers from their sellable products. Serial numbers can, for example, be scanned before the products are sold and used when creating fictitious claims. Service agents can also work in collusion with the sales channel (e.g., retailers or distributors) and obtain serial numbers from them.

▼ Serial Numbers from Resellers' Registers

CASE STUDY

An Apple reseller in Australia, who was also acting as a service agent, was suspected of creating fictitious claims worth over $2.6 million. The scheme worked in the following way:

"If a consumer returned an Apple product for repair and it was not covered under warranty, the consumer was charged a fee for the replacement of parts and the work done in replacing the parts."

"The reseller then found the serial number of an Apple device that was covered under warranty and then submitted the same claim also to Apple. The claims were against customers that the reseller already had on their database" (Gracey, 2008).

---

8. *Serial numbers are from customer products.* Another method is to obtain serial numbers from products in the market. A technician visiting customer premises can scan the serial numbers from other similar products and later use them in claim reporting. Serial numbers may also be taken from the products being maintained or products that customers bring to service agent for diagnostics. Vehicle identification numbers can be obtained from vehicles found in the parking lot.

9. *Serial numbers are from the warranty provider's registers.* In some cases, service agents have access to the warranty provider's registers and can obtain serial numbers directly from the database. This provides a holy grail of serial numbers to be used in fictitious claims.

10. *Serial numbers are from waste bins.* Dumpster diving refers to obtaining discarded proof-of-purchase documents with serial numbers from point-of-sales' waste containers. Claims can then be created with serial numbers shown in the document. Furthermore, the proof-of-purchase document can be attached to the claim if required by the warranty provider.

Conducting Out-of-Warranty Repairs

Out-of-warranty service can be given and warranty provider charged due to sloppiness or unclear warranty status, with the intention to better serve or satisfy the customer, or to increase the service agent's revenue. Numerous ways are available to conduct out-of-warranty repairs:

- The service agent may intentionally or unintentionally fail to verify warranty validity and coverage.
- Customer-damaged products may be given free-of-charge service, although they should be paid by the customer.
- There can be double billing, where both the customer and warranty provider are charged, as illustrated by the following case.

▼ Double-Charging Out-of-Warranty Claims

CASE STUDY

An automotive manufacturer identified that several of its dealers were charging both the customer and the manufacturer for the same repair. This happened when mileage had reached the limit after which warranty expires. These dealers rightly charged the customer, but also sent a warranty service claim to the manufacturer with a somewhat lower mileage, making the repair look like a warranty repair.

- Refurbishment of worn-out products can be done, although not covered by warranty.
- Customer products with expired warranty may be given service for goodwill reasons. If the customer can justify the need for out-of-warranty repair, this way of working may be acceptable in an individual case. When the number of goodwill repairs grows, goodwill becomes overservice, and overservice becomes fraud.

- A manufacturer may authorize its service agents to do out-of-warranty repairs in case of epidemic failures. Often, such authorizations result in misuse and increase in the volume of out-of-warranty repairs across the board.

- Service agents, who are also resellers, may service the products in their sales stock. This activity can be justified, for example, if there is a quality issue with the products requiring action. However, if not authorized by the manufacturer, the activity becomes questionable, as seen in the following case.

 Warranty Claims for Products Not Yet Sold

CASE STUDY

A reseller of consumer electronics products conducted a software update for thousands of products in its stock. The manufacturer was charged for the activity. This activity was identified in statistical analysis. The CEO of the company was contacted and the issue settled. As the reseller was also an important customer of the manufacturer, the case was not taken into court.

Extended warranty contracts can also be abused to earn money from the warranty provider and at the same time from the customers, as illustrated by the following example (AGMA and PWC, 2009, pp. 11–12). "The abuse occurs when a service agent buys a small number of valid service contracts, then resells their own service agreement to several customers. Knowledgeable of product serial numbers or other identifiers, the service agent submits claims to the manufacturers for the covered products, for service work actually done on products sold without valid service plans. In the process, the revenue from service plans is passed from the manufacturer to the fraud-perpetrating service agent. Furthermore, the manufacturer often incurs additional costs due to the replacement of products that are not properly covered under contract."

Inflating the Price of an Existing Claim
The price of an individual claim can be inflated through multiple methods:

- Claiming multiple service activities within the same claim
- Adding new, fictitious cost items or cost components to an individual service activity
- Changing cost components to ones with a higher price

- Increasing quantities of existing cost components
- Increasing unit prices of cost components

Any of the cost drivers within the claim can be manipulated, as these five examples illustrate:

1. *Multiple service activities are claimed.* When a product comes in for repair, the service agent may claim that it has found multiple defects, and consequently conducts several repairs for the same product, even when this is not the case.

2. *New cost items or cost components are added.* Fictitious spare parts that were not used in reality can be included in the claim. The intention can be to obtain either monetary compensation or replacement parts from the warranty provider. In some cases, the volume of fraud can be excessive, as illustrated in the following case.

Excessive Number of Fictitious Claims

CASE STUDY

Data analysis showed that a service agent had been using thousands of highly expensive spare parts in its repair activities in electronics repairs. The number of spare parts used exceeded the number of products sold in that country. If the claims had been valid, the failure rate of the part in question would have exceeded 100 percent, although this service agent covered only a fraction of the products repaired in the country in question.

---

3. *Cost components are changed to ones with a higher price.* The labor charge of an individual service event may be inflated. The repair activity may be changed to an activity with higher labor compensation. Quite often, a strong bias toward higher-priced claims can be observed. It is not rare that 100 percent of the claims submitted by the service agents are in the highest possible price category, although only a fraction of the claims should be there. In a similar way, low-price spare parts can be changed to more expensive ones or to ones that match the manipulated repair activity.

4. *Reported quantity of existing cost components is inflated.* Reported quantities of cost components can be manipulated. More hours can be reported than were actually needed. Working time can be rounded up even when this is not permitted by the contract. In some cases, spare parts quantities can be changed. Field

service can report inflated mileage to obtain compensation for longer distance than actually traveled, as illustrated in the following case.

▼ Mileage Overcharging

CASE STUDY

A countrywide in-house field service network serving electromechanical equipment used in points of sale included dozens of technicians. The technicians used their own cars to travel on-site and received compensation for the mileage driven. When the company started using a fleet of its own cars instead, the average mileage driven dropped by 20 percent overnight. The technicians had either inflated the mileage driven or used suboptimal and longer routes.

▼ Excess Use of Lubricants

CASE STUDY

A compressor manufacturer has a network of service agents. As a part of warranty service, service agents need to use high-cost lubricants. The manufacturer noticed reporting of excessive lubricant usage in warranty claims. While only 1 liter of lubricant should have been needed, claimed quantities of 5 to 10 liters were observed. This significantly increased service cost.

---

5. *Unit prices increased.* Although the cost items included in a claim can be correct, the service agents can apply inflated prices within the claims or in the invoice. This is possible when service-agent-reported prices are used instead of using unit prices from warranty provider's registers, as in the following case.

▼ Inflated Part Pricing

CASE STUDY

A service agent sent a monthly claim worth 130,000 euros to a consumer products manufacturer. When the claims were analyzed, it was noticed that all the claims were as they should be, with one exception. The price of one single spare part was incorrectly declared, increasing the cost almost a hundredfold. Without this deviation, the monthly invoice would have been only 100,000 euros.

In such a situation, the service agent may state that the wrong price was simply a typing error and avoid accusations of fraud unless the occurrence of such errors is excessive.

One method is to utilize changes in price lists. For example, if spare parts prices are periodically updated, the service agent can continue to use the old prices if they are higher and claim to be using parts purchased before the price change. This is possible when transition rules in case of price changes are not clearly defined.

We have also seen cases where service agents have systematically used inconsistent spare part prices and the charged prices have been up to five times the actual price. This is possible if the reported prices are not properly controlled.

Overservicing or Using Too Many Parts

Besides including fictitious cost items or inflating prices used within existing claims, the claim price can also be inflated by including costs that did incur in reality. This can be done, for example, by doing more work and changing more parts than is necessary to get the immediate problem fixed.

- A part may be changed to prevent future failure, although there is no direct need to change it.
- The work may be done as an emergency repair in a few hours, although the customer has paid for a service with longer response time.

As a result, higher costs can be charged from the warranty provider. In these cases, the intent may have been to serve the customer, to increase service agent's own revenue, or both.

 Excessive Parts Usage

CASE STUDY

A government-owned service point maintained and repaired military vehicles. The technicians were instructed to conduct excessive replacement of parts when a vehicle was brought to service. Although there was no immediate financial benefit for the technicians, the service point's management wanted to justify its existence and keep its staff busy.

Using or Reselling Warranty Provider–Owned Parts

When a service agent replaces a defective product, the warranty provider may request the service agent to stock the product in its premises and possibly to return it to the warranty provider later on. Service agents may disassemble the products to obtain spare parts, as exhibited by the following case. These parts can then be sold to third parties or used in repairs and charged to the warranty provider or the customers.

 Cannibalizing Returned Products

CASE STUDY

An electronics manufacturer was piloting a new recycle/reuse concept. As a part of that, it started collecting defective products that had been replaced by a new one to the customer. When the first batch of 10,000 products was received, it became clear that the same reuse strategy had been fully utilized by the service agents already. Each product had been practically disassembled and every part with any value had been removed, leaving only the shell, half-empty circuit boards, and broken parts.

Service Cost Avoidance

Service agents can reduce their costs by not following the service guidelines. At the same time, the warranty provider can be charged the full price as if required procedures were being followed.

Using Counterfeit or Unauthorized Parts or Products

Unauthorized parts or replacement products such as cheaper counterfeit parts, 3D printed parts, used parts or products or parts cannibalized from unrepairable products, or genuine parts that were supposed to be scrapped due to not passing quality controls, can be used in repair while charging the cost of a genuine part or product to the warranty provider. If the warranty provider follows a policy that requires purchase of a genuine spare part against each claimed spare part, the genuine parts can be sold to third parties while unauthorized parts are used in the repairs.

Not Doing All the Necessary Actions under the Service Contract

Costs can be avoided by skipping some of the required service activities defined in the service procedures. For example:

- Only the immediate problem is fixed without diagnosing the product for other problems.
- Product may not be calibrated or tested after the repair.
- Some of the parts that are supposed to be changed may not be changed.

While required service activities are skipped, the warranty provider can still be billed a full charge.

Unnecessarily Changing Parts to Minimize Diagnostics Effort

Effort can also be reduced by excessive parts usage. For example, by replacing a module, a more laborious diagnostics and repair by soldering can be avoided. By doing this, a service organization or an individual technician may reduce his or her own workload while using too many parts. A technician may, for example, know that replacing four particular parts will fix the problem in 90 percent of cases and do that rather than conduct any further diagnostics. In most cases, replacing only one faulty part would fix the problem.

Unnecessary Change of Expensive Parts

CASE STUDY

On average, an expensive display module needed to be changed in 1 percent of the repairs conducted for a consumer electronics product. However, data analysis revealed that one technician in one service company changed the same part in 70 percent of his repairs. Earlier, there had been an epidemic failure with the displays. The technician continued to change the displays long after the issue had been resolved.

Using Unqualified Technicians to Reduce Costs

Service agents may intentionally use technicians who are not certified to work with the product in question to save costs. As a result, product may be damaged or the original problem not be solved.

If the first repair has been done poorly, the product may come back to service shortly after it was first repaired, while the fault is the same as on the first time. Even when there is a different fault, the question is whether the service agent should have noticed and fixed the fault during the first repair or whether the damage has been caused by the first repair.

Customer as the Victim

Earning Extra Revenue from the Customer

Service agents can obtain extra revenue not only from the warranty provider but also at the expense of the customer. Figure 6.6 shows the five categories of service agent fraud. The motivation in each of them is to generate extra revenue. The methods that service agents use in each case are also shown in the figure. We now discuss in detail the methods used.

Overselling Extended Warranties

Service agents can oversell extended warranties with no or limited benefit to the customer. Sales of extended warranties are discussed further in the section covering warranty provider fraud.

Selling Nonexistent Extended Warranties

Also, nonexisting warranties can be sold and its impact is the same as the overselling of extended warranties

Charging the Customer for In-Warranty Service

One trick used by the fraudulent service agents is to charge both the customer and the warranty provider. If the product is still under warranty, a legitimate service claim can be submitted to the warranty provider while the customer is convinced to believe that the product is not covered by warranty, allowing both the customer and the warranty provider to be charged for the same repair. This is possible, for example, in situations when the warranty period is close to expiration and the customer is not sure if the product is still covered. The same applies to situations where the customer cannot prove that his or her product is under warranty. The service agent can use other means to check warranty status, such as using manufacturer's warranty registers. Even when the warranty has expired, the service agent can charge both the customer and the manufacturer if the manufacturer does not properly control warranty validity. An additional method is to tell the customer that the defect has been caused by the customer and the warranty is void.

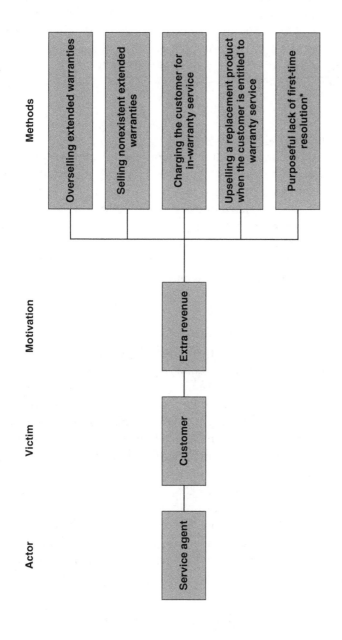

Figure 6.6 Service agent fraud categories (customer as the victim)

161

Upselling a Replacement Product

If the service agent is the seller of the products, the customer can be upsold a similar or better replacement product, although the warranty would still be valid. This is fine if the customer is fully aware of the situation. However, if an ill-informed customer is made to believe that the warranty is not valid or is frightened with high diagnostics costs in case of no-fault-found or customer damage, this practice becomes questionable.

Purposeful Lack of First-Time Resolution

Service can also be done intentionally poorly, requiring the customer to visit the service point multiple times. A single defect can, for example, be diagnosed on the first visit and fixed on the second one, or multiple defects can be fixed one at a time. This can be the case, for example, when the contract between the service agent and warranty provider results in higher compensation for multiple versus single repairs. The customer suffers the loss of time and effort while the warranty provider ends up with higher costs.

SALES CHANNEL FRAUD

Fraud done by the sales channel partly overlaps with the fraud done by the service agents. This is explained by the nature of operations. Both points of sale and service centers act as contact points for the customers. Distributors or dealers can act both as sellers and service agents. This is a typical case, for example, in the automotive industry. Even when the sales channel is not providing service, customers may return products to the sales channel to be replaced or forwarded to an authorized service center for repair.

Figure 6.7 shows the seven categories of sales channel fraud. In three of them the victim is customer and for the remaining four it is the warranty provider. As before, the motivations are different, and these are shown in the figure along with the methods used by the service channel. We now discuss in detail the methods used by service channel.

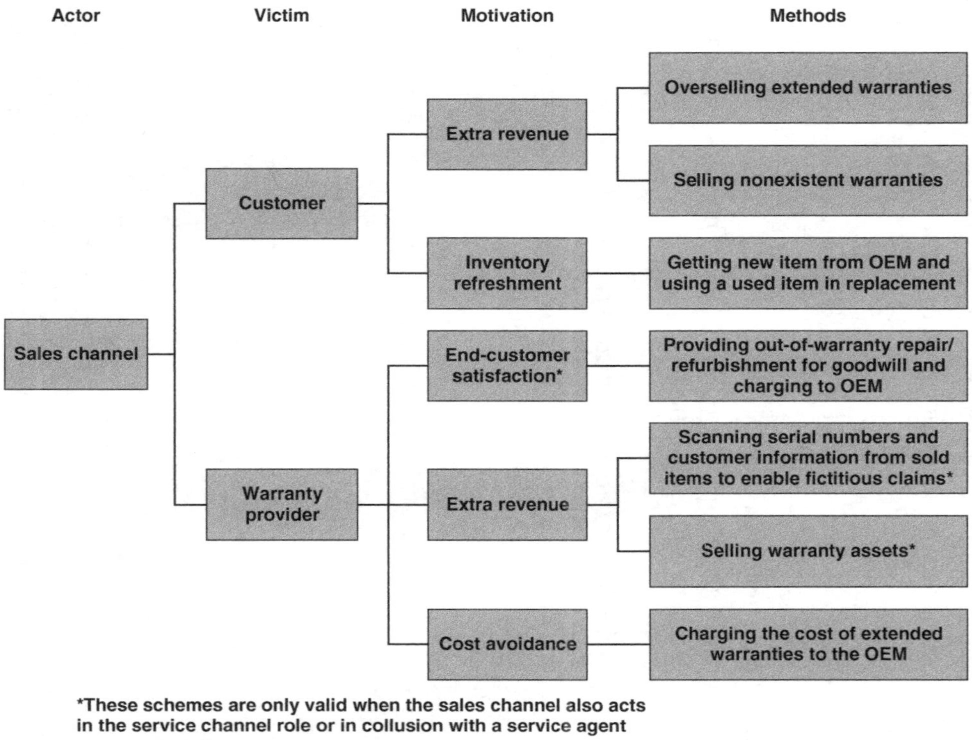
Actor
Victim
Motivation
Methods
Sales channel
Customer
Warranty provider
Extra revenue
Inventory refreshment
End-customer satisfaction*
Extra revenue
Cost avoidance
Overselling extended warranties
Selling nonexistent warranties
Getting new item from OEM and using a used item in replacement
Providing out-of-warranty repair/ refurbishment for goodwill and charging to OEM
Scanning serial numbers and customer information from sold items to enable fictitious claims*
Selling warranty assets*
Charging the cost of extended warranties to the OEM
*These schemes are only valid when the sales channel also acts in the service channel role or in collusion with a service agent

Figure 6.7 Sales channel fraud categories (customers and warranty provider as the victims)

Customer as the Victim

Extra Revenue

Overselling Extended Warranties

Sales channel can act as or represent the warranty provider when selling extended warranties to customers. The sales of extended warranties can be highly profitable for both the sales channel and the warranty provider. As a result, customers can be sold extended warranty contracts with limited value to them. Fraud related to extended warranties is covered in detail under the section on warranty provider fraud.

Selling Nonexistent Warranties

Also, nonexisting warranties can be sold and its impact is the same as the overselling of extended warranties.

Inventory Refreshment through Replacement Fraud

Replacement fraud can be done to renew products in the inventory. This can happen when a retailer has obsolete products in its warehouse. If these are claimed to be faulty, the warranty provider may in some cases replace them with a newer model. This allows the retailer to increase the value of its sales stock, as happened in the following case.

 Refreshing Sales Inventory

CASE STUDY

One of the authors experienced the following case when returning a set of faulty power line Ethernet adapters to a point of sale. Later on, after contacting the warranty provider, the point of sales told the author that they had received replacement units and gave them to the author. However, these adaptors did not work, either. At this point, the author contacted the warranty provider directly. The author was told that the model in question is unreliable and is replaced by a newer model in case of issues. Also, newer units had been delivered to the point of sale. It appeared that the point of sale kept the newer units itself and gave out old products from its stock as a replacement.

Warranty Provider as the Victim

End Customer Satisfaction through Out-of-Warranty Service

Sales channel may do goodwill service or refurbishment at warranty provider's expense. The channel may also fail to do proper entitlement. Products with expired warranty or products damaged by the customer may be let through to service chain. Often, this is done for goodwill purposes. Customers are satisfied with the retailer and the warranty provider pays.

Not all goodwill service is fraud. A global heavy industrial equipment manufacturer has instructed all its dealers to invite the customers to a warranty service just before the expiry of the warranty. Their main motivation is to avoid the unpleasant situations where the customer has a breakdown shortly after the warranty expiration.

Extra Revenue

Creating Fictitious Claims

Sales channel can take serial numbers from products within its stock to create fictitious claims in collusion with an in-house or external service agent. This case was discussed more in detail under the section on service agent fraud.

One form of fictitious claims is bogus product replacements. If the warranty provider does not require the original products to be returned for verification, the retailer may be able to get monetary compensation or replacement units for unnecessary or nonexistent replacements. Based on our experience, the volume of replacement fraud can be excessive and even as high as the volume of real replacements. When preventive methods have been implemented, the volume of replacements has often dropped significantly.

Selling Warranty Assets

Sales channel may also sell various assets given by the warranty provider for warranty purposes instead of using them for warranty service. This is illustrated by the following example. Distributors may be given the warranty obligation for a particular geographical area. To cover the cost of warranty, manufacturers can give the distributors extra products, such as extra 2 percent swap stock to replace the products, which are coming back with a warranty claim from the customer. What often happens is that the distributors sell the additional swap stock at market price. When customers come with claims, distributors hand over any replacement product, independent of model and brand, if it only equals the value. By doing so they are maximizing their revenue by selling attractive devices and using excess stock for warranty instead. This may be acceptable for the customer, but as the distributors are representing the manufacturer they are harming brand reputation and loyalty, which is fraudulent as well.

Cost Avoidance through Charging the Cost of Extended Warranty from the OEM

Out-of-warranty service can also relate to cost avoidance. Sales channel may offer better warranty than what is provided by the manufacturer base warranty. This enhanced warranty can be offered to all customers purchasing a particular product or sold as an extended warranty. Sales channel warranty offering may, for example, have a longer duration than the manufacturer base warranty or even cover service for customer-damaged products that is not typically covered by manufacturer warranty. In such cases, the sales channel may try to charge the manufacturer also for those service events that are not covered by the original manufacturer warranty to reduce its own warranty servicing costs.

WARRANTY ADMINISTRATOR FRAUD

Warranty administrators are in control of service agents and their claims. They make decisions on claims to be approved and rejected and thus determine the value of the payment to be made to the service agent within the boundaries set by the warranty provider. Warranty administrators can also set up vendor master data and price data as the basis for service agent compensation. They can also make decisions to allow customers a refund, replacement, or repair as a part of the RMA process. As representatives of the warranty provider, warranty administrators have the power to make decisions with financial implications. This power can also be abused.

Figure 6.8 shows the four categories of warranty administrator fraud. The motivation for all is extra revenue. The methods that service agents use in each case are also shown in the figure. We now discuss in detail the methods used by warranty administrators.

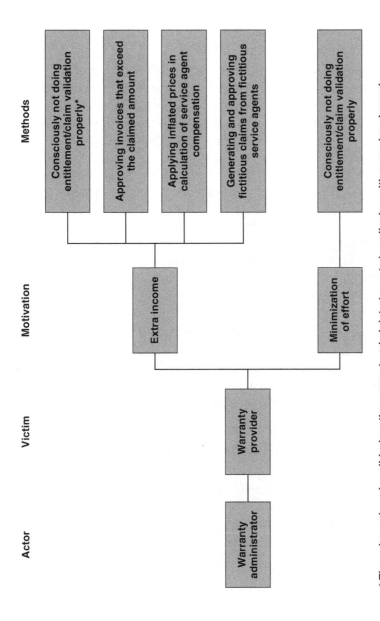

Figure 6.8 Warranty administrator fraud categories (warranty provider as the victim)

Methods

Consciously not doing entitlement/claim validation properly*

Approving invoices that exceed the claimed amount

Applying inflated prices in calculation of service agent compensation

Generating and approving fictitious claims from fictitious service agents

Consciously not doing entitlement/claim validation properly

Motivation

Extra income

Minimization of effort

Victim

Warranty provider

Actor

Warranty administrator

* The scheme is only valid when the warranty administrator acts in collusion with a service channel

Extra Income

Warranty administrators can occasionally conduct fraud individually although our understanding is that the majority of the fraud in this category takes place in collusion with service agents or customers, such as after accepting a kickback or bribe.

Consciously Not Doing Entitlement and Claim Validation Properly

Warranty administrators can intentionally fail to follow warranty control procedures. When working in collusion with a customer or a service agent, they can then share the financial benefit with these parties.

One method is to give RMA for a fictional product helping a customer to obtain a replacement product even when there is no original product to be returned. This newly obtained product can then be sold, providing earnings to be shared by the customer and the warranty administrator.

Another method is to approve claims that should be rejected in claim validation. A less visible method is to fail to conduct further statistical analysis, audits, or further controls for selected service agents.

Approving Invoices that Exceed Claimed Amount

Warranty service claims submitted by and payments made to a service agent are not necessarily reconciled. Warranty administrator can work in collusion with a service agent to approve invoices that exceed the claimed amount. The following case illustrates this method of fraud.

 Validation-Invoicing Inconsistency

CASE STUDY

A major service agent submitted large volumes of warranty claims to a consumer products manufacturer following a monthly reporting cycle. Warranty administrators validated these claims following warranty provider's procedures. Large proportions of the claims were found invalid and rejected. However, the invoice received from the service agent included all submitted claims, even the ones that had been rejected. The warranty provider had paid the invoice in full for a long time and suffered a major excess cost.

Errors and sloppy processes can explain part of such mismatches, but fraud can also be involved.

Applying Inflated Prices in Calculation of Service Agent Compensation

Another method is to work in collusion with a service agent and manipulate prices in the warranty provider's systems, resulting in inflated payments to the service agent. This works when the warranty provider applies self-billing and uses its system to calculate compensation for the service agent. This method can also be used to prevent rejection of service agent claims with wrong prices.

Generating and Approving Fictitious Claims

One method is to set up a nonexistent service company within the warranty provider's systems and generate fictitious claims and payments for this company. If sufficient controls are not in place, this may go unnoticed in a global company with thousands of service agents within its service network.

Minimization of Effort

Consciously Not Doing Entitlement and Claim Validation Properly

In addition to seeking financial benefits, warranty administrators can intentionally fail to follow warranty control procedures to reduce personal work load. We have seen cases where the warranty administrators simply mass-approve warranty service claims on an ongoing basis instead of spending hours in doing thorough validation.

Although the underlying reason can be pure laziness, this behavior can also be explained by excessive workload combined with lack of awareness of the possibility of fraud.

WARRANTY PROVIDER FRAUD

Although warranty provider is typically considered as a victim of fraud, it can also be the party conducting direct fraud or behaving unethically. The fraud can be done (i) by the company at large or (ii) by an individual or a group of individuals within the company. While a company is typically acting by itself to increase its revenues or save its costs, individuals are mostly working with other parties to seek personal gain.

Figure 6.9 shows the seven categories of warranty provider fraud. The victims for four categories are customers, product lines being the victim for two and part supplier and government/shareholders being

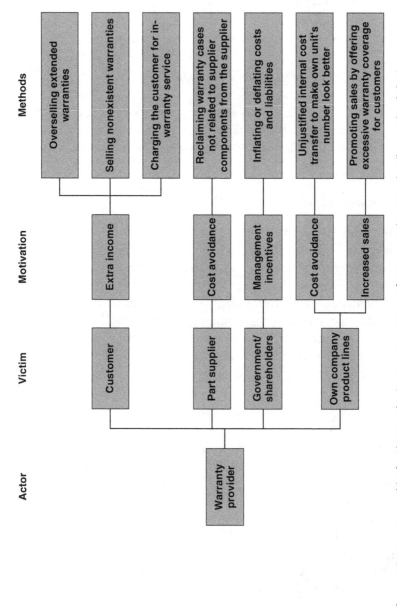

Figure 6.9 Warranty provider fraud categories (customers, part manufacturers, and own product lines as the victims)

the victims for one category each. As before, the motivations are different, and these are shown in Figure 6.9, along with the methods used by the service channel. We now discuss in detail the methods used by service channel for each category.

End-Customer as the Victim

Extra Income

Overselling Extended Warranties

Sales of extended warranties provide several opportunities for fraud. There are numerous examples of third-party companies who sell extended warranties and then go bankrupt. As a result, the customer is left without the warranty coverage that has been paid for. Another questionable practice is to sell an extended warranty and fail to mention that the standard warranty would provide almost similar coverage. A three-year extended warranty can be sold in a region with two-year statutory warranty in practice, offering only one additional year of warranty coverage. Terms and conditions within the extended warranty contracts may significantly differ from the terms in the original base warranty providing only a limited coverage for the customer. As a result, the customer pays an excessive price for the additional coverage.

False or Misleading Extended Warranty Advertising

CASE STUDY

An Australian warranty provider sent out 48,214 letters to purchasers of a dishwasher that had a two-year warranty. The letter stated, "Your dishwasher is now a year old, which means you have 12 months remaining—after that, your appliance won't be protected against repair costs." The letter then offered, for a fee, an extended two-year warranty on top of the original warranty.

However, under Australian consumer law, consumers may be entitled to a repair, replacement, or refund on a product beyond the time period covered by the manufacturer's warranty if the product suffered "major failure" or is not of "acceptable quality."

In court, the statement was ruled to be "false and misleading and the making of it was conduct that was misleading and deceptive." Both the warranty provider and white goods company were fined AUD (Australian dollars) 200,000 (Cauchi, 2014).

Selling of Nonexistent Warranty Service

Failing to follow contractual commitments is another form of fraud or questionable behavior. Extended warranty providers may fail to provide any service at all or try to limit service coverage to a minimum as illustrated by this case.

▼ Aggressive Denial of Customer Claims

CASE STUDY

Magoo's Automotive Consultants Inc. among other services inspects vehicles on behalf of warranty provider before they are repaired. "When I got into this business," Magoo said, "there were a whole bunch of extended service plans out there that were not only duping the consumers by selling them product that they had no intention of paying claims on, but then they would use us inspectors to go inspect the vehicles so they could deny them. And then they wouldn't even pay us!" (*Warranty Week*, Oct. 5, 2004).

Charging the Customer for In-Warranty Service

Warranty providers may also fail to follow statutory requirements. There are well-known manufacturers, who act in ways that are in conflict with local legislation. An example is to limit warranty coverage within the European Union to one year while local legislation requires a two-year warranty. In this case, customers are only informed about the one-year warranty and charged for repairs done in the second year. If the customer complains, they may be granted free repairs in the second year.

Other examples include voiding warranty when a car has been serviced by an independent repair shop or requiring customers to return product to warranty service in person or returning product in its original sales packaging.

Another case is the so-called secret warranty. In the automotive context, Ditlow and Gold (1993) define this as a multibillion-dollar consumer abuse that refers to the practice to pay for repair of defects not covered by the original factory warranty (e.g., due to defects in material or workmanship that appear only after expiration of the written warranty). The manufacturers may call this a "policy adjustment," "goodwill program," or "extended warranty."[4]

Secret warranties share three elements: (1) The existence of a common defect recognized by the manufacturer; (2) the establishment of a policy to pay for all or part of the cost of repair of the defect beyond the terms of the express factory warranty; and (3) the failure of the manufacturer to directly notify vehicle owners about the "warranty" or the policy adjustment. Since the manufacturer does not directly notify vehicle owners, only the consumer who complains loudly enough gets covered by the secret warranty (Ditlow and Gold, 1993). According to the US-based Center for Auto Safety, at any time over 500 secret warranties exist for all auto companies. In 1987, the Center for Auto Safety (CAS) identified 10 exemplary secret warranties covering 30 million vehicles and US$3 billion in repair costs (Center for Auto Safety, 2015).

Part Supplier as the Victim

Cost Avoidance

Reclaiming Warranty Costs Not Related to Supplier's Parts

Manufacturers often recover part of the warranty costs from their part suppliers (i.e., part distributors or part manufacturers). This is a normal and acceptable practice. However, recovery can become excessive.

The warranty provider can be sloppy and fail to validate claims, as the supplier will pay the costs anyhow. The situation is difficult from a supplier's point of view as the visibility to what has actually happened to the products is limited or nonexistent. A manufacturer may utilize its purchasing power and force the part manufacturer to compensate warranty claims where the culpability of the supplier is unclear. As a result, the supplier can end up paying for costs that should have been covered by the manufacturer or the customer.

Government and/or Shareholders as the Victims

Warranty expenses can be used for financial statement manipulation. The target of manipulation can be to either falsely decrease or increase profits. As a result government may lose tax revenue or shareholders receive misguided information about company profitability. One of the beneficiaries of such schemes can be a company's management, if its incentives are linked with the result. In addition to maximizing short-term results, management may want to concentrate all the costs into one period, making company's future prospects look better.

Inflating or Deflating Costs and Liabilities

Warranty accruals are a reasonable estimation of future warranty costs. Uncertain nature of these costs provides an opportunity to inflate or deflate their value. Undervaluation of accrued warranty costs, for example, allows short-term profits to be inflated.

There are also opportunities to manipulate realized warranty costs. Current period's warranty expenses can be shifted to a later period, for example, by utilizing the delays in repair and claim reporting, or the company may fail to write down the value of unrepairable equipment, violating accounting standards.

Own Product Lines as the Victim

The victim of warranty fraud and other questionable behavior can also be another function within warranty provider's own organization through cost transfer mechanisms. This applies especially to the cases where the warranty provider is also the manufacturer of the products.

Cost Avoidance through Unjustified Cost Transfer

Manufacturers often have an internal policy where warranty costs are not covered by sales or country organizations but by the product lines instead. This provides an opportunity for the sales or country organizations to tag nonwarranty costs as warranty costs. These can then be charged from the product lines, making the misbehaving organization's figures look better. In such a case, individuals may obtain monetary benefits if bonuses are linked with the organization's results.

 Inflated Service Effort

CASE STUDY

The in-house services organization within a global industrial equipment manufacturer has the global responsibility for warranty service, getting the reimbursement for the cost from the product lines. "It is an internally sensitive subject, but we have noticed that in certain countries the hours spent per certain specific warranty repair activities are double compared with the global average. Also, the hourly cost rate is high, although the general cost levels in those countries may be low. With this people try to manipulate their own KPIs and show better results. The impact is a lot of internal work and lack of trust between the units."

Increasing Sales through Abuse of Warranty Offering

Sales organization can make unprofitable contracts with their customers by leveraging shortcomings in internal policies and accounting practices. The sales organization may win deals through offering extended warranty periods or maintenance contracts with too tight service levels for the products. If the cost of these arrangements is not acknowledged when assessing sales organization's performance and the profitability of the deal, the sales can get their bonuses while the product lines carry the costs. Sales organization can also leverage internal cost transfer to satisfy its customers. It can allow questionable repairs to be covered under warranty, again at the expense of the product line.

NOTES

1. In the last case, the bank's data analysis system detected the fraud as it occurred, the credit card was deactivated, a new one was issued (the card was never stolen; it remained unclear how the extra withdrawals/purchases had taken place), and all additional deductions were refunded.
2. Warranty administrator can also be understood as a person who works for service agent and, for example, controls the quality of claims being submitted, submits the claims to warranty providers, and monitors that the service agent gets paid for the work done.
3. Buyer's remorse refers to the customer's sense of regret after making a purchase. Legislation or retailer policy may allow the product to be returned without a reason during a short period after the purchase.
4. US Federal Transit Administration (FTA) has certain requirements in relation to critical components and can issue a recall due to design or manufacturing problem. Often, instead of recall, FTA might say that the component needs to be covered for a specified time, which can be much higher than the original warranty duration. This is referred to as secret or hidden warranties.

CHAPTER 7

Warranty Control Framework

We discussed the different actors responsible for warranty fraud and the different fraud categories in Chapter 6. An exhaustive list of them cannot be made, because there can always be new actors and new and unknown methods of warranty fraud. However, we have aimed to cover the most common actors and most common scenarios. Due to the diversity of the scenarios, it is very difficult to develop a one-size-fits-all tool or approach to tackle warranty fraud once and for all. A combination of approaches, tools, and methods is required to detect and prevent warranty fraud. We call this combination the warranty control framework. Having a proper warranty control framework not only improves fraud detection and prevention, but also provides transparency and cost control over warranty management as a whole.

We confine our attention to frauds where the warranty provider is the victim and focus on customer and service agents as the actors of fraud. The framework is composed of four key elements, with two of them having more than one subelement, as shown in Figure 7.1. The four key elements are:

Contracts

This defines the interaction between the warranty provider and the customer, the service agent and other parties in the warranty chain, and the rights and duties of each of them. Contractual rules are the basis for customer claim entitlement and service claim validation.

Transaction controls

These include processes and methods for handling customer warranty claims and warranty service claims, from the customer issue through servicing and financial settlement of the claim. The focus is on customer warranty entitlement, service agent claim validation, and material returns control for defective items.

Analytics

They assist in identifying claims with high likelihood of being unjustified, whether through fraud, abuse, or sloppy processes, and

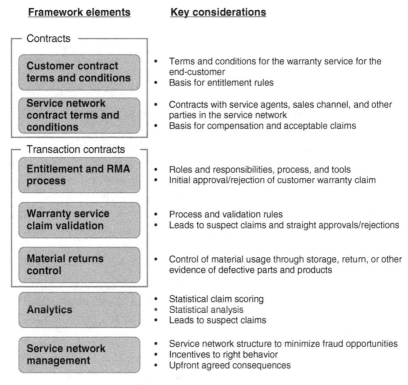

Figure 7.1 Warranty control framework

to identify service agents and/or customers with high propensity to commit fraud.

Service network management

This involves setting up a network structure that minimizes fraud opportunities, incentivizes service agents to right behavior, and provides predefined and clear procedures on actions taken if fraud is detected.

Figure 7.1 lists the key considerations for the various elements. This chapter discusses the key elements and the key considerations in general. Chapters 8 to 10 deal with the details of the framework for controlling customer, service agent, and other parties as the actors, respectively.

CONTRACTS

Having the right contract terms and conditions sets the rules of the game between the warranty provider and the customers and the service agents.

Customer Contract Terms and Conditions

Customer warranty terms and conditions define the warranty service that the customer is entitled to under each warranty offering. It needs to be clear for each warranty offering, when warranty is valid and when it is not, what service and service level the customer is entitled to, and what compensation the warranty provider gets for the service, if any. These rules need to be articulated in a way that all parties (customer, warranty provider, service agent) have the same interpretation of the warranty coverage for every product and failure. The terms and conditions provide a contractual basis for rejecting a customer claim for warranty service when the customer is not entitled to it. Practical rules and checks used in the entitlement process are derived from the terms and conditions in the customer contract.

Service Network Contract Terms and Conditions

Service agent rules and contracts provide a clear definition of terms and conditions for warranty servicing the service agent does on behalf of the warranty provider. The following questions should be addressed:

- What are the services that the service agent is authorized to do?
- How does the service agent report the service activities, and how is the agent compensated for the work?
- In which cases does the warranty provider have the right to reject warranty service claims?
- In which cases is a material return or on-site inspection required for the defective parts/products?
- When is a product considered to be beyond economic repair? What is done with these products?
- What are the circumstances under which extra goodwill refurbishment or other additional service can be offered to the customer?

- When can the service agent claim those expenses back from the warranty provider, and when does the agent need to cover the cost? This is especially relevant in cases where the service agent is also a sales channel partner to the warranty provider.

In a similar way, the contracts with the sales channel need to cover the situation where the sales channel is the contact point for the customer with a product issue. This is discussed in more detail in Chapter 10.

TRANSACTION CONTROLS

It is important to have customer self-help support, such as built-in diagnostics (as part of design), online or over-the-air software updates, problem-solving checklists, and answers to frequently asked questions. This can reduce customer warranty claims through appropriate customer actions to fix the problem instead of the customer exercising a claim for service.

Should a claim result, the transaction controls define the controls to cover the process from the customer issue through servicing and financial settlement. The main control processes for warranty transactions are:

- Entitlement and RMA process
- Warranty service claim validation
- Material returns control

Entitlement and RMA Process

The customer entitlement and RMA process defines the steps of customer entitlement and the controls that are needed before the actual service work can commence. The entitlement rules used within these processes are based on the warranty contracts with the customers. A number of questions need to be answered when designing the process.

- How is warranty status determined?
- In which cases does the customer need an authorization from the warranty provider?
- Is an inspection needed?
- Is there a return materials code required from the call center or an online service?

■ What are the requirements for a proof-of-purchase document?

■ Does the installed base include blacklist information on stolen or black-market products?

Before service execution or as a part of it, a physical inspection of the defective item is done. Is there a failure or does the product actually work (no-fault-found check)? Has the product been used in a proper way, or is the damage due to customer negligence and/or misuse? Is the cause of the failure the same that the customer claims it to be? Does the warranty cover the failure in question?

Warranty Service Claim Validation

The second control process for warranty transactions is claim validation, controlling warranty service claims from service agents and sales channel. Key considerations are claim validation process and rules.

The claim validation process defines the overall approach to claim validation:

■ How much manual validation needs to be done?

■ Are all claims validated, or is there a sample-based approach?

■ Can parts of the validation activities be moved upstream and combined with customer entitlement?

Validation rules define the basis on which service agent and sales channel claims are approved or rejected:

■ How is it verified that the service agent and sales channel claims are valid, based on valid customer warranty claims?

■ How is it confirmed that the right service activities and the right spare parts are provided at the right price?

Real-time transparency and a well-defined warranty data model are needed to support validation and analytics so that deviations and anomalies can be highlighted and potential fraud cases detected.

Material Returns Control

The third main control process for warranty transactions is material returns control. It defines the requirements for local storage of defective materials for service agents and sales channel and requirements for their return for service agents, sales channel, and customers.

Some companies have a strict policy that the service agents and sales channel need to return all defective items when the cost of the part or product exceeds a defined threshold. However, they do not necessarily reconcile the returned materials with the claimed defective parts. The material returns control process defines which materials need to be stored or returned, how reconciliation is done, and what happens with the missing defective parts. The sequence of activities must be clearly defined. Are the spare parts compensated before or after the defective parts have been received? If after, is a refund expected, or are the missing returns deducted from subsequent payments?

Getting defective parts/products back from remote locations is not always feasible. In these cases, other mechanisms to verify the existence of the defect should be implemented (e.g., photographs sent with the claim, obligation for the service agent to store the parts for a certain period and sample checks on these, a trusted third party making the local sample checks).

ANALYTICS

With Bill Roberts, SAS Institute

In Chapter 5, we discussed the importance of warranty data collected in different phases of the warranty servicing process and analytics as a part of a warranty management system, playing a major role in warranty fraud management. In this section, we describe general analytics methods for warranty fraud detection. In Chapters 8, 9, and 10, we will discuss specific analytics methods to detect customer and service agent frauds and fraud by other parties directed at the warranty provider.

It is clear that any service agent can generate a fake claim, which is technically and content-wise correct and indistinguishable from a valid claim by looking at the one individual claim only. Analytics can be used as a tool to identify customer warranty claims and service agent claims that have a high probability of being incorrect, whether through fraud, waste, or abuse. When used in conjunction with automated claims processing, analytics can enable the identification of suspicious claims and target auditing efforts and specific actions within specific service agents. Unlike the warranty business rules set in the contract, analytical models are more difficult to be mastered by service agents. In fact, it is the other way around—advanced analytics can learn from the service agents, evolving to meet the changing ways a warranty system can be compromised.

There is no single analytic approach that detects all fraud. Because of the scope of the problem, including the sheer number of claims submitted, the large number of ways fraud is committed, and the fact that those who conduct fraud are constantly changing and learning, a combination of analytic approaches is most effective. This *hybrid analytic approach* includes business rules, and adds anomaly detection, advanced analytics including predictive models, and social network analysis, as indicated in Figure 7.2.

Anomaly detection is the search of unknown patterns. The idea is that over time, legitimate warranty repair activity would fall into regular patterns or baselines. A baseline is not a simple threshold. Thresholds represent a hard limit, typically managed in the business rules engine. For example, for a given repair type, the system can use a range of statistical techniques to establish baseline characteristics, making it easy to identify anomalies, or outliers, that might suggest mistakes or training issues, or even fraud. An example of an anomaly is when a

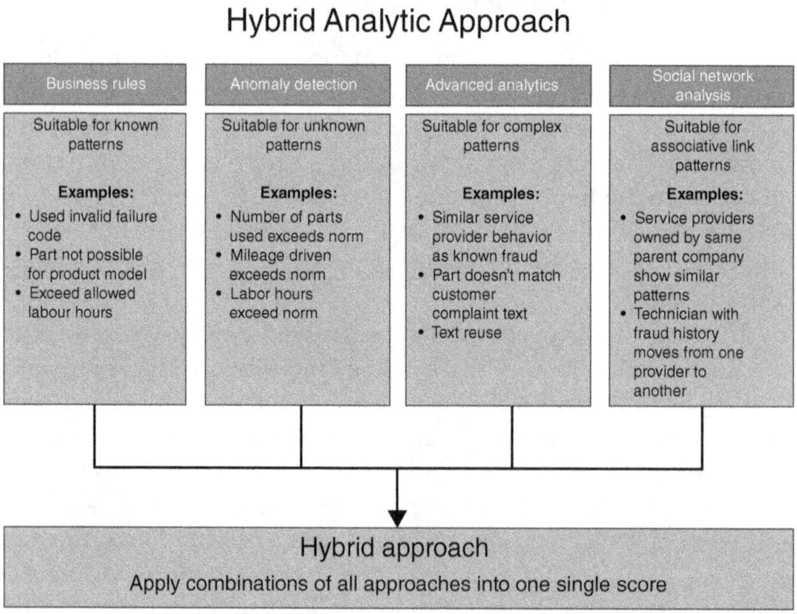

Hybrid Analytic Approach

Business rules	Anomaly detection	Advanced analytics	Social network analysis
Suitable for known patterns	Suitable for unknown patterns	Suitable for complex patterns	Suitable for associative link patterns
Examples: • Used invalid failure code • Part not possible for product model • Exceed allowed labour hours	**Examples:** • Number of parts used exceeds norm • Mileage driven exceeds norm • Labor hours exceed norm	**Examples:** • Similar service provider behavior as known fraud • Part doesn't match customer complaint text • Text reuse	**Examples:** • Service providers owned by same parent company show similar patterns • Technician with fraud history moves from one provider to another

Hybrid approach

Apply combinations of all approaches into one single score

Figure 7.2 Hybrid analytic approach (SAS Institute 2015)

technician consistently uses three or four parts when most others use two for a specific repair. Or perhaps there's a limit on the number of hours allowed for a specific repair. These techniques would identify service technicians who are under the allowed hours, and therefore pass a business rule, but regularly push the limit when compared to the baseline. Results can be improved by considering the population used in computing baselines. You can certainly build baselines on individual service technician history, comparing current work to their historical work. Baselines can also be built using a broader population of "like" service technicians, to get a better estimate of normal variation, flagging anomalies that are more likely to be pervasive issues.

Advanced analytics is used to search for complex patterns in the data. Predictive analytics leverages historical audit data to learn the patterns that have been adjusted in the past. New claims are then scored based on how closely they resemble the historical pattern. There is a large range of predictive techniques that can be leveraged, from regression to decision trees, to neural networks and beyond. Which model, or combination of models, is most effective at identifying any given pattern, is based on the data.

Text analysis uses machine-learning techniques to efficiently and consistently cluster comments into groups or categories that can then be analyzed with structured data. Text analysis can be used in a number of ways. For example, it can detect when the work performed or part used does not match the customer complaint. An example would be an oven part being ordered when the customer claim was for a defective refrigerator. Text analytics is also useful for detecting the reuse of text, often a sign that someone is cutting and copying text in order to submit a higher number of bad claims.

Fraud is not always a one-to-one proposition, where an individual customer or service agent is attempting to exploit the system. Customers, service agents, and claim validators can work together to commit fraud. Even organized crime might participate. Social network analytics is looking for relationships between the participants in the warranty process. For example, network analytics may find a group of customers that exhibit similar behaviors, and share a piece of information, like a cell phone or address. That information might help uncover additional associations that indicate the group is acting as one entity. Another example is where multiple service providers show similar behaviors, and it turns out they are all part of the same parent company.

In the hybrid analytic approach, each claim and service provider can be scored using several different models and methods of analysis. Many organizations do this, and carry out the analysis using data from their *paid claims* database. Although they will detect anomalies, and perhaps see where fraud was committed, the best practice is to operationalize the analyses within the processing system. Each claim can be analyzed in real time by dozens of models. Each claim can be given a score—a composite probability based on all the analyses run can then be highlighted to a business rule. Depending on its likelihood to be fraudulent, the decision can be made to reject, review, adjust, or pay the claim in full. Running these models in real time as part of the claims processing system will prevent organizations from paying fraudulent claims, saving the money on the front end rather than trying to recover the funds after the fact.

There are other value drivers to leveraging analytics in the claims processing system. Organizations find that they increase the percentage of claims they pay automatically, with no human intervention, because they have removed the subjectivity of their claims processing resources to interpret claims. Their auditing and service engagement activities are far more targeted and effective. They recover more money and they drive improvements into the service network that has a positive impact on customer satisfaction. Finally, many organizations leverage warranty data to understand product quality. By removing the inaccurate, fraudulent claims from the system altogether, companies get a much clearer picture of how their products are performing in the field.

 ## Analytics-Based Fraud Reduction

CASE STUDY

A major home appliance manufacturer had over a million claims annually handled by a large third-party service network. It leveraged a robust claims processing service that managed its warranty programs and offered a rules engine to help ensure claims were accurate before they were paid.

It was clear that service agents were exploiting the system by learning the business rules to facilitate quick, automated payments. Auditors were at a disadvantage because they could only audit a subset of claims, chosen almost at random. They could not see larger patterns, and there was little consistency in how to analyze claims between auditors.

The company introduced a robust hybrid analytic approach, developing over 30 models that looked at all information on the claim and ranked both the claims and service agents based on the likelihood of fraud—in near real time.

> The company saw dramatic results almost instantly and saved over US$5 million in the first six months of operation. It saw dramatic improvements in auditor productivity as well, as they leveraged the analytics to focus their activities and greatly reduced the subjectivity with which claims were reviewed. In the end, the auditors were so effective the company was able to redeploy a number of them to other areas like service education.

In addition to well-functioning analytics solutions, a right attitude and competencies with both analytics and business understanding are needed. The authors have, time and time again, been in situations where people running the analytics have been unable to focus on the right issues and see the fraud in the results of their analysis. In such a situation, analytics has become a mechanistic exercise focusing on wrong types of analytics or reports that are not understood or acted on, bringing no value. It is as important to be able to interpret the results as it is to do the number crunching. Actually, truly high-performing warranty fraud analysts are relatively rare, even among the more experienced ones.

SERVICE NETWORK MANAGEMENT

In Chapter 5, we discussed service network management in general. It has a significant impact and needs to be taken into account in warranty fraud management. It has two main elements:

- Service network structure
- Service agent management

The right *service network structure* enables the warranty provider to:

- Prevent fraud through a structural setup (fraud prevention).
- Identify suspicious claims and anomalies with analytics over the entire service network (fraud detection).

An effective *service agent management* process enables the warranty provider to:

- Encourage the right behavior from the service agents (fraud prevention).

Service network management and the impact of the right service network on warranty fraud management will be discussed further in Chapters 9 and 11.

CHAPTER **8**

Customer Fraud Management

he four types of customer fraud (based on motivation and methods indicated in Figure 6.3) introduced in Chapter 6 are as follows:

Refund or replace

Unjustified return claiming the product to be faulty, although there is nothing wrong with it, or bringing in a fake to get replacement or refund not entitled as per the warranty terms.

Service cost avoidance

To get an out-of-warranty service that the customer is not entitled to.

Extra products or earnings

Claiming and reselling replacement parts or products.

SLA improvement

Claiming better service level than the customer is entitled to.

In this chapter, we look at detection and prevention of these types of fraud using one or more of the four elements of the warranty control framework discussed in Chapter 7. The link between the control elements and the types of fraud is shown in Table 8.1. When applying these control mechanisms, customer satisfaction needs to be taken into account, and sometimes unjustified claims accepted to retain the customers.

CUSTOMER CONTRACT

Warranty contract with a customer or warranty terms and conditions for consumer products define the boundaries of warranty provided

Table 8.1 Fraud Detection and Prevention Activities against Different Types of Customer Fraud

	Customer fraud categories			
	No failure return	Service cost avoidance	Claim and resell	SLA improvement
Customer contract	✓	✓	✓	✓
Customer entitlement	✓	✓	✓	✓
Materials returns control		✓	✓	
Analytics	✓	✓		

by the warranty provider to the customers. The need for these to be precise is a prerequisite for effective warranty cost control and fraud prevention. The terms need to be explicitly stated—what is the warranty coverage (e.g., warranty length in terms of usage and/or time, is the warranty for the whole product or a part of it, are there limitations in usage), what kind of services and service levels is the customer entitled to receive, and what compensation the warranty provider is getting, if any. It is important that all parties (customer, warranty provider, service agent) have the same interpretation of warranty coverage for any product failure. If the terms and conditions are ambiguous or do not exist, the borderline between in- and out-of-warranty situations becomes unclear.

Warranty terms and conditions for consumer products may be in conflict with the local legislation. In such a case, the legislation takes precedence over warranty terms and conditions and sets the minimum level for warranty coverage.

Warranty coverage provided by the manufacturer may also exceed the statutory coverage. This is often the case with automotive warranties where manufacturers may offer three-, five-, or seven-year warranty coverage as a part of their offering, thus exceeding a typical one- or two-year statutory requirement.

Another difference between the terms and conditions of a manufacturer's warranty and that of the legislation is that the former is often more specific while the latter is more generic.

The warranty contract should define the terms related to:

- The warranty period—start and end
- Proof-of-purchase
- Product usage limitations
- Warranty for spare parts and repair
- Coverage for parts, labor, and logistics
- Transfer of ownership
- Warranty provider right to review the product during the warranty period
- Time limits to report a product issue
- Regional limitations, remote/dangerous locations
- Customer damage and alterations
- Cosmetic issues, wear and tear, consumable parts

- Unauthorized service
- Replacement items
- Original parts usage
- Preapproval requirements
- Included services and related service levels
- Repair and replace options
- Time limits for getting an extended warranty

Warranty Period

The unambiguously defined warranty period is perhaps the most important term of the contract. The contract should define when the warranty period starts and when it ends. There is no uniformity across companies, as illustrated by the following cases:

- Apple (2016)[1]: The warranty starts from the date of original retail purchase by the end-user purchaser.
- Ford UK (2015): A new car warranty starts from the moment of delivery.
- Volkswagen UK (2015): Defines it to start at the date of registration.
- Cisco (2007): Refers to the longer of the date of shipment by Cisco or the period set forth in the warranty card accompanying the product.

In many B2B cases, the warranty starts after the customer acceptance test, start of commercial use, or when another agreed project milestone is passed. To avoid situations where the milestone triggering warranty start is delayed (e.g., due to extended storage), the warranty provider can define a maximum lead time between delivery from factory and start of warranty. Extended warranty contracts may also have a "cooling period" between the extended warranty purchase and the warranty period start, to avoid the warranty provider covering any pre-existing failures in the product.

The contract should specify how the customer can prove the existence of the warranty. Proof of purchase is required as an evidence of purchase date, for example in Apple's and Microsoft's warranty terms.

- The Swatch warranty for watches comes into force when the warranty certificate is dated, fully and correctly completed and stamped by an official Swatch dealer (Swatch, 2015).

▨ Apple sets requirements for the proof of purchase. It should be legible, include a clear description of the product, the product's date of purchase, an invoice or receipt number, the product's price, the reseller's contact information, and if possible, the reseller's company seal or logo. Also, the proof of purchase should include the product's serial number, if the reseller normally lists serial numbers on their invoices (Apple, 2015b).

Furthermore, both Apple and Microsoft state that warranty is not valid if serial number—or as in Microsoft's warranty terms, mobile accessory date code—is illegible (Microsoft, 2015).

Warranty period, its calculation rule, and the required evidence is the basis for segregating in- from out-of-warranty items.

Availability of serial number allows the manufacturer to compare warranty start date in the proof of purchase with its own records (e.g., factory shipping date or usage data remotely obtained from connected products).

If there is a requirement to have the serial number printed in the proof of purchase, there is a possibility to verify that the proof of purchase relates to the product in question. Our recommendation is to require a serial number in the proof of purchase if local legislation and market situations allow this. Having the serial number in the proof of purchase eliminates the possibility of claiming warranty for an older product using the proof of purchase of a newer product of the same model.

Product Usage Limitations

The design reliability is based on an expected usage. The contract needs to list the limitations explicitly, whether it is on usage intensity (average load, peak load), locations, temperature, or mode of usage (professional versus personal use, etc.). For some products, the contract explicitly states that the product is meant for use in domestic homes and not in commercial buildings (such as hotels and motels).

Warranty for Spare Parts and Repair

Warranty terms and conditions should define if there is a new specific warranty covering the installed spare parts or if they are covered by the original warranty.

Warranty contract terms should also define how a warranty repair affects the remaining warranty period.

- Apple states: "A replacement part or Apple Product, including a user-installable part that has been installed in accordance with instructions provided by Apple, assumes the remaining term of the warranty or ninety (90) days from the date of replacement or repair, whichever provides longer coverage for you."

- Swatch states: "The warranty for the replacement watch ends twenty-four (24) months after the date of purchase of the replaced watch"—that is, the replacement does not extend original 24-month warranty.

Coverage for Parts and Labor

Warranty may cover parts or labor only or both, which should be defined. The type of labor to be covered should also be defined. If warranty service only requires minor effort (e.g., tightening or change of settings), such work can be excluded from warranty coverage.

The contract should also clearly state, who is responsible for the logistics costs and risks of transport, when the product needs to be returned to the service center or travel costs, when field engineers need to come to the site.

In B2B context, the customer may need to independently carry out the warranty repair in case of urgency, when no consent and service is available from the warranty provider. In such cases, the warranty terms and conditions should define the compensation the customer is entitled to.

Transfer of Ownership

The contract needs to state specifically if the warranty coverage is limited only to the original purchaser. If the product is resold, the warranty may cease:

- Cisco has a term in the contract that limits its certain US router warranties. It states, "This limited warranty extends only to the original user of the Product."

- Ford UK states in its passenger car warranties that "the warranty is not affected by any change in ownership of the vehicle."

Warranty Provider Right to Review the Product

In some cases, the warranty provider may want to review the product during the warranty period to ensure that proper maintenance activities are done and either suggest or execute appropriate preventive maintenance actions.

Time Limits to Report a Product Issue

It is in the warranty provider's interest to learn about product issues as soon as possible. The warranty contract may include clauses on the time limits to report a product issue. This also supports the overall transparency and fraud control.

When the warranty period has expired, the customer may argue that the defect appeared before the end of warranty. To avoid such situations, terms on reporting of the defects can be set.

- Volkswagen states: "Any defect must be reported to a member of the Volkswagen Authorized Network as soon as it is discovered. This must of course be within the warranty period."

Regional Limitations, Remote/Dangerous Locations

As a result of market situation and differences in legislation, warranty duration and other terms may vary across countries. In some countries, consumer products may be sold without any manufacturer warranty or the warranty may be valid only within the country in question. This allows the manufacturers to sell the products to distributors in such countries at a lower price than to the distributors in other markets.

- To prevent utilization of cross-country differences, Volkswagen requires that "After the first two years of your warranty, your vehicle will be covered by a third year warranty if the vehicle has not exceeded 60,000 miles and the vehicle was imported by Volkswagen UK and supplied through the United Kingdom Volkswagen authorized network."
- Apple has a local rule that states that it "may restrict service for iPad and iPhone to the EEA (European Economic Area) and Switzerland."
- An example of Microsoft's regional limitations for warranty is to provide warranty to products "which Manufacturer has released for sale in the European Union, Iceland, Norway, Switzerland, and Turkey."

The terms should also include a clause allowing the warranty provider to charge the customer if field service is needed in a remote location not covered by warranty provider's normal service operations, and exclude dangerous locations from warranty coverage.

Customer Damage and Alterations

Based on our experience and various studies, a significant percentage of repairs under warranty period are to fix failures due to customer misuse and/or damage. In portable electronics, for example, liquid damage is a common issue. If not controlled for, many of these cases get charged from the manufacturer as in-warranty repairs. Consequently, manufacturers should reserve the right to exclude damage caused by the customer from warranty coverage.

The appropriate terms vary, depending on the nature of the product and the environment the product is used in.

- Apple's warranty terms for MacBooks state: "Warranty does not apply to damage caused by accident, abuse, misuse, liquid contact, fire, earthquake or other external cause." The terms and conditions also limit Apple's responsibility on damage arising from failure to follow instructions relating to the Apple Product's use. Furthermore, Apple states that products should not be opened unless instructed by Apple.

- Microsoft warranty terms for Lumia phones state: "Errors or damage caused by misuse or not using your Product in accordance with the user guide, such as if the Product has been exposed to moisture, to dampness or to extreme thermal or environmental conditions or to rapid changes in such conditions, to corrosion, to oxidation, to spillage of food or liquid or to influence from chemical products" is not covered by warranty. Also, "damage or errors caused by hacking, cracking, viruses, or other malware, or by unauthorized access to services, accounts, computer systems or networks" are excluded from warranty coverage.

- Swatch excludes defects in watches caused by lack of care, abnormal or abusive use, and accidents from warranty coverage.

- Cisco includes abnormal physical or electrical stress and abnormal environmental conditions in the list.

- Volkswagen's automotive warranties do not cover damage caused by failure to prevent mechanical damage from occurring (e.g., when warning lights appear), not having the vehicle serviced as recommended, improper use, neglect and use of vehicle for motor sports, accident damage, damage to paintwork caused by climatic, thermal, chemical, or industrial pollution, and windscreen or glass breakage.

Another similar limitation relates to damage caused by use with another product.

- Microsoft Lumia warranty excludes defects caused by connecting the product to any product, accessory, software, or service not manufactured or supplied by Manufacturer and any products combined with your Product by a third party.

An increasing amount of defects in various products are software related. As connectivity of the products improves, these issues can often be solved by software updates provided by the manufacturers. If the customer fails to conduct a software update, the issues are naturally not resolved. Warranty coverage can be limited in such situations.

- Microsoft, for example, states: "The warranty is not valid if you have not installed the latest software updates that are publicly available for the purchased product within a reasonable time of their release."

Manufacturers also have a possibility to limit warranty coverage in cases where the product has been altered.

- Cisco states that its hardware warranty and limited warranty for selected routers in the United States do not apply if the product has been altered, except by Cisco or its authorized representative.
- Apple states that the warranty does not apply to an Apple Product that has been modified to alter functionality or capability without the written permission of Apple.

Cosmetic Issues, Wear and Tear, Consumable Parts

Consumable parts have a lifetime shorter than the warranty period. Limiting their warranty coverage allows the warranty provider to avoid unnecessary costs.

▦ Ford limits the duration of warranty of items with a limited service life or that are subject to damage. These items include wiper blades, certain light bulb categories, and remote control batteries.

Sometimes, service agents refurbish products that do not have defects affecting functionality, but are cosmetically damaged. As such issues are not caused by the warranty provider, they should be ruled out.

▦ Apple's warranty terms for MacBooks express the limitation in the following way: "Warranty does not apply to cosmetic damage, including but not limited to scratches, dents and broken plastic on ports." Furthermore, Apple states that warranty does not apply to defects caused by normal wear and tear or otherwise due to normal aging of the Apple product.

▦ Swatch states that warranty does not cover normal wear and tear and aging—scratched crystal and alteration of the color in the material and peeling of the plating.

▦ In addition to normal wear and tear, Microsoft excludes reduced charging capacity of the battery resulting from its natural end of product life, or pixel defects in "your Product's display that are within the scope of industry standards from warranty coverage."

Likewise, in B2B operations, defects or faults—such as dents or surface scratches—that have no significance to the operation can be excluded from warranty coverage.

Unauthorized Service

In addition to damage caused by the customer, damage caused by unauthorized service should be excluded.

▦ Apple states that warranty does not apply to damage caused by service (including upgrades and expansions) performed by anyone who is not a representative of Apple or an Apple Authorized Service Provider.

Replacement Items

Customer products and parts are often replaced in the service network instead of being directly repaired. Sometimes, a replacement unit is delivered to the customer before the original product is returned to minimize the downtime or discomfort caused to the customer. Replacement fraud where the original product is not returned to the warranty provider or where the original product never existed, can be a multimillion-dollar issue.

- Both Microsoft and Apple state that replaced items become their property. Apple additionally reserves the right to require a credit card as security for the retail price of the replacement Apple Product or part and applicable shipping costs.

Original Parts Usage

Customers may change the parts included in the original product or add new parts. For example, additional memory can be added to personal computers and many other products. Various accessories can be added to cars. When these parts fail or cause defect in the main product, the warranty provider should be able to exclude warranty coverage.

- Volkswagen's passenger car warranty in the United Kingdom denies warranty coverage from "components or equipment, which are not part of the vehicle at the point of original manufacture."
- Apple limits warranty coverage by stating that warranty "does not apply to any non-Apple branded hardware products or any software, even if packaged or sold with Apple hardware."

Preapproval

Repairs can be costly and not always done in the interest of the warranty provider. Preapproval can be used to control work done in the service network before the costs have already incurred.

- Volkswagen, for example, "reserves the right to appoint its own or an independent consultant engineer to inspect the vehicle prior to repair or replacement of the part(s) covered."

Included Services and Related Service Levels

The warranty contract terms need to define the services included in the warranty offering, their availability and service levels for service logistics (on-site service, pickup and return, customer returns the product), access to online and technical support (cost, availability times, number of calls), replacement parts, field engineers on-site, and potential performance or uptime guarantees.

Repair and Replace Options

The warranty provider needs to state in the contract which service options are available for the customer. Typically, the warranty provider keeps the options to repair the defect or replace the defective part or product.

Time Limits for Buying an Extended Warranty

Depending on the warranty provider and the product, an extended warranty and/or maintenance service contract may be purchased:

- At the same time with the product purchase
- After the product purchase, before the base warranty expires
- After the base warranty has expired (with diverse limitations)

With the latter alternatives, the warranty provider may want to inspect the product before making the contract to rule out any material preexisting defects. Also, if the product fails rapidly after signing the extended warranty contract, that may be assessed to be a preexisting failure. These statements are needed to avoid the cases where someone has:

- A product with a preexisting defect that is repaired or
- A unrepairable product that is replaced with a new or working one with the price of the extended warranty.

CUSTOMER ENTITLEMENT

The goal of the entitlement process is to verify the validity of a customer warranty claim based on warranty terms and conditions:

- The product in question is under warranty.
- There is a failure.
- The failure is covered by warranty.
- The cause of the failure doesn't void the warranty coverage.

Additionally, the type of warranty coverage (e.g., which share of the failure costs is covered by base warranty, which by extended warranty, which by the customer, and what type of service is covered) and the service level the customer is entitled to are verified. The purpose of entitlement is not to avoid the cost of legitimate customer claims, but to ensure that only valid customer claims are covered by warranty service.

To a certain extent, entitlement can be done remotely (checking the validity of the product warranty coverage, inclusion of the claimed failure type and through remote diagnostics) over phone or online. However, a more thorough verification of the cause of the failure may require physical inspection of the product and can only be done once the product is returned to the service channel, or when a field engineer or an inspector is on-site in customer premises.

The first step is to verify that the customer product or part is under warranty. If the warranty provider has a warranty register or contract database, the warranty status data can be retrieved online. Many retail chains have their own registers where the warranty period is entered when the product is sold. In case of two-dimensional warranties, odometer reading, running hours, or other usage values need to be obtained from the product. If the item is out of warranty based on warranty provider's registers, the customer can still have an in-warranty repair by presenting a proof of purchase or an extended warranty certificate. A copy of such documents is taken and filed. Furthermore, it needs to be verified that this document is legible, includes serial number, and does not appear to be fake.

If the item is out of warranty, it may still be repaired for goodwill purposes in exceptional cases. A case-specific preauthorization or an approval from a preauthorized limited quota should be used. Use of goodwill approval is reported with the claim.

Additional warranty provider–defined policies can also be applied. One printer manufacturer applies a policy that denies printer ink cartridge replacement if the claim is made more than two weeks after the purchase.

Customer entitlement should also be the first step in no-fault-found filtering. In here, basic checks are conducted with the customer to verify that the item is faulty. The purpose is to minimize the proportion of no-fault-found products. At the same time, information required later in the service process can be obtained. This is done following a checklist provided by the warranty provider. The customer can, for example, be requested to repeat the problem with the customer service representative and explain the symptoms. The product can be reset and the user can be provided instructions in the usage of the product.

The purpose of entitlement is also to eliminate cases where the customer wants to return a working product and claims it to be faulty, or cases where the customer is trying to use the product in a wrong way and thinks it is not working. One way of reducing the likelihood of unnecessary returns is a handling charge for no-fault-found returns to cover the cost of diagnostics and related handling.[2] A customer just wanting to return a product or replacing a product with a newer version may need to think twice—does the benefit of getting the product returned outweigh the risk of paying the handling charge (and not getting a new product) and the claim being rejected? Ideally, the handling charge should be charged in advance. The following case illustrates the issue, although it relates mainly to out-of-warranty repairs.

 Handling Charge Not Charged in Advance

CASE STUDY

A service agent repairing televisions conducted diagnostics before starting the repair. After diagnostics, the customer was informed about the cost of repair if the repair was not covered by warranty. If the cost was high and the customer decided not to have the product repaired, the service agent returned the defective product and charged a handling charge to cover the cost of diagnostics. To avoid the charge, customers often simply left the defective product to the service agent. The service agent ended up with a large stock of defective televisions and no compensation for diagnostics.

Ensuring that the customer knows how to use the product through training, product usability design, and easy-to-use product manuals can help in reducing the unnecessary usage-related returns.

 Reducing Unnecessary Returns

CASE STUDY

A telecommunications service provider established a new procedure where every customer, who had bought a smart phone for the first time, received an outbound call from the service provider's contact center within 48 hours from the purchase. The customer was asked if everything is all right with the new purchase and if any assistance is needed in product configuration or installing new apps. The outcome of the new procedure was a significant reduction in customer returns for the product categories in scope.

Receipt or evidence of the purchase price should be requested to eliminate cases, where the customer has bought the product at a discount and tries to get a refund with a higher price. If price information can be retrieved from sales channel or warranty provider database, this is not necessary.

Installed base and customer contract data with accurate information and broad coverage play a crucial role in customer entitlement. They help in answering the following questions:

- Is the product under warranty?
  - Warranty start date is checked from manufacturing, shipment, sales, installation, or activation data in the installed base.
  - Length of warranty is obtained from records with length of base warranties or customer contract database in case of extended warranties, maintenance service contracts, or other customer contracts.
  - Existence of possible repair warranty is checked from service history.
- What is the service level the customer is entitled to?
  - Checked from the warranty master data or contract database with data on extended warranties, maintenance service contract, and or other customer contracts.
- Is the failed part under warranty?
  - Part-specific warranty duration is checked from warranty contract database.
  - Other part- and product-related data are checked in the installed base.
- Does the product exist? Is the product stolen, scrapped, or a prototype that should not be on the market?
  - Checked from manufacturing registers or installed base and serial number–level registers on stolen, scrapped, and prototype products
- Was the product sold to the customer/country from where the claim is coming?
  - Checked from serial number, location, and customer information in installed base or shipment registers
- Has the defective part been included in the original product configuration?

- Checked from component-level traceability and configuration data in the installed base or the manufacturing registers
- Does the claimed part exist or is it a fictitious part or a part that should have been scrapped?
  - Checked from component-level serial number traceability database in the installed base or the manufacturing registers
- Has the product been used in line with the intended usage?
  - Checked from the usage data in the product or the usage data uploaded earlier to the installed base (physical inspection may also be needed):
    - Is the usage limit exceeded?
    - Is the usage pattern in line with the contract?
    - Is there sensor-based evidence of user damage?

Physical inspection can complement the entitlement process and provide information that cannot be obtained remotely. The aim is to obtain additional information about the defect before making a final decision on the claim—is it covered by warranty, or should the customer pay for the service? Physical inspection includes product failure analysis, and analysis of the scope and cause of the defect. A proper diagnosis done as a part of the physical inspection confirms that the product has not been damaged or altered by the customer. The checks that are done are based on instructions from the warranty provider. Any signs of tuning are checked. A photograph confirming the identity of the product and the defective parts may be required. In certain products, it should be checked that the defective part being changed is the original part that came with the product. Computer hard drives are an example of parts often changed or added by the customers after the original purchase. The hard drive should be covered only if it is the one originally sold with the product.

Physical inspection can be done by the service agent, a third-party or warranty provider's inspector, a field engineer, or a service engineer in the warranty provider's repair facility. For instance, auto inspectors will look at a claim and attempt to discover whether it might have been caused by low oil levels or perhaps continued driving in an overheated state. If this is the case, the defect is classified as owner abuse or negligence, and the claim will not be covered under the service contract (*Warranty Week*, 2004). Physical inspection should check damages caused by:

- Individual incidences caused, for example, by liquid damage or dropping the product. Portable electronics manufacturers have introduced physical indicators, which help in detection of liquid damage, and acceleration sensors indicating if the product has been dropped or used too heavily (see, e.g., Oh et al., 2015).

- Customer continues to use the product after a minor failure, which leads to a major failure.

- Continuous usage outside the limitations set by the contractual warranty terms (excessive power, speed, acceleration, or load). To enable checking continuous usage, the product needs to have means to store the relevant usage data.

▼ Excessive Usage/Speed

CASE STUDY

An industrial equipment manufacturer had installed power limiters to prevent their engines from being run at too high speed. The customer wanted to have warranty break-fix service. The manufacturer noticed that the customer had removed the power limiter and the part typically failing with excessive speed had failed. After a lengthy discussion with the customer, it was concluded that the item was not covered by warranty.

If the customer has a fleet of identical products covered with different warranty periods and with different maintenance service contracts, the entitlement check needs to include the service levels attached with the warranty.

▼ Expensive Overservice for Demanding Customers

CASE STUDY

Industrial manufacturer had several maintenance service contracts with diverse contract terms and SLAs. In many cases, the customer called them requesting a next-day delivery for a spare part, which in fact had a longer SLA, up to two weeks. After improving the entitlement process, such cases could be detected and excessive expediting costs avoided. Additional revenue could also be obtained in part of the cases by providing the customer the expedited service for a fee.

The entitlement rules need to be in line with the customer warranty policy, and clearly communicated to the service agents and the sales channel who often conduct the entitlement. Typically, the manufacturer provides the tools and procedures for the service agent to support customer warranty entitlement.

One specific decision in the entitlement phase is whether the service can be executed or spare part shipped to the customer before the customer has returned the defective part or product. The reason for this process may be the urgent need of the customer for the product to be in functioning operational state, but this may also provide an opportunity of fraud. This decision can be supported by analytical scoring (What is the likelihood of the customer claim being fraudulent?) and conducting the following checks before making the decision:

- Is this a known customer who owns the product according to the installed base information?
- Is the customer a one-off customer or a customer with a long-term relationship with us?
- Does the customer have a history of above-average numbers of warranty claims or suspected fraud?
- How many such cases are there in this region where the defective part or product has not been returned?
- What does our contract say about advance shipping of spare parts?
- What is the value of the part?
- What is the cost of returning the defective part compared to the part cost?

Verma and Rajendran (2015) have listed the following issues as potential symptoms for spare parts dispatch fraud:

- Same customer asks for replacement parts frequently.
- Incorrect customer name and contact details are provided.
- Customer refuses to give the faulty item back, stating it has been thrown away or already returned by mail, etc.
- The serial number is valid, but the product is still in channel inventory and has not been sold yet to any customer.
- Shipping and invoicing addresses are different.

If the decision for the advance shipping of the replacement part or product is made, it is essential to ensure that material return happens, as will be discussed in the next section. In addition to that, for example, in B2C business, customer credit card number can be requested and customer charged if the defective product or part is not returned. Apple (2016) applies this policy.

MATERIAL RETURNS CONTROL

As discussed in Chapter 3, material returns are used to:

- Get the defective item back for further processing (repair, refurbishment, recycling).
- Do technical analyses as a part of the product quality feedback process.

Material returns from customers also provides opportunities for warranty fraud control, as it does the following:

- It enables physical inspection—for example, for customer damage.
- It allows warranty provider to control that the claimed item exists and is defective.

The returned materials should be tracked and matched against the customer warranty claims. Follow-up actions should be taken on claims where the material returns have not taken place in due course.

Typically, the contract terms state that the defective products or parts are the property of the warranty provider and should be returned when exchanged. We have seen two issues in this area:

- The cost of returning the item is much higher than the cost of the replacement item.
- There is a policy of requesting the returns, but they are not monitored and matched against the customer warranty claims.

When the cost of returning the item is too high, it is natural that requesting a return doesn't necessarily make sense. Getting a photograph of the product/part with the serial number visible will at least ensure that the customer has had the product and potentially the defect is visible as well. If the product has self-diagnostics features, the diagnostic report can be used as well. The other option may be to have a local inspector check that the item under consideration exists, it is defective, and it is disposed of in a proper way and not sold or used as a spare part.

The material returns should be tracked and matched against the open customer warranty claims. Proper actions should be taken on claims where the material returns have not happened in due course.

ANALYTICS

Various analytics methods can and should be used to get alerts of potential customer fraud. Based on these alerts, further verification activities can be taken before the customer is provided with the service, sent a replacement part or product, or given a refund. Also, in the B2B context, the customer service team can be given specific instructions for specific customers or customer locations about things to watch out for.

Analytics can be grouped into two categories—general and targeted. The objective of general analytics methods is to provide transparency of the warranty claim history across customers and enable benchmarking and comparisons between customers. Targeted analytics are used to detect specific methods of customer fraud.

General Methods for Identification of Anomalies

Excessive *repeated repairs for the same product item* can be related to the customer usage of the product (overloading, mishandling) or using an in-warranty product to replace defective parts originating from out-of-warranty products. In consumer products, it may be unfeasible to report all individuals, but having a list of those customers whose claim history exceeds specific thresholds can assist in eliminating more systematic attempts of fraud.

Excessive *repeated replacements for the same family of products* can be related to an issue in the way the customer uses these products.

High *customer-specific claim rates* or abnormal failure patterns can generally focus the activities on selected customers. These patterns can be caused by various methods of customer fraud. Tighter warranty controls can then be applied to the customers whose claim rate exceeds a threshold value. Table 8.2 exhibits the comparison of customer claim rates. In this example, customer 4 stands out with clearly higher claim rate than the other customers.

Table 8.2 Claim Rate by Customer

Customer	Claim rate, %
Customer 1	1.9%
Customer 2	1.5%
Customer 3	4.8%
Customer 4	**14.2%**
Customer 5	6.1%
Customer 6	5.0%
Customer 7	6.5%
Customer 8	6.9%
Customer 9	1.6%
Median	5.0%

 Detection of Hotspots

CASE STUDY

A manufacturer of industrial electronics measures failure rates by customer and customer location. Customer locations with above-threshold failure rates are called hotspots. When such cases are identified, the site is visited and reasons for high failure rate analyzed. In one case, the quality of air was observed to be inferior, causing electronics to fail.

Targeted Analytics Against Specific Methods of Customer Fraud

In this section we describe how analytics can be used to detect the four types of customer fraud listed at the beginning of the chapter.

No-Failure Returns

Looking at the claim history of the customer may reveal a pattern where the customer is systematically extending the product lifetime or upgrading the product by claiming an intermittent failure. By producing alerts of the number of earlier no-failure returns, customer entitlement can take the potential behavioral pattern into account to make proper decisions.

Service Cost Avoidance

If a customer has a history of demanding warranty service for out-of-warranty products, that should be made visible as an alert for the people doing customer entitlement.

Table 8.3 illustrates the comparison of number of claims, no-fault-found claims, and rejected claims per customer. In this example, customers 5 and 8 have more claims per product, customers 4 and 7 have larger share of rejected claims, and customers 2 and 8 have larger share of no-fault-found claims than other customers.

Analyzing the usage data may reveal usage-related information, which voids the warranty, like in the following case.

CASE STUDY

▼ Sensor Data Revealing Serious Overloads

Industrial manufacturer has a number of sensors in their products, primarily for condition monitoring services. The same information is analyzed and used for alerts in customer warranty entitlement. In one case, the product was in-warranty, the failure would normally be covered, but the sensor history revealed more than 20 overload situations during the previous year, leading to the customer warranty claim rejection.

Analyzing the service history and the related usage pattern may also reveal tampering of the usage figures. This can be identified if the usage goes down or if there is a sudden flattening of the usage figures, as shown in Figure 8.1, which indicates the odometer readings at service time instants for two cars with a 7 years/50.000 miles base warranty and annual service. Car 1 has suddenly less miles than the previous year and car 2 is driven very little between the two most recent service events. For car 2, there can be perfectly valid reasons, but it is worthwhile verifying.

Analyzing product data can also reveal cases where the product operating system, other software, or usage parameters have been hacked to enhance product performance or to implement new features, and this might be causing the damage. Resets to factory setup can also be a sign of hiding the evidence of the unauthorized tuning of the product.

If the customer has a fleet of identical products, some of them in-warranty and some of them out-of-warranty, monitoring the field failure rate for both and comparing that with other customers may

Table 8.3 Claims per Product, No-Fault-Found Claims, and Rejected Claims per Customer

Customer	Number of Products under Warranty	Number of Claims	Claims per Product	Number of Rejected Claims	Ratio of Rejected Claims to All Claims	Number of NFF Claims	Ratio of NFF to Claims
Customer 1	32	74	2.3	6	8%	9	12%
Customer 2	12	24	2.0	—	0%	8	**33%**
Customer 3	54	224	4.1	39	17%	6	3%
Customer 4	120	444	3.7	80	**18%**	33	7%
Customer 5	6	43	**7.2**	6	14%	5	12%
Customer 6	19	40	2.1	1	3%	—	0%
Customer 7	11	55	5.0	14	**25%**	4	7%
Customer 8	78	593	**7.6**	16	3%	137	**23%**
Customer 9	15	74	4.9	3	4%	12	16%
Median			**4.1**		**8%**		**12%**

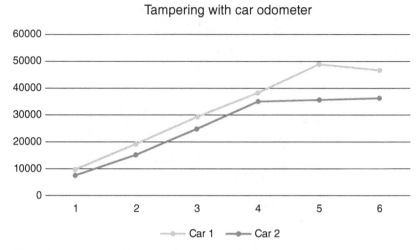

Figure 8.1 Tampering with automotive odometer figures

be used to identify cases where parts from out-of-warranty products are swapped into in-warranty products to get the service for free. This requires visibility on out-of-warranty repairs, which is not always the case. If the manufacturer has component-level serial number traceability, this type of fraud can be detected already during customer warranty entitlement.

Comparing the servicing location with the product delivery information may reveal occasional or systemic fraud where the product is purchased in a country with shorter warranty coverage and then brought to service in a country with a longer warranty period.

Comparing the manufacturing date with the purchasing date of the product may reveal cases where customers are using a false proof-of-purchase or they have been given one without the date. If the channel lead time from the date of manufacturing to the date of purchase indicated in the proof-of-purchase document is materially longer for products in some region, with some service agent, or some customer, than with others, there is a potential issue the root cause of which should be verified.

To reveal cases where the customer is approaching different service agents to get the warranty entitlement accepted by one of them, the following data can be analyzed:

- The records on customer interactions in the CRM system
- Claims, that are opened, but no service is done against them

▦ The number of warranty entitlement checks for the same customer and the same product

If it is detected that the customer warranty claim relates to a counterfeit item, it needs to be recorded for later use. That can be used later to identify customers who have a tendency to use counterfeit items to save costs and still try to get them repaired under OEM warranty.

Claim and Resell

Cases where the customer claims replacement products or parts to resell them can be tricky to detect, since the customer may use several names and addresses for the claims. The analytics to detect these cases should include:

▦ Analyzing any common denominators on cases where the customer has not returned the defective parts.

▦ Analyzing cases where the same customer is continuously asking for advance replacement parts.

▦ Checking the existence and correctness of the customer name, address, telephone, and other contact details. Specific attention should be paid when the customer is using a P.O. box as the address.

▦ Checking the installed base status of the product in the customer warranty claim.

▦ Determining if there is an increasing number of customer warranty claims within the region where shipping and invoicing addresses are different.

NOTES

1. When referring to these companies, the same references are applied throughout this chapter, unless stated differently.
2. A similar charge can be applied if the customer has damaged the item.

CHAPTER 9

Service Agent Fraud Management

Chapter 6 introduced the following types of fraud conducted by service agents:

- Creation of fictitious claims
- Conducting out-of-warranty repairs
- Inflating the price of an existing claim
- Giving overservice or using too many parts
- Using or reselling warranty provider–owned parts
- Using counterfeit or unauthorized parts
- Not doing all the necessary actions under the service contract
- Unnecessary change of parts to minimize effort
- Using unqualified technicians to save costs

Chapter 7 discussed the overall warranty control framework to detect and prevent fraud. This chapter deals with service agent fraud with warranty provider as the victim and looks at methods that assist the warranty provider to detect and prevent fraud. These involve the following elements from the warranty control framework:

- Service agent contract
- Entitlement and repair authorization processes
- Claim validation process
- Analytics
- Material returns control
- Service network management

The link between the control elements and the types of fraud is shown in Tables 9.1 and 9.2.

SERVICE AGENT CONTRACT

Chapter 3 discussed the need for, and the importance of, contracts between the warranty provider and the different parties including the service agents. In addition to general terms in the service agent contracts, there are specific sections and terms and conditions that are needed to control warranty fraud. This section will discuss the recommendations related to warranty contracts.

Table 9.1 Fraud Detection and Prevention Activities against Different Types of Service Agent Fraud to Obtain Extra Revenue

	Types of service agent fraud to obtain extra revenue				
	Creation of fictitious claims	Conducting out-of-warranty repairs	Inflating the price of an existing claim	Giving over-service or using too many parts	Using or reselling warranty provider-owned parts
Service agent contract	✓	✓	✓	✓	✓
Entitlement and repair authorization	✓	✓			
Claim validation process	✓	✓	✓	✓	
Analytics	✓	✓	✓	✓	✓
Material returns control	✓	✓	✓	✓	✓
Service network management	✓	✓		✓	✓

Table 9.2 Fraud Detection and Prevention Activities against Different Types of Service Agent Fraud to Avoid Service Costs

	Types of service agent fraud to avoid service costs			
	Using counterfeit or unauthorized parts	Not doing all the necessary actions under the service contract	Unnecessary change of parts to minimize effort	Using unqualified technicians to save costs
Service agent contract	✓	✓	✓	✓
Entitlement and repair authorization				
Claim validation process	✓	✓	✓	✓
Analytics	✓	✓	✓	✓
Material returns control	✓	✓	✓	
Service network management	✓	✓	✓	✓

From a warranty cost control and fraud management perspective, a good service agent contract must motivate the service agent toward high performance and operational excellence, and must highlight the consequences of undesired performance. The contract needs to:

- Provide a clear definition and segregation of acceptable and unacceptable claims eliminating possibilities of intentional or unintentional misinterpretation.
- Provide contractual basis for rejecting unacceptable claims.
- Allow contract termination and legal actions to be taken against service agents breaching the terms of the contract.
- Act as a deterrent for fraud.
- Set requirements for a standardized claims process.
- Establish cost elements and pricing mechanisms that can be controlled.
- Provide incentives that reward the service agents for integrity and desired behavior.
- Standardize claim reporting and pricing so that service agents' claims and costs can be compared with each other.
- Set requirements for service agent operations and reporting.
- Give the warranty provider the right to audit the service agents.

The terms applied in the contracts made with different service agents should be identical. Only if there are legal requirements in different countries or specific requirements from customers should deviations be allowed.

When proper contracts and related controls are not in place, the warranty provider is likely to face the following issues:

- A gray area (i.e., a contract that leaves too much room for interpretation by the service agent) between acceptable and unacceptable claims exists, resulting in excess costs to the warranty provider. For example, is a service agent entitled to compensation if the same product has been repaired three times within a month to fix the same failure?
- The warranty provider trying to reject dubious claims faces lengthy disputes with and a possibility of being sued by the service agents.
- Claims process and pricing lack standardization, hindering the ability to control and compare service agents.

Table 9.3 Key Sections in Service Agent Contract from a Warranty Fraud Management and Cost Control Perspective

Service Agent Compensation	Spare Parts and Other Materials
Pricing models Chargeable costs	Spare parts and other materials to be used Ownership, storage, and/or return of replaced parts and products
Claim Reporting and Payment	**Rules for Acceptable Claims**
Claims process, information systems, and data Frequency of claim reporting Payment process	Repair warranty Validity of serial numbers Proof of physical presence In- and out-of-warranty service
Servicing-Related Requirements	**Service Agent Management**
Service according to guidelines Competence requirements Service levels Approvals needed	Warranty provider's right to audit Actions if fraud is detected Incentives

▪ The warranty provider is unable to set requirements on service agent operations—e.g., on information sharing, material returns, or right to audit.

Table 9.3 summarizes the six key sections, and the important issues in each that are needed in a contract between the service agent and the warranty provider for effective warranty cost control and fraud management. We will discuss the contents of each box in more detail.

Service Agent Compensation

The role of contract terms relating to service agent compensation is to (i) define and limit those cost components a service agent is entitled to be paid for, (ii) establish a compensation model that is easy to control, (iii) ensure that compensation is fact based, (iv) ensure that it does not incentivize fraud, and (v) allow service agent activities and costs to be compared with each other.

While aiming to keep costs down, the compensation paid for the service agents should not be too low, but adequate and such that it fosters high performance and operational excellence. An unprofitable service business may contribute to service agent fraud. If prices are too low, honest service agents may find it impossible to make a profitable contract with the warranty provider. Instead, the warranty provider gets a pool of service agents whose plan is to accept an unprofitable contract and then offset their low prices with fraud.

Like the contract in general, the compensation model should be standardized across the warranty provider's service agent base to the extent possible. This allows the service agents to be compared within and across different countries and regions. This is a key enabler for identification of anomalies through analytics. Standardization can also reveal and prevent warranty provider's pricing errors as illustrated by the following case.

 Harmonization of Service Pricing

CASE STUDY

Each country organization within a global company had organized its warranty services independently. The global organization had not set standards for warranty management, and the practices applied by different countries varied greatly. The same applied to service agent compensation. Some countries paid by hour, but did not set maximum durations. Some paid by hour with set durations for defined groups of activities. Some had fixed fee for all repairs. As a result, the costs in different countries were not comparable. Following a project to standardize warranty management practices, also the pricing was harmonized. As the old prices were converted into new, harmonized prices, it appeared that the service agent prices in some Eastern European countries with relatively low general cost levels had been higher than in Switzerland, one of the most expensive countries in the world. As a result, it was possible to significantly reduce the costs in Eastern Europe.

Pricing Models

The starting point in the design of service agent compensation is the selection of the pricing model. Alternative pricing models were introduced in Chapter 3 and include the following:

1. Fixed price
2. Cost/resource based pricing
3. Hourly charge
4. Transactional pricing
5. Value-based pricing
6. Hybrid model

The selected pricing model directly affects service agent incentives. In the following, the impact of different pricing models on service agent behavior and fraud management is discussed.

Fixed Price

From the manufacturer's perspective, the benefit of a fixed-price model is that it largely eliminates possibilities of fraud that would increase service agent compensation per claim. The fixed fee covers all cost components and there are no other charges. Due to uncertainties related to estimation of future failure rates and types of failures, the party conducting servicing may need to add contingency to the service price increasing the costs. Furthermore, the service agent may optimize its costs by offering only minimum services to the end-customers, affecting customer satisfaction.

Cost/Resource-Based Pricing

The benefit of the open-book model is that it allows very small margins to be achieved. Its shortcoming is that it incentivizes inflation of expenses. The more there is to bill, the higher the absolute margin the service agent obtains. Contractual incentive mechanisms can be built to reduce such incentives. Another shortcoming of cost-based models is the difficulty of control when (i) the service agent is doing work for multiple warranty providers or (ii) the service agent is doing both in- and out-of-warranty repairs. As a result, costs related to out-of-scope services might be charged to the warranty provider. Like the open-book model, a full-time employee (FTE)–based model also incentivizes inflation of costs.

Hourly Charge

A shortcoming of the hourly model is the difficulty of controlling the number of hours actually worked. It also incentivizes inefficiency. The more time is spent for work, the more can be charged from the warranty provider.

Transactional Pricing

When compared with an uncapped hourly charge, fixed transactional fee reduces possibilities to inflate costs through reporting excessive durations. It also allows service agent prices to be compared with each other. It suits clearly defined, repetitive activities like large-scale repair operations and easily scales with the volume of servicing.

Value-Based Pricing

As discussed in Chapter 3, in value-based models, the service agent compensation depends on the outcome of the service. If the warranty provider is able to reliably measure the outcome without a risk of service agent manipulating the figures and there are no additional charges, this model largely eliminates the opportunities for fraud. What the service agent has done is no longer relevant, as the focus is on what has been achieved. This model can be applied, for example, in B2B maintenance service contracts where the installed base is well known. However, this model is an unlikely candidate for warranty repairs with large volume of low- or medium-priced consumer products where location and state of installed-base is not known.

Hybrid Models

Hybrid models combining elements from different pricing models can be used to ensure the desired behavior.

Chargeable Costs

Another key decision is to define those cost components the service agents are allowed to charge within the selected pricing model. Service agents often apply the following cost components in their billing:

- Labor
- Material costs
- Travel costs
- Shipping costs

The cost components that can and cannot be charged to the warranty provider need to be defined and stated in the contract. This depends on the applied principles and pricing model. For example, in the open-book setup, rent can be charged while in a transaction-based pricing model, and rent needs to be included in the price of the transaction. If a fixed price is used, cost components are only relevant when setting the fixed price.

Labor

The contract should define the labor activities the service agents are to be paid for. Having a clear definition of acceptable activities prevents service agents from inventing and including additional items into their billing.

In a transactional pricing model, tasks with similar costs and effort—e.g., different types of soldering activities—can be grouped together under one service activity instead of having them separately priced. Grouping allows the length of the price list to be limited. There are industry-specific differences in the suitable number of activities. In warranty repairs for consumer electronics, 10 to 20 service activities may be sufficient, whereas in more complex systems like cars or machinery, the number of activities can be counted in hundreds or thousands.

Before entering pricing discussions with the service agents, the warranty provider should exactly know the time and costs involved with each service activity. This allows fact-based price negotiations and estimation of resource requirements.

Experienced in-house service experts can measure the durations of each service activity. The measured time should include not only direct service time but also the time required for indirect service activities. For example, the administrative work of entering repair data after the service activity should be acknowledged.

When the time required by each service activity is known, compensation can be calculated by multiplying it with the hourly cost. Differences in labor costs in different countries need to be acknowledged by applying local hourly cost rates. The assumption is that the hourly charge covers service agent margin and other overhead costs like management and investments.

Material Costs

Besides labor costs, spare parts and other materials are another key component of service costs. Alternative pricing methods can be used, such as:

1. Material cost included in transactional price
2. Service agent–defined price list

3. Warranty provider–defined or negotiated price list used with
   a. Cost-plus approach
   b. Cost only
   c. Cost and fixed material handling fee
4. Provision of parts

Including material costs within the transactional price may work in some clearly defined transactions with little variation in material requirements. However, if the same service transaction, for example, soldering work, can involve the change of a highly expensive spare part, a low-value part, or only fixing with no parts requirements at all, this model does not work.

Service agent–defined price lists are not recommended, as this results in price variations across service agents and makes controlling difficult.

In a cost-plus model, the service agent can buy the parts from an authorized source at a price known by the warranty provider and add a jointly agreed margin.

When provision of parts is used, service agents are not compensated monetarily for parts usage. Instead, they are delivered as many parts as they have used, either based on reported parts usage in warranty repairs or in exchange for returned replaced parts.

Both service agent–defined prices and cost-plus model incentivize excess spare parts usage, as the service agent can earn more by using more parts. To eliminate such incentives, a zero-margin approach can be used. In this case, the service agents are only paid as much as they have paid for the spare parts themselves. Alternatively, the warranty provider can supply parts to the service agent in exchange for faulty parts returned by the service agent. The warranty provider can also own and maintain a stock of spare parts at the service agent location, which is then used by the service agent. In a zero-margin approach, the labor cost of a service activity is assumed to cover the costs of related spare parts handling. Alternatively, a small fixed spare part handling fee can be paid to the service agent for service activities with spare parts usage. Consequently, service agent compensation is not increased even when higher-value parts are used.

Our recommendation is to use zero-margin or fixed-fee-based approaches, as they are easy to control and minimize the incentives for excess parts usage. This is also the case when provision of parts is used.

Furthermore, the spare part compensation should not cover low-value consumable materials like screws where the administrative cost of claim handling exceeds or is close to the value of the materials used. Instead, these should be included within the transactional compensation.

Travel Costs

In field service operations, the time and expenses incurred from traveling need to be covered. Different options include:

- Fixed charge or fixed charge by distance zone
- Charge for mileage
- Charge for mileage and travel time

Fixed charge is easy to control and provides less room for manipulation. However, fixed charge is an average and less accurate than variable, mileage-based charge. When mileage-based charge is used, a common reference for travel time and distance should be agreed. For example, travel time and distance provided by Google Maps could be used as a reference.

Shipping Costs

The pricing options for shipping costs are similar to the ones applicable for spare parts. One approach is that the transportation company directly charges the warranty provider and the service agent is given a fixed handling fee, making the service agent costs easy to control. Another method is to have a common transportation price list on top of which a fixed handling fee is added.

Claim Reporting and Payment

Claims Process, Information Systems, and Data

The claim reporting process, information systems used, data content, and format are central to warranty provider's ability to control warranty expenditure:

- Claim-specific data with a set of required data fields enables claim validation and analytics. If individual claims are not separately reported, claims cannot be validated and there is no possibility to reject unacceptable claims.

- It is important that the same data are available and used at different phases of the warranty chain. The contact center RMA process, service agent customer entitlement process, and claim validation process should use the same data to decide whether a certain customer warranty claim is covered by warranty.

- The standardization of processes, tools, data content, and format enables the same validation tools and the same analytics methods to be easily used across the service agent base. If different service agents are sending claims in different formats, automated claim validation and data analysis cannot be done with a reasonable effort.

Surprisingly, we have seen cases where service agents send their warranty claims as a monthly invoice that only shows the aggregate amount of warranty repairs done within the month. This approach provides almost no possibilities for fact-based fraud detection.

Claim Reporting Data and Format

Needless to say, service agents should deliver warranty claims in an electronic and standardized format. Each individual repair should be separately reported to enable claim validation. The mandatory data to be included in the warranty claim is a very important part of contractual requirements as it largely determines how warranty claims can be controlled.

The data to be included in a claim vary across industries and products. According to Figueora (2009), automotive warranty records typically have 20 to 50 fields. Data that can be derived from company's own databases should not be required unless they are needed for cross-checking purposes. Chapter 5 described the main categories of data collected during a warranty repair. A detailed list of data fields and the reason why each field is needed is described in Appendix A. Not all of these fields are needed in every company, and additional specific data fields are needed in some companies. For example, data related to traveling and customer location are relevant in field service only.

Claim Reporting Systems and Integration Options

Chapter 5 discussed alternative claim reporting systems and integration options between the service agents and the warranty provider. Real-time claim reporting provides improved opportunities for claims control—e.g., through reduced possibilities for repair date and time manipulation. Consequently, the selected system and integration approach should minimize the delay between a repair and is being reported to the warranty provider and, when possible, support real-time reporting.

Frequency of Claim Reporting

If the requirements for the frequency and the acceptable period for reporting claims are not defined, multiple issues may arise:

- Claims may come with long intervals.

- Additional claims from earlier periods may suddenly pop up, although the warranty provider assumed that all claims would have been received.

- Service agents may report claims with varying intervals.

This has several consequences from the cost-control point of view:

- The patterns detected within the data are not reliable, as all claims are not yet received.

- Comparison between service agents cannot be properly done, as their reporting follows different cycles.

- Out-of-warranty repairs can become in-warranty repairs if a past date is used as the repair date. In a similar way, other fictitious claims may be created using past dates, making them more difficult to observe.

- Time stamps within the warranty data may become unreliable from the analytics point of view, as the service agents may report date and time of claim submittal instead of the date of actual repair.

 Consequences of Missing Deadlines

CASE STUDY

A manufacturer did not contractually define deadlines for submission of claims. Service agents submitted their claims infrequently, many of them only once a month. Furthermore, very old claims could be submitted. For example, in October, additional claims related to repairs done in June could be received. Accounting period had long been closed and adjustments were needed. Identification of out-of-warranty repairs also became difficult. Service agents were able to apply old repair dates to make the out-of-warranty repairs appear as in-warranty repairs.

The ideal approach is to require warranty service claims to be submitted in real time as the repair process proceeds—for example, when a product has been received for a repair, when the repair has been started and completed, and when the product has been returned back to the customer. If this is not possible and the claims are, for example, reported only once a day, the claim should include time stamps for key phases of the process indicating both the date and the exact time of the activity.

The exact time stamp helps in data analysis. It is not easy to invent fraudulent warranty service claims with a statistically plausible distribution, as will be discussed in the Analytics section of this chapter. Consequently, the approach used by some of the service agents, where an administrator reports warranty claims once a week or once a month without time stamps, should be avoided.

Payment Process

The traditional invoice-based invoicing and payment process provides service agents opportunities for fraud. Typically, this process involves the following steps:

1. The service agent submits claims, including price for labor, parts, and other cost elements.
2. The warranty provider approves claims and may reject a part of them.
3. The service agent sends an invoice based on the approved claims.
4. The warranty provider pays the invoice.

The prices applied in step 1 may be incorrect. Also, the value of the invoice sent in step 3 may not match the value of the approved claims. To eliminate these loopholes, the warranty provider should require self-billing to be used instead of invoicing. In a self-billing process:

1. The service agent submits claims with information on conducted activities and parts used, but without a price.
2. The warranty provider approves claims and may reject a part of them.
3. The warranty provider calculates the payment value using price data in its own database. This ensures that only approved claims are included and the payment value is correctly calculated.
4. The warranty provider pays the service agent.

As a result, the service agent can no longer manipulate various unit prices and send invoices in which the value does not match the sum of the value of the approved claims. However, in this case the validation burden is on the service agent side—to verify that the warranty provider compensates the right amount for the servicing work done.

Servicing-Related Requirements

Servicing According to Guidelines

The guidelines on servicing aim at achieving a consistent quality of service, preventing cost inflation through overservice and service agent cost minimization through underservice at the expense of quality. The following items are to be considered in the service agent contract:

- The service agent carries out the servicing following the service guidelines defined by the warranty provider.
- Compensation is limited to labor and materials suggested in the guidelines. Additional labor activities and materials usage is not paid for.
- The service agent should not be entitled to compensation, should it not follow the service guidelines and skip required activities and part replacements.
- The service agent should also diagnose the product to identify possible hidden problems and fix them, together with the primary fault.
- The service agent is not compensated for mass modifications of products, mass software updates, or other similar service activities unless separately requested by the warranty provider. This issue is illustrated by the following case.

 Mass Software Updates

CASE STUDY

A consumer electronics distributor imported products to its home country and then exported them to other countries. As the language versions of the products needed to be changed to match the needs of new destination countries, the distributor conducted a software update for the exported products. The manufacturer was then charged for the software update. As the need for update was not caused by a defect and this activity was not preapproved, the manufacturer rejected the claims.

Competence Requirements

To ensure the quality of service, the warranty providers set varying degrees of requirements for the service agent employees conducting the service activities. Otherwise, the service agents could use unqualified personnel in order to save on labor costs.

- Apple Inc. (2015a), for example, states: "Service Providers are required to use Apple Certified Macintosh Technicians when conducting diagnostics, covered repairs, modifications, alterations and upgrades on Apple products. For every thirty Apple repairs conducted each week, a service provider should employ at least one Certified Technician."

In the contract, the warranty provider can require that (i) the technicians conducting the services are certified, (ii) the technician ID of the person who has conducted the service is reported in each warranty claim, and (iii) warranty provider has the right to reject the claim if an unauthorized technician has conducted the service.

Service Levels

Service agents can intentionally fail to meet service level targets to minimize their costs of service delivery. On the other hand, customers can be given and the warranty provider charged for service levels that the customer has not paid for. For example, the duration of warranty repair can be excessive or the customer can be given emergency service, although the customer is not entitled to service with such service levels.

To provide contractual means for managing these issues, the service agent contract should:

- Define service levels to be applied.
- Establish controllable mechanisms for following up service level fulfillment.
- Allow compensation to be reduced if service levels are not met.

When customer service levels vary, the contract should also:

- Require the service agent to verify the service levels the customer is eligible for.
- Allow the service agent to be paid only in accordance with customer service levels, not for overservice.

Approvals Needed from the Warranty Provider

Certain repair and replacement activities are very costly. Engine repair or replacement, transmission replacement, head gasket repair, and replacement of air conditioning compressor are listed among the most expensive car problems (Rawes, 2014). To control costs related to such repair and replacement activities, warranty providers can set a requirement for preapproval. The service agent needs to seek approval from the warranty provider before selected service activities or part replacements can be done. Furthermore, the warranty provider can reserve the right to physically inspect the product before it is repaired or require additional information about the faulty product (e.g., photograph of the defect).

Spare Parts and Other Materials

Spare Parts and Other Materials to Be Used

Service agents may try to avoid costs by buying parts from alternative low-cost sources while charging the warranty provider as if genuine parts were used. To avoid this scenario, the contract can include requirements specifying sources from where parts are to be purchased. The warranty provider can require that only approved parts are to be used and that the service agents buy their parts from the warranty provider, the manufacturer, or authorized parts distributors. Furthermore, use of repaired parts or parts cannibalized from beyond economical repair (BER) products can be prohibited.

Ownership, Storage, and/or Return of Defective Products and Spare Parts

When an item—a product or a spare part—is replaced at the warranty provider's cost, the warranty provider can assume ownership of the defective items. Additional contractual requirements for storage and return of defective, replaced items can be set. This helps the warranty provider to reduce opportunities to report fictitious product replacements and parts usage. Even when items have been used, storing them allows them to be diagnosed to verify if they really were faulty and if the replacement was necessary. In the contract, the service agent can be required to store the items locally, to ship them to the warranty provider at request, or to ship them by default to a warranty provider–defined location. When items are stored or delivered to the warranty provider, they should be clearly identified in a way that allows them to be matched with warranty claims, as discussed in the section on auditing. Warranty provider can also reserve the right to postpone service agent payment until the defective items related to a claim have been returned to the warranty provider.

Rules for Acceptable Claims

Repair Warranty

When the quality of service is inadequate, the serviced product may fail again. As a result, the product in question needs to be serviced multiple times, which means that the customer needs to interact with service and the warranty provider potentially needs to pay multiple times for a single defect. Customer satisfaction decreases and costs increase.

To manage the issue, there should be a clause that:

- Establishes a service agent repair warranty during which the service agent needs to repair the product free of charge
- Defines the duration of repair warranty—for example, to be two months from the date of repair
- Defines the rules for handling cases where another service agent conducts the subsequent repair
- Defines whether the repair warranty covers only the original defect or any defect detected during the repair warranty period

The recommendation is to extend the repair warranty coverage to all defects instead of the original defect only, at least when the product in question is relatively small, allowing full diagnostics to be conducted with a reasonable effort. The reasoning is that the service agent (i) needs to carefully diagnose the product, detect and repair also those defects the customer has not identified herself/himself and (ii) needs to conduct the repair in such a way that no additional damage is caused during the repair.

In addition to eliminating claims resulting from a sloppy service, repair warranty reduces opportunities to reuse serial numbers from own and other service agents' earlier repairs to create fictitious claims. Cost avoidance through skipping of service activities also becomes less lucrative as this may result in repeated service work at the expense of the service agent.

Carriage return

Introduction of repair warranty increases the risk that the service agents do unnecessary repair activities and part replacements during the first repair to minimize their risk of needing to carry the cost of warranty repair. Warranty providers can for example apply material returns and no fault found diagnostics for received parts to mitigate this risk.

Validity of Serial Numbers

If a warranty claim does not have a serial number or the serial number is not valid, the warranty provider cannot verify from its databases if the product is in warranty and whether a product with this serial number exists. The contract (for serial-numbered products) should require that (i) each claim needs to have a serial number and (ii) the serial number needs to be valid. This means that the serial number needs to be manufactured or sold by the warranty provider or a serial number of a product included in the service or maintenance contract. Claims without a valid serial number can then be rejected. If the serial number in the customer product is illegible—for example, due to scratching—the service agent needs to deny the customer from having the warranty service, as the service agent is not to be compensated, either.

Proof of Physical Presence

If the service agent is able to obtain valid serial numbers from other service agents, to generate them through known serial numbering logic, or using other methods, the requirement on serial number validity alone does not prevent fictitious claims. One effective method of verifying that a product has actually been in service is to require a proof of physical presence at the time of service.

There are alternative solutions that can be used for providing a proof of presence, as illustrated by the following examples:

- Taking a photograph with the product and its serial number visible and submitting it with the claim is a basic although not a watertight method.

- Attaching a label to the product with a unique code that differs from serial number and requiring technicians to scan and submit these codes with the claim in addition to the serial number. This prevents the use of serial numbers generated through a known numbering logic, as it is practically impossible to generate the second code that matches the serial number without having the product physically at hand.

- Reading a unique code, which changes over time, from the memory of the product itself. This is a more advanced solution that prevents the reuse of claim data obtained earlier.

- A smart connected product can independently or through a diagnostics application communicate with the warranty provider and provide information about itself and its location. This information can be compared with the data in service agent claims.

Such technical solutions should be designed as a part of product development and made secure enough to minimize the risk of tampering. Even when a technical solution is not in place, the service agent contract should reserve the right to require such information in the future and allow the warranty provider to reject claims without a proof of presence.

In- and Out-of-Warranty Service

A key requirement in the service agent contract is that the agent carefully verifies warranty validity before servicing the customer product. If this requirement is fulfilled, the warranty provider is not charged for out-of-warranty repairs. If the service agent fails to verify warranty status although the product is out of warranty, the warranty provider can reject the warranty service claim even when the customer has received the service.

The following requirements are recommended to be included in the contract. They form the basis for checks to be done as a part of service agent's entitlement process:

- *Product is in warranty.* The service agent needs to verify that the product is in warranty, following the criteria and steps defined in the contract.

- *Proof-of-purchase document or extended-warranty certificate is submitted.* If the warranty status is determined by a proof-of-purchase or extended-warranty certificate, the service agent needs to store it and, if required, deliver a copy of such document to the warranty provider with the claim. To minimize customer and service agent effort, this should only be required if validity of warranty cannot be determined through other means.

▦ *Proof-of-purchase document or extended-warranty certificate is legible.*
The service agent needs to check that the mandatory information required by the warranty provider is legible and is not
tampered with by the customer.

▦ *Authorization for goodwill service is available.*[1] Out-of-warranty
products can be serviced for goodwill purposes at the warranty
provider's expense only by following predefined procedures.
Preapproval or quota of preapprovals is to be obtained from
the warranty provider and reported with the claim.

▦ *No customer damage, misuse, or alterations.* If the customer has
caused the defect, the warranty is not valid. The service agent
contract should set a requirement for the agent to check for
possible customer damages, signs of misuse, and alterations
when receiving the product and when conducting the repair
and charge the customer instead of the warranty provider, if
the product has been damaged by the customer. The verification should be done following the warranty provider–defined
procedures. Further evidence, for example, photograph, status
of liquid damage indicators, acceleration or other sensor or
other diagnostics data read from the product, can be required
as additional information.

▦ *No cosmetic repairs.* The warranty provider does not compensate
warranty claims related to cosmetic repairs that are not covered
by warranty.

▦ *No compensation for no-fault-found products.* The warranty
provider may exclude compensation to service agent for diagnostics costs in case no fault is found in the device. Instead, the
service agent can be requested to charge the customer instead.
As this policy is likely to affect customer satisfaction, the
decision on applying it should depend on the overall targets
set for warranty management.

Service Agent Management

Warranty Provider's Right to Audit

The right to audit the service agent is one of the key enablers of
warranty fraud detection and prevention. In addition to having a
clause giving the audit right to the warranty provider, the service agent
contract should set additional requirements to ensure that access to
the required information, people, parts, and products is attainable and
the scope of the audit is not limited by the service agent.

Actions if Fraud Is Detected

Suspecting fraud and trying to get additional information to confirm or reject the suspicion is a delicate matter and often difficult to act upon. Having the actions defined in the service agent contract acts as a pre-warning and makes it more a standard procedure and less threatening or personal against the service agent. Once there is a situation, the warranty provider actions are backed up by the contract. It is important to proactively define and communicate actions the warranty provider will take if service agent fraud is suspected or confirmed. This is particularly essential when the warranty provider is the manufacturer and the service agent is a part of the sales channel—that is, manufacturer's customer. When the same procedures apply to all service agents and the procedures are jointly agreed before fraud is suspected, taking action is easier even in a politically challenging situation. The contract can—for example, give examples of indicators or anomalies based on which unwanted behavior can be suspected. In such a case, the service agent can be required to provide clarification or to open the records, so that an audit can be conducted. Based on preagreed criteria, a warning can be given to the service agent, refund requested, the service agent contract terminated, or legal actions taken against the service agent. A clause allowing the warranty provider to terminate the service agent contract for any reason is desirable as it helps to manage cases, where there is a high probability of fraud, but watertight evidence cannot be provided.

Incentives

The contract includes the compensation mechanism definition, including prices and incentives. The incentive and compensation schemes as a part of service network management are discussed in more detail later in this chapter.

ENTITLEMENT AND REPAIR AUTHORIZATION PROCESSES

Entitlement

The primary purpose of entitlement is to verify (i) warranty coverage and eligibility for service under warranty, (ii) the scope of coverage, and (iii) the service level that is allowed. Although this process primarily focuses on the customer, the service agent may be the party that conducts the entitlement. As illustrated in Chapter 6, the service agent can conduct fraud at the expense of the warranty provider by servicing out-of-warranty products.

The first decision to be made is whether:

- Entitlement can be done by the service agent or
- Entitlement and service are separated

The risks of a service agent doing the entitlement process include the possibility of creating fictitious claims and intentionally conducting out-of-warranty service, while marking the service as in-warranty and invoicing the warranty provider. Out-of-warranty service can relate either to the product being out of warranty or the failure not being covered by warranty.

In the latter case, the service agent is allowed to repair or replace the product only after the customer has obtained a return material authorization (RMA) from the warranty provider. This involves extra effort, but is a powerful method in preventing service agents from creating fictitious claims. To be able to claim nonexistent cases, the service agent would need to act in collusion with a warranty administrator working in the RMA process or pretend to be a customer requesting authorization.

The warranty provider needs to define the entitlement process and procedures for the service agents and have a mechanism to verify that they are followed in a prompt manner. The checks the service agent is required to do as a part of entitlement process were defined in the subsection on in- and out-of-warranty service in the section on service agent contracts.

Methods to detect fictitious claims are discussed in the Analytics section in this chapter. To detect out-of-warranty failures falsely approved by the service agent, the warranty provider should request sample copies of the customer proof-of-purchase documents or extended-warranty certificates to be verified. Furthermore, sample technical analysis of the defective parts and products can be done, as well as service agent auditing, mystery shopping, and customer verification calls (discussed in more detail later in this chapter) to verify that the service agent is not double-invoicing both the customer and the warranty provider. Good candidates for sample verification are cases where the customer purchase date according to the service agent is much later than one would expect based on the product manufacturing date and the expected channel lead time.

Long Channel Lead Time from Manufacturing to Customer

A service agent submitting a substantial amount of claims had a normal distribution of the time between production date and the date claimed to be the customer purchase date (5 percent of products sold within one year and 95 percent of products sold within two years). However, the remaining 5 percent included both cases where the customer purchase date was recorded to be before the product was even manufactured or there was a very long lead time between the customer purchase and the manufacturing date. The lead time could be five to seven years. Both extremes were flagged and acted upon.

Repair Authorization Process

As discussed in the section on service agent contract, expensive repairs and replacements should not be allowed without advance authorization even if the product is under warranty. For example, in heavy machinery, the cost of an individual spare part may be thousands or even hundreds of thousands of dollars.

As a result, the service agents should be required to seek advance approval, especially if the repair is highly expensive. Preauthorization can be requested by contacting either warranty provider's contact center or warranty processing unit. The warranty provider may wish to send an in-house or third-party inspector on site to verify the necessity of repair and its cost estimate. Many extended warranty providers use this practice with automobile warranties.

CLAIM VALIDATION PROCESS

Warranty claim validation can be defined as a process of verifying whether each warranty service claim meets the criteria set for an acceptable claim. A typical claim validation process has the steps illustrated in Figure 9.1.

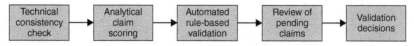

Figure 9.1 Steps in a typical validation process

The activities involved are as follows:

1. The service agent electronically submits the warranty service claims to the warranty provider.

2. Warranty provider's claim validation system verifies the claim file or claim data for technical consistency.

3. Analytical claim scoring analyzes the likelihood of fraud for each service agent and claim. This topic is further discussed in the section on analytics.

4. Automated rule-based validation verifies claims against the warranty provider's specific set of claim validation rules and applies the score obtained from analytical claim scoring.

5. As a result of validation and the score, each claim is either approved, rejected, or becomes pending.

6. A pending claim can be approved or rejected based on warranty administrator's judgment. Further information or actions may be required before the claim can be approved (e.g., return of the replaced part to the manufacturer and inspection of the part, delivery of a proof-of-purchase document or further information about the service done from the service agent). When completed, the claim either becomes approved or rejected.

7. The warranty provider sends purchase order with all approved claims to the service agent.

8. The service agent issues an invoice based on the purchase order and gets paid.

9. A possible dialogue between the service agent and the warranty provider is conducted on claims that are not approved.

Validation can also be done before the service activity starts.

- Apple does the majority of validation in this way via their warranty system. They, for example, validate eligibility, compare described failure with parts ordered, and check technician certification for the repair upfront. Practically the only part to be validated after repair is the returned defective material.

Claim validation can be automated by implementing validation rules in the system. Even then, the validation system typically handles the claims one by one. Based on the validation rules, the validation tool verifies if an individual claim is acceptable. In analytical claim scoring, the individual claims are compared with the overall claim population to identify service agents and claims with the highest probability of fraud. This allows limited claim validation resources to focus on the areas with the highest probability of fraud, instead of randomly going through claims from any service agent. Claim scoring can also directly impact automatic approval/rejection of claims. For example, a claim that would otherwise become pending can be directly approved if the claim gets a positive rating in the claim scoring. Claim scoring is further discussed in the next section.

User judgment plays a critical role in complementing automated claim validation. Human intervention is required when claims cannot be directly approved or rejected by the system. For example, if two service agents appear to be repairing the same product items within a very short time interval, the warranty administrator can evaluate if this is a random occurrence only or a repeating pattern. Cases appearing to be random incidents can be approved. If fraud is suspected, further actions—for example, request for additional information, analytics, and audit—can be taken before making the decision on whether to approve or reject the claims. Supervisors' role is to ensure that warranty administrators follow the validation procedures and do not optimize personal workload. We have seen cases where validation is done in minutes by simply approving all the claims. User training and incentives are also needed to avoid validation becoming a routine. At the same time, sufficient claim validation resourcing needs to be available to avoid skipping checks due to shortage of time. The amount of manual work depends on the level of automation of the rules in the claim validation system and the ability to prioritize. As fraudulent service agents continue to invent new methods of fraud, it is important that somebody keeps an eye on the claims. Often, a professional warranty administrator can detect new patterns simply by looking at the claim data.

It is important to validate the claims and make the required adjustments to the payment amount before the payment is made. The second alternative is to make the deductions from the subsequent payments. In some cases, this does not work. The service agent may not accept the deduction without a lengthy battle. A single service agent company may even ramp down its operations and avoid refund as illustrated by the following case.

A Cluster of Companies Doing Fraud

In one case, about 10 service agents were identified as belonging to the same ring of fraudsters. Some of the companies were submitting clearly fraudulent claims while others were acting normally. When actions were taken against one company, it changed its behavior. However, another company in the cluster then started submitting large amounts of seemingly fraudulent claims. In some cases, a service agent ramped down its operations altogether. This went on several rounds before the whole cluster was acted upon.

If service agent's claims become pending or are rejected, the warranty provider can expect a fast response from the service agent, requesting further information on reasons for not accepting the claim. An audit trail between the rejections and underlying facts and decisions needs to be kept.

The warranty provider needs to make a policy decision on how much it wants to reveal about the reasons for rejection. On one hand, the service agent has the right to know the reasoning behind the rejections. On the other hand, revealing the reasons and underlying rules in detail allows fraudulent service agents to circumvent the rules.

Technical Consistency Checks

The purpose of technical checks is to ensure that the delivered claim data are valid and match warranty provider's specifications. The relevance of some of these checks depends on the integration method the service agent uses to deliver claim data to the warranty provider. For example, if data are directly entered to warranty provider system, the format of individual fields is checked when the data are entered and the file format check is not necessary. The technical checks include the following:

- File format is correct.
- Data fields are of correct format and length.
- All mandatory fields are reported.
- The claim has been sent by a valid service agent.

- The reported codes (e.g., service agent ID, labor and part codes) are valid.
- The reported dates and times are valid and in the right sequence (e.g., not in the future or repair not done before warranty start date).

These checks prevent, for example, nonwarranty data, old file versions, incomplete claim data, and nonexistent parts from being uploaded to warranty provider's system.

Rule-Based Validation

Validation rules vary from industry to industry and company to company. Checking the mileage threshold is relevant for automobiles, but not for mobile phones. Distance traveled is relevant in field service, but not if the repairs are done in a service center.

The validation rules used in claim validation should mirror the (customer) warranty terms and the rules for acceptable repairs in the service agent contract.

In the following, typical claim validation rules used by the warranty providers are introduced.

Checks for Duplicate Work Orders and Repeated Repairs

The checks for duplicate work orders and repeated repairs within a defined time period verify that claims related to the same product are not charged multiple times:

- Multiple repairs from the same service agent with the same work order ID do not exist.
- Same product has not been repaired at the same time or within too short a time interval by two service agents.
- The equipment in question does not fall under repair warranty as such cases should be repaired at service agent's cost.

Entitlement Checks

The purpose of the entitlement checks is to verify that the product exists and is under warranty. If the product is not under warranty, the service agent needs to be specifically authorized to conduct the repair (e.g., for goodwill reasons). The key entitlement checks include the following:

- The reported serial number is valid and the product exists.
- The warranty period has not expired, taking into account differences in base warranty durations in different countries and for different parts and possible extended warranty and maintenance service contracts.

 Serial Number Checking with No Impact

CASE STUDY

A consumer products company had a rule that every warranty claim needs to include a valid serial number. In a data analysis we noticed that many of the serial numbers were violating the generation rules and failed the automatic check. All of those claims were still paid in full.

 Out-of-Warranty Claims Detected

CASE STUDY

A company manufacturing televisions conducted an assessment to identify opportunities to reduce warranty costs. In the assessment, it was observed that validation did not include check for warranty status in one of company's major markets. When this control was turned on, warranty costs dropped by more than 20 percent overnight.

- The product usage does not exceed set limits (in two-dimensional warranties).
- The product has not been damaged by the customer—as indicated by the customer-reported symptoms, the technician-reported fault, sensor, or the diagnostics data obtained from the product.
- The product appearing to be out-of-warranty in warranty provider's registers has a valid proof of purchase, an electronic copy of which is delivered by the service agent together with the claim. If the proof-of-purchase document has not been delivered, the claim remains in pending state until the document has been received. After it is received, it is to be checked by the warranty administrator. If it is illegible, appears

to be counterfeit, or if the purchase date in the proof of purchase differs too much from the date information available in warranty provider's registers, the claim can be rejected or subjected to further investigation. Similar checks can be applied to verify existence of extended-warranty certificates.

- Out-of-warranty repair is conducted only if the repair has been preauthorized by the warranty provider. The authorization can, for example, be in the form of approval code delivered with the claim data, approval associated with the product's serial number, or approval quota associated with the service agent in warranty provider's systems.

- The product has not been stolen or scrapped and is not a prototype.

 Stolen Products Caught During Repair

CASE STUDY

Finding a stolen product may allow the culprit to be caught as witnessed by one of the authors. Hundreds of high-value products had been stolen during distribution from the manufacturer to a distributor. The serial numbers of stolen products were updated to manufacturer's entitlement system. Some of the stolen products ended up in repair. During the entitlement check, the products were identified to be stolen. As a result, the persons who had stolen the products were identified. They were employees working in the distributor's warehouse.

Servicing-Related Checks

The purpose of the checks related to servicing is to verify that the service data are coherent and the service agent is authorized to conduct the activities it has reported. The checks include the following:

- The service agent is certified to conduct the service activity claimed. Only specialized service centers may be allowed or have the capability to conduct certain types of repairs.

- The product has physically been in service. Physical presence is validated using a reported code (e.g., read from product's memory, code shown on the label of the product, information directly reported by connected products during repair, or location data reported by connected products).

- The technician is certified and the certification covers the product and service activity in question. This is to avoid use of technicians who have not been trained and certified to conduct repairs in general or certain types of repairs for certain products.

- The product has been sold to the customer referred to in the claim (when up-to-date installed base data are available).

- The customer reported within the claim is a valid customer. Customer's address and telephone number exist and are valid for this customer.

- The primary fault and/or part causing the damage has been reported.

- The claim is not reported as a no-fault-found case. (Not to be applied if the service agent receives products from third parties, such as point of sale or service agents on lower tiers. In such case, the service agent in question is not able to prevent no-fault-found products from entering the service chain.)

- Spare parts used in the repair are such that they can be a part of this particular product's configuration (i.e., they belong to its bill-of-materials).

- Labor activities and spare parts match the customer-reported symptoms, technician-reported fault, or diagnostics data reported by the product before and after the repair.

- Labor activities requiring parts usage have parts reported with them.

- The travel charges (e.g., time, distance, or zone) do not exceed predefined claim-specific and daily limits and match the location and measured distance to customer site.

- The service is done within service level. For example, the repair lead-time service level can be checked by comparing the customer-reported issue date and time with the time of completion reported by the service agent.

- The warranty provider has authorized the repair, when preauthorization is required or required inspection has been conducted. As in the case of goodwill repairs, this check can be based on an approval code submitted with the claim or approval information stored in the warranty provider's system.

- Replaced parts or products have been returned to the warranty provider before the claim is approved. If the return has not been registered, the claim remains in a pending state until the part has been returned.

Billing-Related Checks

The purpose of billing-related checks is to verify that correct prices are used in the claims and the claims have been sent within contractually agreed time limits:

- Correct prices have been used in the claim. The checks include verification of all separately priced cost elements like labor, spare parts, and travel costs contractually agreed with each service agent in the latest valid price list. This is only needed if the service agent delivers prices with the claims. Instead, the recommended approach is to maintain the compensation data and calculate the payment value in warranty provider's system.
- The maximum values for different cost elements have not been exceeded.
- The claim has been delivered within predefined time limits from the date of repair. For example, if weekly reporting schedule is applied, claims with repair date older than one week are not accepted. This prevents service agents from submitting claims related to past periods and partly limits the methods available for creation of fictitious claims.

Prerequisites and Recommendations for Claim Validation

The ability to conduct claim validation has several prerequisites:

- The validation process and rules are defined and implemented both within the company itself and within its service agent base.
- The organization responsible for validation is assigned and the importance of thorough validation perceived.
- Claim data format and content and validation systems are standardized.
- Access to data needed in claim validation is provided.
- The method for obtaining claims from service agents is defined.

Claims Accepted without Proper Validation

CASE STUDY

A warranty provider had distributed claim validation responsibility to its country organizations. Claim validation was an additional piece of work assigned to people mainly responsible for other activities. As a result, these persons neither had sufficient amount of time to conduct their responsibilities adequately, nor were they able to build the required competencies. As a result, the claims were, in many cases, simply approved in mass to save time.

It is possible to use nonstandard formats and multiple claim validation systems, but in this case, the results of claim validation are likely to be compromised. Differences in data content prevent the use of best practice validation rules.

Another prerequisite is that the data needed in claim validation exist and are available in one database or otherwise accessible by the validation system. Claim validation cannot be adequately conducted if the warranty provider does not have all the data needed (discussed in Chapter 5)—for example, information on active service agents, warranty start dates, warranty contracts, service levels, granted repair authorizations, product configurations, bill of repair materials, authorizations given for technicians, scrapped and stolen materials, travel distances, and price lists.

ANALYTICS

Claim validation focuses on individual warranty service claims. When evaluating claims, it largely works in a binary manner. If a claim meets the criteria set for an acceptable claim, it is accepted; if not, the claim is rejected. For example, the product is either in warranty or not in warranty, spare part is applicable for the repair in question or not, or a preapproval has been given for an out-of-warranty repair or not. In between, there is an area where claims are pending until the results of further investigation are obtained.

However, claim validation has its limits. This is illustrated by the following example. If a valid spare part is used in a repair, the claim is accepted. If there are multiple claims with the same spare part, each of the claims is also accepted. Even if the same part has been used in all of the repairs, claim validation still considers each of the individual claims to be acceptable, even if such a widespread failure in one part would be highly unlikely. No differentiation is made between cases where the part has been used in 1 percent, 20 percent, or 100 percent of the repairs. What looks like a valid claim at individual level can appear fraudulent when seen at an aggregate level. Analytics is needed to evaluate claim validity across individual claims.

Various analytics methods can be used to address different methods of fraud. It is important to understand the methods of fraud to ensure that analytics methods are available to address each type of fraud. Also, methods bringing up anomalies are needed to detect previously unknown methods of fraud.

Methods used in detecting service agent fraud vary from simple reports to advanced analytics. Benchmarking of service agents is one of the key tools to identify abnormalities. If the behavior of a service agent clearly differs from other service agents, this can be a sign of fraud. Benchmarking can be done using various attributes of warranty service claims. Cost of repair, proportion of different types of repairs, and proportion of specific spare parts used in repairs are some of the examples.

Use of statistical distributions is another key method in fraud detection. This approach is based on the fact that it is difficult to create fraudulent claims in a statistically consistent manner, as illustrated by the following case.

Heads, Tails, and Difficulty of Plausible Fraud

CASE STUDY

If one flips a coin 100 times, one gets a series of heads and tails that appear randomly in the series. There are few successive heads or tails in a row as the probability of several repeated heads or tails soon becomes small. For example, the probability of getting 15 tails or 15 heads in a row within a sequence of 100 flips is around 0.5 percent, whereas the likelihood of getting 10 tails or heads in a row is around 15.3 percent and getting at least 5 in a row is almost certain, with the probability of 99.8 percent. If one would manually add individual heads or tails to a random series, this could be statistically detected as the random distribution of heads and tails would soon get distorted.

If one considers warranty service claims, the difficulty of inventing statistically consistent fraudulent claims multiplies. Instead of being able to consider only one dimension of data (head or tail), a fraud perpetrator needs to consider a large number of attributes from serial number to fault codes and spare parts used. They all need to be statistically consistent within the overall claim population.

Although statistical analysis is an important tool for fraud detection, it also has its limitations. Not all methods of fraud can be detected with analytics. Use of fake parts as an example is not directly visible in the analytics, although indirect hints of it can be obtained. Another key limitation is that analytics best applies to high-volume operations. Analytics applied to data from service agents with a small number of service activities may not yield statistically significant results. Industries, where the size of the installed base is limited, cannot fully benefit from analytics either. This is often the case in B2B operations. Also, small-scale fraud is hard to detect. The following subsections discuss different analytics methods available and how they can be used to address different methods of fraud. The discussion is divided into three subsections:

- Analytical scoring of service agent and of claims
- General methods for identification of anomalies
- Targeted analytics against specific methods of fraud

Analytical Scoring of Service Agent and Claims

Analytical scoring of service agent and of claims complement rule-based claim validation and can reduce the number of claims requiring user judgment by separating high-risk claims from the ones with low risk of fraud.

Burke (2014) divides scoring into service provider (i.e., service agent) risk score and claim anomaly score. Each is given a score from 1 to 100. A higher score indicates a higher likelihood of fraud. Burke continues by stating: "A service provider's risk score is based on analyzing and benchmarking dealers on many factors like costs, frequency, repair profiles, parts/labor, etc. The score is also impacted by how many times claims were manually adjusted or rejected in the recent past. The claim anomaly score is used by manufacturers based on past claim patterns and audits in new claims."

General Methods for Identification of Anomalies

General methods include advanced and other analytics that can be used to bring up anomalies in the service agent data, suggesting that something is wrong with the particular service agent's claim reporting. However, these analytics methods do not highlight the use of any particular method used in fraud, but are the starting point for further analysis.

Self-Organizing Maps

According to Germano (1999), self-organizing maps (SOMs) are a data visualization technique that reduces the dimensions of data through the use of self-organizing neural networks. The dimensions are reduced by producing a map with usually one or two dimensions. The map plots the similarities of the data by grouping similar data items together. This allows complex data sets with large number of variables to be visualized.

Self-organizing maps can be applied to cluster service agents with similar claim characteristics together on a two-dimensional map. One practical example relates to variations in claim attributes. We have seen that service agents with fraudulent claim reporting typically use smaller number of attribute values than is present in other service agents' data. This applies, for example, to use of symptom and failure codes, service activities, and parts usage. When fraudulent claims are generated or adjusted manually, the imagination of the person manipulating the claims normally does not match the variations present in real life. When service agents are put on a map based on the variation in claim attributes, those service agents that are located close to the ones with known fraud can be identified and subjected to further analysis as illustrated by Figure 9.2.

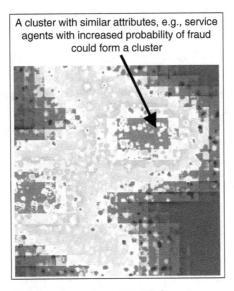

Figure 9.2 An example of a self-organizing map (Köpf, 2013)

Benford's Law in Serial Number Analysis

Benford's law is named after Dr. Frank Benford, who noticed in 1938 (Kristensen, 2012) that for a very diverse set of naturally occurring data, some numbers appear much more frequently than others when looking at the first digits in the number sequence. Intuitively one would expect the first nonzero digits to be random, and there would be an equal chance for the first digit to be between 1 and 9 and for the first two digits to be between 10 and 99. However, the first digit is far more likely to be 1 than it is to be 9. More specifically, approximately 30.1 percent of the numbers have 1 as the first digit, falling down to 4.6 percent for the numbers having 9 as the first digit. The first two digits from 10 to 99 follow a similar pattern, starting from 3.6 percent for 10, falling down to 0.39 percent for 99. If the data set in question follows Benford's law, it can be used in fraud detection, which has been researched and applied quite extensively during the past 15 years.

Kraus and Valverde (2014) tested Benford's law with sample data reflecting two years of warranty claims from dealers of an automotive manufacturer. They did not find any fraudulent cases, but did separate a case, relating to a product recall campaign, involving the replacement of a large number of faulty parts and a significant deviation from the expected distribution.

We have used a similar approach in analyzing the last two digits of the product serial numbers in warranty claims and noticed that some cases are visually quite easy to identify, as highlighted in the following example. Figure 9.3 shows the empirical frequency graph of the numbers (00 to 99) based on the data from service agent 1. Here every pair of digits from 00 to 99 has roughly the same frequency (hovering around 1 percent), as is to be expected from an honest service agent.[2] Figures 9.4, 9.5, and 9.6 show the empirical frequency graphs using data from three other service agents—2, 3, and 4, respectively. These differ significantly from Figure 9.3. The shapes indicate the different ways the numbers for nonexistent claims were created. In all three cases, the service agents had invented a significant number of nonexistent claims.

Targeted Analytics Against Specific Methods of Fraud

The different fraud methods that service agents use are discussed in Chapter 6 and can be seen in Figure 6.6. This section introduces a set of analytics methods that can be used to test the existence of

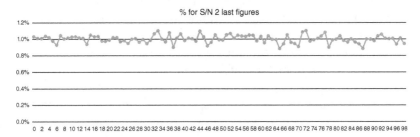

Figure 9.3 Service agent 1: Uniform distribution of serial numbers' two last digits

Figure 9.4 Service agent 2: Skewed distribution of serial numbers' two last digits

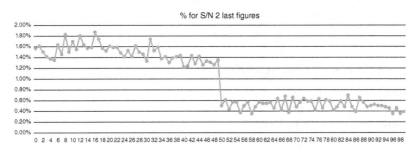

Figure 9.5 Service agent 3: Skewed distribution of serial numbers' two last digits

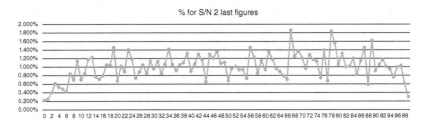

Figure 9.6 Service agent 4: Skewed distribution of serial numbers' two last digits

specific methods of fraud. These methods can be adjusted and additional attributes included, depending on the situation. Individual analytics methods may be applied for detection of multiple types of fraud. Various methods can and should be used in combination with each other to obtain further information on suspected fraud. Running the analytics, combining results of multiple methods, calculation of statistical significance, and highlighting the deviations can be automated. In the following, we look at methods to detect:

- Fictitious claims
- Out-of-warranty servicing
- Inflated claim prices and excess parts usage
- Cost avoidance

Detection of Fictitious Claims

If the service agents invoice their warranty service claims as a total quantity without claim-level breakdown or if individual claims are reported but they are not serial numbered, the possibilities available for analytics are limited. When applicable, claim-level reporting on serial number level should be set as a requirement in the contract between the warranty provider and the service agent.

Claims without Serial Numbers

Some of the analytics methods can be used in detecting fictitious claims even when serial numbers are not available. One option is to look at claim volumes by product and type of repair. The volumes can first be looked at using longer time intervals, for example, monthly volumes. The drill-down can then continue to weekly, daily, and hourly figures. Use of graphs and comparison to other service agents allows easy observation of suspicious peaks and other anomalies in the shape of the graph. For example, repair volume on certain week, day, or hour can be much higher than on others and exceed service agent's estimated repair capacity as indicated in Figure 9.7. Volume data can also be delivered to the auditing team, who can compare claimed volume with service agent capacity. The team can verify whether the repair capacity is sufficient to handle the highest reported daily or hourly volumes. A prerequisite for analyzing distribution of claim volumes

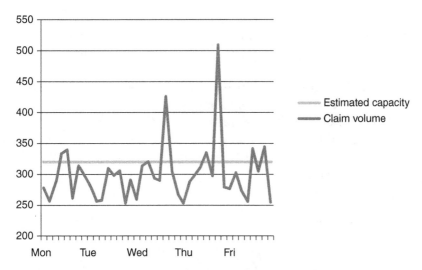

Figure 9.7 Daily/hourly distribution of reported work versus capacity

over time is that service agents are required to report the exact time of servicing the product, not, for example, to create claims once a week on Fridays using Friday as a servicing date.

It is often very difficult to create fictitious claims where the ratios of different attributes match the similar ratios based on the overall claim population. Not only distribution of the time of service, but also the distribution and sequence of serviced products, fault types, service activities, parts usage, and all other attributes need to match. Do certain products or certain types of repairs have a different volume distribution than others? How does the service agent being analyzed compare with other service agents?

Claims Generated When the Serial Numbering Logic Is Known

When serial numbers are generated using a known numbering logic, the service agents can create serial numbers that are assumed to be valid. As the service agents typically do not know the boundaries of serial number ranges and distribution of serial numbers related to the real-life defects within this range, the serial numbers of fictitious claims tend to be close to each other. This provides an opportunity for analytics. As real serial numbers are randomly distributed across the overall serial number space, generated serial numbers are often clustered around known valid serial numbers. This can be made visible by sorting claim data by serial numbers and calculating the differences between subsequent serial numbers.

Table 9.4 illustrates serial numbers from generated and normal warranty service claims. Serial numbers are sorted and the difference between subsequent serial numbers is calculated. In this example, and also often in real life, generated serial numbers have very small differences, while normal serial number data have larger differences and larger variations.

Table 9.4 Serial Numbers from Generated and Normal Warranty Service Claims

Generated serial number data		Normal serial number data	
Serial Number	Difference	Serial Number	Difference
4115852	-	1840416	-
4115894	42	1840651	235
4117241	1347	1840677	26
4117243	2	1840992	315
4117247	4	1841004	12
4117249	2	1841043	39
4117271	22	1841057	14
4117313	42	1841305	248
4117322	9	1841398	93
4117323	1	1841457	59
4117324	1	1841496	39
4117327	3	1841776	280
4117328	1	1842155	379
4117330	2	1842264	109
4117332	2	1842367	103
4117333	1	1842517	150
4117336	3	1842599	82
4117339	3	1842869	270
4117342	3	1843104	235

CASE STUDY

Serial Number Distribution and Fictitious Claims

A consumer products manufacturer with high-volume repair operations had a pool of 150 service agents. Contracts with many of the service agents had been terminated due to suspected fraud. New service agents had been selected to replace the expelled ones. The remaining service agents were assumed to be relatively honest, and no major issues had been identified with the available control methods.

When serial number distributions in the claims submitted by each of the service agents were analyzed, additional cases surfaced. By looking at the graphs, it was visually possible to detect that some of the service agents were conducting fraud in a large scale and many others had some levels of fraud through serial number generation only.

Actions were taken, resulting in major savings for the warranty provider.

The clumsiest service agents have had long rows of serial number differences of 1. Slightly more advanced service agents have differences varying between 1 and 10, and still more advanced ones are using a wider range of differences.

CASE STUDY

Probability of Identified Patterns

A high number of claims with sequential serial numbers were identified in a service agent's claim data. The probability of products with the detected sequence of subsequent serial numbers ending up at the same service location on the same day was calculated to be 0.0000000000000001 percent. After initial denial, the service agent later admitted fraud.

There are also other indicators of fictitious claims being created through known serial number logic. A service agent creating fictitious claims may want to verify that the serial number really exists and the respective product is under warranty. Warranty provider's entitlement system can be used for this purpose. If the service agents need to log into the system and if the system keeps search history, the warranty provider can study the patterns of queries conducted by different service agents. Service agents with high percentage of queries made with nonexistent serial numbers are possibly probing the system when creating serial numbers. Low ratio of approved claims to entitlement system queries and low ratio of in-warranty versus out-of-warranty within submitted warranty service claims are similar indicators.

In Table 9.5, service agent 3 has an unusually low ratio of approved claims to queries. Only 42 percent of the queries relate to approved warranty service claims, indicating use of entitlement system to verify validity of fictitious serial numbers. At the same time, the service agent has entered 1,872 invalid serial numbers to the entitlement system. This suggests a possibility of serial number fabrication. Service agent 8 also has relatively high number of queries with invalid serial numbers.

Another indicator of fictitious warranty service claims is overrepresentation of products originally delivered to countries other than the country of repair. This is caused by the fact that the service agent does not normally know where the manufacturer has originally shipped each of its products. In the same way, products shipped to other states, an other part of the same country, otherwise differing geography, or unusual customers can be detected with this method.

Table 9.6 illustrates the issue. In a normal situation, claims include a small percentage of products originally shipped to another country. This can, for example, be explained by tourist imports or Internet purchases. In this table, service agent 6 stands out by having an anomalous percentage of claims with a product originally shipped to another country.

Table 9.5 Entitlement System Queries

Service Agent	Number of Approved Claims	Number of Entitlement System Queries	Ratio of Approved Claims to Queries	Queries with Invalid Serial Number	Queries with Invalid Serial Number of All Queries
Service agent 1	779	884	88%	33	4%
Service agent 2	412	492	84%	11	2%
Service agent 3	1,592	3,781	**42%**	**1,872**	**50%**
Service agent 4	913	1,224	75%	23	2%
Service agent 5	488	558	87%	22	4%
Service agent 6	22	25	88%	1	4%
Service agent 7	79	116	68%	1	1%
Service agent 8	449	734	61%	**101**	14%
Service agent 9	114	134	86%	1	1%
Median ratio			84%		4%

Table 9.6 Percentage of Warranty Claims with a
Product Shipped to Another Country

Service Agent	% of Products Shipped to Another Country
Service agent 1	3%
Service agent 2	2%
Service agent 3	1%
Service agent 4	2%
Service agent 5	3%
Service agent 6	**26%**
Service agent 7	2%
Service agent 8	1%
Service agent 9	3%
Median %	2%

Claims Generated by Dumpster Diving

Obtaining serial numbers from proof-of-purchase documents taken from points of sales' trash cans and cars parked in parking lots were raised in Chapter 6 as examples of obtaining serial numbers. If the number of such claims is small, they may be difficult to identify through analytics.

Some hints on dumpster diving can still be obtained, especially if the volumes created using this method are bigger. These include excessive proportion of claims related to products sold through a particular distributor and biased age distribution (discussed later in this chapter) resulting from the fact that serial numbers obtained from proof of purchase are typically only a few weeks or a few months old, while real product failures distribute more evenly across warranty period.

Serial numbers obtained from parked vehicles may pop up as the proportions of claims relating to different car models, cars sold through different sales channels, or to different geographies—e.g. certain zip codes—gets overrepresented and do not match the proportion in overall claim population from all service agents.

Serial Numbers from Own Earlier Repairs

Taking serial numbers from own earlier repairs is perhaps the easiest method to generate fictitious claims. At the same time, this is also very easy to detect, as the proportion of repeated serial numbers is higher than in the benchmark population. Also, the product age distribution of claims becomes biased, as the average age of products at the time of repair is by definition higher than within normal claims if the reported date of repair is later than in the original claim. When repair warranty is in place, a part of the claims is directly rejected in validation.

Table 9.7 illustrates the percentage of those claims where a product with the same serial number has been repaired by the same service agent two or more times during the reporting period. In this example, 9.7 percent of service agent 5's claims have products that have been repaired more than once within three months.

The same method also applies to products that are typically repaired multiple times during their warranty period, e.g. cars. In this case, the rate of repeated repairs is likely to be higher for all service agents. The fraudulent ones stand out with higher than average repeat rates.

In addition to comparing serial numbers, one can also compare other details of the claims. Sometimes, the claim attributes and free text descriptions are directly copied from earlier claims, sometimes invented by the person creating the fraudulent claim. When claim attributes are invented, the variation of different values used in the claims may get reduced. The person generating the claims may not have the imagination to generate claims matching the variety of real events. When the claims are then statistically compared with the overall claim population, a deviation in proportions of claim attributes can be observed. Also, identical or suspiciously similar free text

Table 9.7 Rate of Repeated Repairs

Service Agent	Repeated Repair, 1 Month	Repeated Repair, 3 Months	Repeated Repair, 6 Months
Service agent 1	0.9%	1.8%	1.9%
Service agent 2	1.7%	2.5%	2.7%
Service agent 3	0.1%	0.6%	0.8%
Service agent 4	1.5%	1.5%	2.0%
Service agent 5	0.8%	**9.7**%	**10.7**%
Service agent 6	0.4%	0.6%	1.1%
Service agent 7	1.7%	2.4%	2.5%
Service agent 8	0.5%	0.9%	1.2%
Service agent 9	0.1%	0.3%	0.6%
Median %	0.8%	1.5%	1.9%

descriptions may appear. Often, when an amateur has conducted the fraud, this becomes apparent by simply looking at the claim data without conducting any analysis.

Serial Numbers from Other Service Agents

Claims fabricated using serial numbers obtained from other service agents can be detected using largely the same methods as claims created using the service agent's own earlier repairs. In addition to looking at the percentage of repeated repairs from the service agent itself, the analysis is extended to cover repeated repairs from other service agents. If the number of repeated repairs is higher than in the benchmark population and if a small number of service agents seem to have repeated repairs between each other, further analysis is probably needed. The repeated claims not being evenly distributed in time, but appearing in clusters, can provide further supporting evidence.

Table 9.8 highlights the repeated repairs between two service agents. Columns show the number of claims where another service agent has repaired the same product already earlier during the reporting period. In this example:

- Service agent 5 has 87 repairs that have been done by service agent 8.
- Service agent 8 has 135 products earlier repaired by service agent 5.

As similar patterns do not exist between other service agents, there is a possibility of serial number exchange between service agents 5 and 8.

Serial Numbers from Own Sales Stock

As discussed in Chapter 6, one method of obtaining the serial numbers required in claims is to scan the serial numbers from the stock of sellable products. This works if the service agent is or acts in collusion with a distributor or a retailer.

A shortcoming of creating claims using own sales stock is that timing of fraudulent claims is not in conformance with the timing of warranty repairs. Benchmarking to other service agents or statistical methods from reliability theory can be used to detect this method of fraud.

Table 9.8 Repeated Repairs between Service Agents

	Service agent 1	Service agent 2	Service agent 3	Service agent 4	Service agent 5	Service agent 6	Service agent 7	Service agent 8	Service agent 9
Service agent 1		–	–	12	–	–	–	–	–
Service agent 2	–		–	–	4	–	2	–	–
Service agent 3	1	–		–	–	–	–	–	9
Service agent 4	–	–	–		–	–	3	–	–
Service agent 5	–	3	1	–		–	–	**135**	–
Service agent 6	2	–	1	–	–		–	–	1
Service agent 7	–	–	–	–	–	2			2
Service agent 8	–	1	–	6	**87**	–	–		–
Service agent 9	–	–	–	–	–	–	3	–	

First, an empirical graph of failure rate (discussed in Chapter 2) is obtained using the ages of products at failure for the overall service agent population. This is used as the benchmark value.

Second, a graph of the actual service agent claims/repairs over time is done for the service agent under investigation. If this does not match the benchmark value, the deviations can be a result of fraudulent behavior on the part of the service agent. Fraud can be easily detected, as the claims to be repaired tend to be younger in age than typical repairs unless the service agent waits before submitting the claims. Often, the deviations appear in the form of peaks or other abnormal shapes.

Figure 9.8 shows two plots of the number of claims (normalized as a percentage) as a function of the age of the product at the time of failure. The first corresponds to service agent X. The second is the average distribution across all service agents. As can be seen, the two differ significantly. Service agent X used serial numbers from the stock to create fictitious claims soon after the inventory was restocked. As a result, the failure rate shows a peak at an early age.

The graphs shown in Figure 9.8 can be used to detect other fraudulent activities as well. If there is a peak with older products, close to the end of the warranty period or even beyond, the service agent may issue claims using serial numbers from products with recently expired warranty and double invoice the customer and the warranty

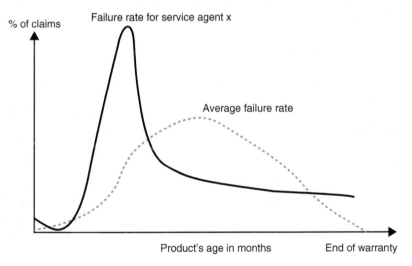

Figure 9.8 Age of the product at the time of service

provider. Other peaks may be visible when other serial number generation methods are used by the service agents (see Accenture, 2011, for reference).

Serial Numbers from Customer Products

Scanning serial numbers from customer products is one of the methods used when creating fictitious claims. Serial numbers can be scanned from nonfaulty products when visiting the customer. Analytics provides some possibilities for detecting such cases. If the end customer of the products is known, those customers from whom serial numbers have been scanned can be overrepresented among the claims. Their claims may also be clustered time-wise.

Serial Numbers from Warranty Provider's Registers

In the previous cases, fictitious claims were centered on a source from which serial numbers were obtained, like another service agent or a distributor. If the warranty provider gives access to its installed base database, a wealth of product and serial number data become available for the service agents. In this case, detection of fictitious claims is somewhat harder than in the other cases as there is no single factor around which fictitious claims are grouped. Even in this case, analytics can give hints on fraud. If, for example, the serial numbers selected for the claims to be submitted do not follow the average failure rate as a function of time, fraud can be uncovered. In a similar way, other attributes of claims can be analyzed to detect the fabrication of bogus claims.

Detection of Out-of-Warranty Servicing

A significant proportion of warranty service claims can relate to out-of-warranty products if warranty status is not controlled. Validation can reject clear cases, but claims can still be approved—for example, for goodwill purposes or if a customer has a proof of purchase showing a purchase date that is later than the one derived from warranty provider's registers.

The starting point for out-of-warranty analytics is to report the percentage of cases where product's base warranty or extended warranty has expired, but the claim has been approved due to aforementioned exceptions. The percentage of such cases should be small and in line with other service agents.

Table 9.9 presents the percentage of out-of-warranty claims by service agents. It shows that service agents 2 and 4 differ from other

Table 9.9 Proportion of Out-of-Warranty Products Approved in Claim Validation

Service Agent	Out of Warranty Total, %	Approved with Proof of Purchase	Goodwill Approval
Service agent 1	5.3%	4.7%	0.6%
Service agent 2	**9.2%**	**6.4%**	2.8%
Service agent 3	3.5%	2.1%	1.3%
Service agent 4	**8.0%**	1.5%	**6.5%**
Service agent 5	2.9%	2.6%	0.4%
Service agent 6	2.6%	1.4%	1.2%
Service agent 7	2.6%	2.5%	0.1%
Service agent 8	1.3%	0.6%	0.7%
Service agent 9	3.4%	3.2%	0.2%
Average	4.3%	2.8%	1.5%

service agents in the percentage of out-of-warranty repairs. Service agent 2 has an exceptionally high proportion of repairs approved with proof of purchase. This can be a sign of improper service agent entitlement control. Service agent 4 has an exceptionally high percentage of cases approved for goodwill reasons, which can indicate careless or fraudulent use of goodwill approvals. Further actions are needed to analyze these cases—for example, requesting service agent 2 to deliver copies of proof-of-purchase documents or a review of cases approved for goodwill reasons with service agent 4.

Other variables to monitor include the volume of repairs done just before the base warranty expires and just after the start of the extended warranty. If there is a possibility to report the claim using a date that is earlier than the actual repair date or register an extended warranty contract with a delay, out-of-warranty repairs can be made to look like warranty repairs. Differences in the volume distributions across service agents can reveal such arrangements. However, one should acknowledge that there often is a real peak in warranty repairs just before warranty expires, as customers rush to have their products repaired before the warranty expires (see, e.g., Rai et al., 2009). Some manufacturers even encourage their customers to have their products repaired before warranty ends.

Figure 9.9 illustrates a similar peak in service agent repair activities just before the car's mileage limit of 60,000 miles is reached, after which the warranty expires. In addition to customers wanting to have

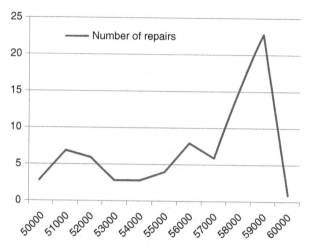

Figure 9.9 Number of repairs and mileage

their cars repaired before the warranties expire, service agents may report lower odometer reading so that the repair qualifies as a repair under warranty.

A product damaged by the customer is not covered by warranty. Servicing such products under warranty can be detected if the service agent has honestly reported customer damage as a reason code in the claim. If not, analytics can look for signs of customer damage in the claim data. These include customer description of symptoms reported within the claim, parts used, and the types of service activities done for the product. Self-diagnostics or sensor data read from the products can also reveal customer damage. For example, acceleration sensor can reveal that the product has been dropped.

Apple's Consumer Abuse Detection System

CASE STUDY

Apple Inc. has a patent titled "Consumer abuse detection system and method." The patent covers one or more sensors that detect an event of abuse and store it in the memory of the product. Available sensors include liquid, thermal, continuity, and shock sensors as well as an accelerometer (Johnson, 2010).

Like customer damage, refurbishment of worn-out products should not be covered under warranty. Excessive use of cosmetic parts like covers suggests existence of refurbishment activities. In particular, this can be the case if the volume differs from the volumes of other service agents.

Detection of Inflated Claim Prices and Excess Parts Usage

As discussed in Chapter 6, service agents can use a variety of methods to inflate their claim price, including the following:

- Inflating the price of an existing claim through various methods like reporting fictitious service activities or fictitious parts usage
- Intentional overservice or using too many parts

We now discuss methods to detect these kinds of fraud.

Cost Benchmark Table

Like benchmarking in general, benchmarking of costs is a powerful, yet simple method to observe signs of fraud and other deviations. The starting point is to:

- Calculate average cost per claim.
- Break it down to cost components such as labor, parts, and travel.
- Benchmark each individual service agent within the overall service agent population.

Service agent costs are then presented in a tabular format so that costs of different service agents can be compared with the average cost for all service agents. Table 9.10 is an illustrative example where the costs of service agent 3 and 7 clearly exceed the average.

Actions can be targeted at the service agents with the highest costs as illustrated by the following case.

 Applying Average Repair Cost Analysis

CASE STUDY

A warranty provider compared the average repair cost across a large number of service agents. The service agent with the highest average cost was selected for an audit. It was a relatively small repair shop run by a father and a son. The audit team did not even need to go inside to detect that something is wrong. The owners had highly expensive cars parked in front of the repair shop that were not in proportion to the income expected from a small-scale business. During the audit, major fraud was confirmed.

Table 9.10 Service Agent Cost Benchmarks

Cost by service agent	Total, $	Labor, $	Parts, $	Other, $
Average cost	105	66	22	16
Service agent 1	103	733	16	13
Service agent 2	101	64	20	18
Service agent 3	**140**	**90**	**36**	14
Service agent 4	90	55	18	18
Service agent 5	82	46	18	18
Service agent 6	90	49	25	15
Service agent 7	**147**	**115**	14	19
Service agent 8	94	56	21	17
Service agent 9	95	48	33	14

It is important to allow data to be filtered, for example, by product model and type of service agent. This allows detection of issues within subsets of data and natural reasons for deviations appearing as fraud to be ruled out. Drill-down can also reveal issues, for example, by bringing up inconsistencies in spare part prices.

Costs can also be benchmarked across countries. If price level differences between different countries are normalized, benchmarking can be extended to global service agent base.

Service Activity Benchmark Table

Another benchmarking-based method is the comparison of the distribution of service activities. This method highlights cases where expensive service activities are overrepresented, resulting in inflated service billing. Like with cost benchmarking, proper structuring of data is important as it allows ruling out valid product or service agent–driven reasons for the differences.

Table 9.11 shows a simplified distribution of automotive service activities by service agents. In this example, high-cost engine, heating and cooling, and transmission repairs are overrepresented within service agent 7's claims. The issue can be analyzed by drilling down to subcategories of service activities and individual claims, and in dialogue with the service agent.

Table 9.11 Distribution of Service Activities by Service Agent

Service Agent	Total, %	General	Electrical	Electronic	Engine	Heating and Cooling	Steering and Suspension	Transmission	Other
Service agent 1	100%	29%	4%	12%	0%	2%	11%	5%	37%
Service agent 2	100%	42%	13%	13%	1%	5%	7%	2%	17%
Service agent 3	100%	20%	1%	22%	6%	3%	3%	0%	44%
Service agent 4	100%	30%	10%	11%	5%	5%	9%	1%	30%
Service agent 5	100%	28%	2%	18%	2%	8%	8%	9%	25%
Service agent 6	100%	38%	6%	27%	5%	5%	8%	3%	8%
Service agent 7	100%	32%	10%	15%	9%	9%	10%	13%	3%
Service agent 8	100%	26%	7%	27%	4%	3%	4%	6%	23%
Service agent 9	100%	32%	10%	30%	3%	1%	3%	3%	19%
Average, %	100%	31%	7%	19%	4%	5%	7%	5%	23%

▼ Only One Type of Service Activity

CASE STUDY

When the distribution of different service activities has been analyzed, it is surprisingly commonplace to find that some of the service agents claim to be doing only one type of service activity. Amazingly, this service activity almost always happens to be the most expensive activity on the price list.

In addition to fraud, the service activity benchmark can highlight other issues requiring action. In some cases, the service agent or specific technician may need additional training. In other cases, the conclusion might be that a new service bulletin with more detailed instructions is required from the manufacturer.

Spare Part Usage Benchmark

One method to detect excess claiming of spare parts is to compare spare parts usage in repairs. To visualize deviations, spare parts usage can be presented in a tabular format. The comparison can, for example, start from the spare part forming the highest proportion of spare part billing and continue down to the lowest.

It is also worth looking at the usage of spare parts with the highest unit cost, as these are often the ones that fraudulent service agents prefer to use when inflating claims. Thus, another variant of this method is to organize the table based on spare part unit price, in descending order. Parts that have not been used or parts with trivial importance can be excluded from the analysis to avoid an excessive number of parts being included.

Table 9.12 illustrates how this benchmarking method can be applied. The percentage of repairs where a particular part (or module in this case) has been used is compared across service agents, highlighting the deviations. In this example, service agent 5 has excessive amount of motherboard replacements. Also, the ratio of power supply replacements stands out.

The product age at the time of service can be used to graph empirical failure rate as discussed earlier in this chapter. Similar graphs for individual spare parts can be used to detect fraud. If a service agent includes a significant number of fictitious spare parts in the servicing,

Table 9.12 Percentage of Repairs Where a Part Has Been Used

Service Agent	Motherboard	CPU	Hard Drive	Memory	Graphics Card	CD/DVD Drive	Power Supply	Fan
Service agent 1	1%	3%	5%	0%	1%	1%	6%	1%
Service agent 2	2%	2%	0%	1%	0%	0%	3%	1%
Service agent 3	2%	3%	6%	3%	4%	1%	0%	1%
Service agent 4	1%	3%	6%	1%	1%	0%	5%	2%
Service agent 5	**27%**	3%	2%	5%	2%	1%	**8%**	0%
Service agent 6	5%	3%	2%	1%	0%	1%	3%	2%
Service agent 7	4%	1%	3%	3%	0%	2%	1%	1%
Service agent 8	13%	0%	4%	1%	4%	1%	6%	1%
Service agent 9	2%	0%	4%	4%	2%	1%	0%	1%
Average, %	6%	2%	4%	2%	2%	1%	4%	1%

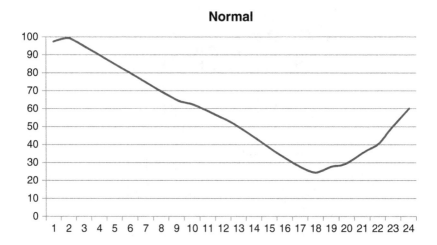

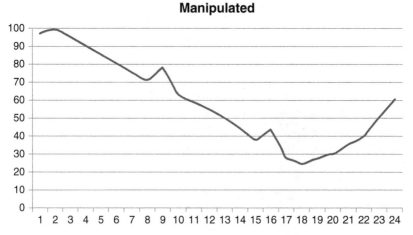

Figure 9.10 Failures of a given part over time—Normal and manipulated spare parts usage data

this alters the graph, results in a deviation from normal, and can be detected as illustrated in Figure 9.10.

Figure 9.10 shows a simulated example. The upper graph is the number of claims (normalized as a percentage) across service agents as a function of the age of the defective part under servicing.

The bottom graph corresponds to the case where the service agent has added extra bogus spare parts around months 9 and 16, resulting in the small peaks that can be seen in the figure—the bogus spares are only 1.6 percent of the actual spare parts used, but still visible in the graph. In real life, detecting the deviations is somewhat more difficult, as there are natural fluctuations in the claim data that hide small amounts of fraud.

Number of Parts Used

Number of parts used for a particular repair can be used as one indicator of excess usage. Service agents can be compared against the average parts usage. If a service agent is using more parts than required for a repair, this can indicate doing trial and error repairs, excess claiming of parts, and/or using the parts for out-of-warranty repairs.

Parts Used versus Parts Purchased

When parts are supplied by, or through, the warranty provider, the volumes purchased by each service agent are known. This allows comparison of the volumes of purchased versus claimed parts. Further investigation is required if the volume of claimed parts exceeds the volume of parts purchased. This can be a sign of fictitious reporting of spare parts usage, cannibalization of parts from warranty provider–owned products, or purchase of spare parts from unauthorized sources.

As some of the spare parts are used in out-of-warranty repairs that are not reported to the warranty provider, the ratio of claimed versus purchased parts should be less than one. Comparison of claimed versus purchased parts ratio across service agents allows the ones with the highest ratio to be picked up for further analysis. If reporting is manual, focus can be on parts with high monetary value. Automation allows more systematic comparisons.

Table 9.13 is an example with PC modules to illustrate this issue. Service agent 5 has a suspected issue with excessive claiming of motherboards and power supplies. Comparison of purchased versus claimed parts shows that the service agent has claimed more motherboards and power supplies than it has purchased. The ratio of purchased versus claimed parts for motherboards is 242 percent, but should be clearly below 100 percent to allow motherboard replacements in out-of-warranty repairs.

Table 9.13 Purchased vs. Claimed Spare Parts—Example from PC Repairs

Service Agent 5	Motherboard	CPU	Hard Drive	Memory	Graphics Card	CD/DVD Drive	Power Supply	Fan
Purchased parts	12	8	7	14	6	2	24	1
Quantity of parts claimed	29	6	5	13	3	1	28	1
Ratio	**242%**	75%	71%	93%	50%	50%	**117%**	100%
Difference	17	-2	-2	-1	-3	-1	4	0

Mismatch of Reported Activities

The validity of reported service activities can be verified by comparing the claimed service activities and parts usage with data available from other sources. These include:

- Symptoms reported by the customer when contacting customer service
- Symptoms reported by the customer at service point
- Fault diagnostics done by service agent technician him/herself
- Self-diagnostics data reported by the product
- Usage data reported by the product

 CASE STUDY

▼ **Mismatch between Claims and Diagnostics Data**

An automotive manufacturer utilized data read from the cars' on-board computers in fraud detection. Diagnostics data were compared with the service activities reported by the service agents. Clear mismatches were identified. Service agents had clearly not done those repair activities they had reported. A number of service agents were caught indulging in fraud.

Reported service activities and parts usage should match the data available from other sources. If the customer has complained about headlights, the service activity should not be to change the gearbox.

Distribution of Reported Activities

When fictitious service activities or parts are added to a claim, the fraudulent technician also needs to manipulate related data. For example, the fault code needs to match the service activity. Earlier, we discussed how to detect deviations in distributions of service activities and parts usage. Additionally, we can look at other attributes in the claim data and compare their distribution with the benchmark population of service agents. For example, the occurrence of different fault codes can be compared with other service agents. Table 9.14 illustrates a case where service agent 5 has abnormal distribution of fault codes. The percentage of no-fault-founds, software, and other faults is clearly higher than for other service agents.

One method of detecting fraud is to identify those service agents whose claims have common faults underrepresented.

Table 9.14 Distribution of Fault Codes Reported by Different Service Agents—Example from Mobile Phone Repairs

Service Agent	No Fault Found	Microphone Fault	Speaker Fault	Charging Fault	Display Fault	Customer Damage	Software Fault	Other Fault
Service agent 1	1%	3%	5%	0%	1%	1%	6%	6%
Service agent 2	2%	2%	0%	1%	0%	0%	3%	3%
Service agent 3	2%	3%	6%	3%	4%	1%	0%	0%
Service agent 4	1%	3%	6%	1%	1%	0%	5%	5%
Service agent 5	**27%**	3%	2%	5%	2%	1%	**8%**	**8%**
Service agent 6	5%	3%	2%	1%	0%	1%	3%	3%
Service agent 7	4%	1%	3%	3%	0%	2%	1%	1%
Service agent 8	13%	0%	4%	1%	4%	1%	6%	6%
Service agent 9	2%	0%	4%	4%	2%	1%	0%	0%
Average, %	6%	2%	4%	2%	2%	1%	4%	4%

Detection of Missing or Excessive Preauthorizations

When preauthorization for a repair is required, a reference code should be either reported within the claim data or associated with product serial number or other identifier. This allows the claims lacking authorization to be rejected during claim validation. Analytics comes into the picture if claim validation is not rejecting unauthorized repairs. Furthermore, analytics can be used to compare the volumes of repairs with preauthorization. This allows service agents with excessive usage of preauthorizations to be identified for possible further investigation and leakages in the preauthorization process to be detected.

Detection of Cost Avoidance Affecting Service Quality

As discussed in Chapter 6, service agents can skip service activities required by the warranty provider to save time, effort, and materials. Another method to save costs is to use unqualified technicians. The likely outcome of this behavior is poor service quality and increased probability of repeated product failure.

One sign of issues in service quality is repeated repairs for the same product. This can be measured as a percentage of repeated repairs within a time period, as indicated earlier. The analysis should include repeated claims from any service agent in the service network. Service agents with excessive repeat repair rates are then subjected to further investigation.

In principle, use of uncertified technicians can be monitored with a report that indicates the technicians who have conducted different repairs. The report can compare the data against the certified technicians. However, if the service agent intentionally breaches warranty provider policies and uses uncertified technicians, it is likely that the claim data indicating the identity of the technicians are also falsified. Claims done by uncertified technicians are reported using the identity of certified technicians. Some further investigation is needed to identify such cases. A basic check is to report repair volumes by each certified technician as a function of time. There should not be too many repairs compared to available working time or multiple repairs conducted at the same time. However, a limitation of this method is that service agents also conduct work for other warranty providers and do out-of-warranty repairs, blurring estimates on maximum capacity per technician.

Products themselves may also be able to report their status before and after the service, helping to reveal skipped activities with built-in sensors and logging facilities. For example, it is possible to compare changes in configuration, software, and diagnostics results with the claim data reported by the service agent.

MATERIAL RETURNS CONTROL

As mentioned in Chapter 6, excess claiming of spare parts within warranty service claims can be caused by:

- Overservice
- Unnecessary change of parts
- Fictitious claiming of spare parts
- Claiming but not replacing all required parts

Additionally, excess costs can result from unnecessary product replacements.

Requirements for handling replaced items can reduce excess parts usage. We have seen significant reductions in the volumes of claimed spare parts after implementing storage and return policies.

The requirements can be divided into two categories:

1. Storage at service agent premises
2. Return of parts to warranty provider–defined location

Cost–benefits analysis should be applied when making decisions on the scope of storage and/or return requirements. The requirements can be applied to replaced products and to most expensive spare parts only or to a wider set of parts. If certain part categories form a major proportion of the costs or if fraud is suspected in certain part categories, storage and return policy can be applied. The policy may also vary across service agents. Service agents with suspicious claim reporting may be required to store or return a wide set of parts while service agents with no observed anomalies can be relieved from this requirement.

Storage at the Service Agent Premises

Replaced parts and products can be stored at service agent premises. This allows the warranty provider to audit the inventory of used parts as a routine procedure, or if issues requiring clarification or alarming patterns are observed in service agent behavior and claims.

To add value, a set of requirements must be applied to stored parts. The parts need to be:

- Stored and sorted by the type of the part and claim period
- Separated from other parts used in the service agent's business
- Scrapped with warranty provider's approval or after a specified time limit only
- Scrapped in a way that allows their scrapping to be verified

This allows counting the parts and matching their volumes with the claimed part volumes in a given claim period. If parts are serial numbered, the validity of the serial number can be checked against the serial number of the part originally used in the product.

If parts used in in-warranty repairs are mixed with parts from nonwarranty repairs or with parts from different periods, it is nearly impossible to match stored parts with claimed volumes. If scrapping of parts is not controlled, service agents can simply state that old parts have been scrapped and reuse the old parts, as an evidence of parts usage on later periods. To avoid this issue, scrapping can be done by a certified third-party company that is able to provide an audit trail to the scrapping event, such as videographic evidence.

Storage of complete products and subassemblies also allows the auditor to verify that they have not been cannibalized by removing parts. It also allows parts and products to be taken for diagnostics.

Return of Parts to a Warranty Provider–Defined Location

An alternative to storage is to require the service agents to return defective parts to a warranty provider–defined location. A set of requirements also applies to material returns:

- The returned items need to be sorted in a way that they can be matched with claims from a particular reporting period.
- The return needs to take place within a set time period matching the needs of claims process and its schedule.

Despite the requirements, the returns process can get uncoordinated. Service agents may return a messy pile of parts and products. In such a situation, matching them with claims can become overly laborious. A communicated policy of not compensating the service agent before the parts have been returned and matched with the claims can bring discipline to the returns process.

Material returns provide more control options than storage at the service agent site. Parts and products can be:

- Counted and matched against claim volumes
- Diagnosed to find unnecessarily replaced products with no fault found
- Diagnosed to identify customer- and service agent–damaged products
- Visually inspected to detect signs of parts cannibalization

Furthermore, material returns provide other benefits beyond warranty control. Diagnosis can provide valuable information on root causes of issues for product development. Returned parts can be reused or sold to be recycled as material.

It is important that the material returns process is integrated with the claim validation and analytics processes. The results of counting and diagnosing parts need to be made available to warranty administrators so that they can do the following:

- Approve justified claims to be paid.
- Reject or keep incomplete claims pending.
- Get further evidence that potentially confirms the findings obtained in analytics.

Although parts are returned, not all of them need to be diagnosed or even counted. The possibility of control as such already reduces the likelihood of fraud. Diagnostics can be costly and sampling may be enough to meet the control targets. Frequency of sampling and sample size can depend on the outcomes of earlier diagnostics done for the parts and products returned by a given service agent.

SERVICE NETWORK MANAGEMENT

Service network management has two main elements that help in fraud detection and prevention:

- *Service network structure:* This has a significant impact on the scale of warranty fraud. Certain structural arrangements can greatly reduce or even eliminate fraud.

▨ *Service agent management:* This serves two purposes: warranty fraud prevention (reduce service agent need, motivation, and opportunities for fraud) and warranty fraud detection (which confirms or invalidates suspected cases and takes actions if fraud is identified).

In the following subsections we will discuss these two in more detail.

Service Network Structure

Naturally, there are many other factors than warranty fraud that need to be considered when designing the service network. From warranty fraud avoidance and control perspective, the key elements for consideration are:

▨ In-house versus outsourced warranty servicing

▨ Level of centralization

▨ Structure of material and information flows

▨ Having reliable comparison points for benchmarking

In-House versus Outsourced Warranty Servicing

Warranty servicing can be outsourced to service agents or done in-house. When a company conducts warranty servicing by itself, the financial benefits obtainable through fraud are reduced. Extra revenue gained through fictitious claims or inflating the price of claims becomes an internal cost transfer within warranty provider's accounting. Doing warranty service in-house can largely, but not entirely, eliminate warranty fraud. A statement from a service manager in a sports equipment manufacturing company highlights the issue: "Based on my experience of the excessive fraud in my previous company, I will never outsource repair."

Although outsourced service operations provide opportunities for fraud, there are other benefits of outsourcing that often overweigh the impact of fraud. Global in-house service network would require major investments and move focus away from company's main business. The efficiency of outsourced operations can be higher. Third-party companies can combine service volumes of multiple brands increasing productivity.

Furthermore, even when service is done in-house, some opportunities for fraud and misconduct still remain. Employees can still seek for personal gain—for example, in the form of workload minimization or bonuses. Service activities can be skipped to reduce own effort. Employees can take parts from spare part storage, claim to have used them in repairs, and then sell the parts. Field service employees can inflate mileage driven to increase travel allowance.

One important issue in outsourced service network structure is that a service agent should never be the sole party controlling its own work or, in a structure with multiple tiers, be the only party controlling the lower-level service agents it also manages. In a similar way, a warranty administrator should not have connections with the service agents it controls. Service agent being a part of sales channel is unavoidable in many industries. The connection needs to be taken into account and monitored for warranty control.

Level of Centralization

Having everything centralized into one service center location may be beneficial from productivity and management perspective, if the logistics costs can be kept reasonable. However, it is very difficult to find anomalies against the norm if there is only one service agent whose unwanted behavior is the only comparison point.

If warranty service is outsourced to one global or regional service agent with multiple locations, it is important that service agent claims still include information of the corresponding service center location and service technician. This provides comparison points for benchmarking across the service agent locations and technicians, if not between service agents. On the other hand, if the warranty service network is totally distributed, opportunities for benchmarking exist, but volumes for many service agents may be so small that any anomalies found are within the margin of error and statistical analyses are not very meaningful. Also, the cost of auditing a large number of small service agents may exceed attainable savings.

Structure of Material and Information Flows

The way the service network is organized and products and information managed within it can also affect the amount of fraud.

Customers can be instructed to always call warranty provider–owned call center to order service. Serial number of the product requiring service, symptoms, product issues, and required service activities can be logged in the call center. Alternatively, customers can be requested to physically send the products to the warranty provider, who diagnoses the fault and then sends them to different service agents to be repaired. These approaches reduce the opportunities to inflate claim volumes and to some extent the opportunities to inflate claim prices as well. As the warranty provider knows beforehand which products are to be serviced, the service agent cannot include additional service activities within its warranty service claims. Also, as the warranty provider knows the symptoms, the reported repairs cannot be too far off from the work that was actually conducted.

Segregation of duties between different players in the service network also has a similar impact. If field service engineers, smaller service points, or points of sale only collect products to be repaired and separate centralized service centers conduct the repairs, then possibilities for fraud are reduced as information reported by collecting and repairing parties needs to match. A service center cannot do more repairs than it has received from the network feeding it. Points collecting the products coming for service can also collect information on symptoms from the customer or diagnose the products, reducing service centers' opportunities of reporting repairs that have no connection with the actual work done.

Even in this setup, there is a possibility of collusion between different parties. Also, if the warranty provider's processes are sloppy, this approach loses its value. This can happen if only a part of the required information is collected or information delivered by different parties is not crosschecked to identify anomalies.

Having Reliable Comparison Points for Benchmarking

If the warranty provider does a part of warranty servicing in-house, those cases should be documented with the same structure and level of detail as the ones done by external service agents. This provides a reliable baseline and a comparison point on frequency of different types of repairs and the time required to conduct each type of service.

If that is not the case, there should be a service agent who has sufficient volume and is audited to a level that can be considered to be a reliable benchmark.

Service Agent Management

Service agent management serves two purposes in warranty fraud management: warranty fraud avoidance and warranty fraud investigation. In warranty fraud avoidance, the main target is to understand and reduce the service agent need, motivation, and opportunities for fraudulent activities. In warranty fraud investigation, the main target is to confirm or invalidate suspected cases and take actions if fraud is detected.

Warranty Fraud Avoidance

Warranty fraud avoidance is done mainly through the overall governance and management of the service agents. The key elements for consideration are the following:

- Setting the rules of operation
- Empowering the right people
- Driving performance
- Executing consequence management

Setting the rules of operation includes the timing and process of reporting service agent claims, the expectations in terms of clarity of reporting, and obligation on providing further information if suspicious claims or other anomalies are identified. It also includes the mutual expectations on how often the service agents are visited normally and what types of audit activities may be carried out.

Empowering the right people includes both the service agent employees and the warranty provider employees. The people executing the service in the front-line need to know the decisions they are allowed to do and the evidence they need to produce to allow the correctness of the decisions to be verified afterward.

There should also be a channel for service agent employees to report abnormal behavior, such as suspect customer claims or malicious activities inside their own company. In some of our projects, service agent employees have contacted the warranty provider to inform about fraud done by their employer.

The warranty provider's expectations toward the service agent (the voice-of-the-customer) must be communicated to the supervisors, customer-facing people, and service technicians within the service agent organization. As this is not always the case, it is important that the warranty provider ensures that it takes place.

Not all suspect cases are related to warranty fraud. Solving the issue might also require additional service tools or training for the service agents, or additional or more detailed information delivered through service bulletins, written in a clear way.

Driving service agent performance in the right direction includes compensation and incentivization schemes. For example, the following questions need to be answered:

- Is the compensation structure clear and understandable?
- Is it considered to be fair, or does it provide an excuse for the service agents to "try to make a living and recover what is rightfully theirs"?

The compensation structure may also include incentive schemes rewarding the right behavior and penalties on undesired practices.

One of the key problems in warranty fraud management is that service agents can increase their earnings through small-scale fraud without a risk of losing revenue or other negative consequences. If fraudulent claims go unnoticed, the service agent obtains extra earnings. If fraudulent claims are detected, the only consequence may be the rejection of these claims. In other words, a fraudulent service agent can only gain, but not lose. This is the case when fraud is not happening on a large scale and there is no threat of contract termination or legal actions. If the compensation scheme includes incentives for disciplined and high-quality warranty claim reporting, small-scale fraud becomes dis-incentivized, which reduces fraudulent activities.

An incentive system can change the behavior of a service agent and prevent indulging in fraud. For example, the following incentive mechanisms can be used:

- *The base price for warranty servicing can be relatively low.* Additional compensation applying to all claims is paid only if claims are consistently of high quality measured by a scorecard of fraud indicator metrics. This provides a penalty on probable fraud even when waterproof evidence is not available. As a result, adding fraudulent claims reduces the bonus available for the service agent and offsets the earnings obtained through fraud.
- *Penalties can be used to reduce compensation in case of suspected or confirmed fraud.* If the local legislation permits, the penalty can be set to be so high that it exceeds the earnings from fraudulent

claims even if part of them go undetected. For example, penalties that are 5 to 10 times the value of the fraudulent claim are being used (when not prohibited by local legislation).

 Incentivizing the Right Behavior

CASE STUDY

A global manufacturer had a large number of service agent claims with suspicious claim reporting, but had difficulties providing concrete evidence of fraud. It crafted an incentive scheme where a part of the service agent compensation was tied to the quality and consistency of the claim reporting. Having too many anomalies would reduce the variable part of the compensation. The motivation for fraud fell as the additional revenue earned by fraud would be lost, as the variable compensation would be reduced.

We have seen cases where the warranty provider catches a service agent for fraudulent behavior and is then quite abashed as to how to react. The principles of consequence management should be decided upfront, before fraud is found. These principles should be communicated very clearly within the warranty provider organization and across the service agent network. They should also be included in the service agent contracts answering the following questions:

- What are the different levels of fraud?
- What are the consequences on each level, such as just rejecting the claims, demanding credit notes, subtracting the overpayments from future claims, applying penalties or reducing performance incentives, termination of service agent contract, or legal actions? There should be an option for dialogue, audit, and warning before more determined actions are taken.
- What is the process for corrective actions?
- How is it verified that the service agent has taken the agreed actions?
- What is the expectation in terms of clarity of reporting and obligation for providing further information if suspicious claims or other anomalies are identified?

Policies that have been communicated in advance make the actions easier, especially if the service agent is also acting as a sales channel partner for the warranty provider.

The consequence management policy should also apply to suspicious behavior when there is no direct evidence of fraud. Even if the warranty provider cannot request direct remedies, it should be able to demand the service agent make changes to abolish the suspicious behavior.

Warranty Fraud Investigation

Claim validation, analytics, and material returns control bring up suspected cases of fraud. In such cases, existence of fraud can be validated through:

- Auditing
- Mystery shopping
- Customer verification calls

Auditing

Service agent audits can be divided into two categories:

1. Regular audits where warranty control is one element among the other topics to be handled
2. Focused audits that aim to obtain further evidence on possible fraud identified through claim validation, data analysis, material returns control, or other means

Regular audits are a part of the normal vendor management process, including the verification of the operational effectiveness, customer service, and the accuracy of financial transactions. That process should include methods to verify the existence of the service agent as an operational company with plausible operations, the correctness of warranty transactions, the service agent claim process, sample checking of proof-of-purchase documents, and the existence of the stored defective items. The service agents need to be aware that these audits will occur regularly and that they need to be able to demonstrate evidence supporting the claims they have made. The process audit should include:

- *Customer entitlement:* How is the entitlement executed and what options are the customers given when they bring a product to service? What is the consistency of customer experience?
- *Diagnostics:* How are the issues with the product analyzed? How are no-fault-found and customer-damage cases excluded from being covered by warranty? How are the in- or out-of-warranty decisions done?

▪ *Storage:* Storing the defective parts and products waiting for repair appropriately and scheduling the service activities.

▪ *The service process and compliance with warranty provider service guidelines:* The actual process, discipline of executing the entire service plan, available people and machine capacity, certifications of the service technicians, control of parts usage during the process, packing and dispatch of the products to the service center on a higher tier, if the product can't be repaired in the service center being audited.

▪ *Data collection and information systems:* The process of collecting data during and after the service process. Who are involved? What data are entered by the technicians and what by the administrative staff? What information systems are used? Can the data be manipulated afterward? How are changes logged?

▪ *Customer delivery:* Handing the serviced product back to the customer, registering the appropriate repair warranty. Consistency of the customer experience.

▪ *Claims creation:* Structure of recording the service activities and parts used.

The regular audits should also give the warranty provider a clear picture of the capability of the service agent to provide additional information on claims submitted in the past and the type of information systems the service agent uses for repair management and claim reporting.

The audits triggered by suspected fraud should primarily focus on verifying the suspect cases. Therefore, the scope depends on the nature of each case. However, in these cases it might make sense to execute a more thorough data analysis to define the full scope of the audit.

An effective execution of the service agent audit includes the following phases, as shown in Figure 9.11.

1. *Select the service agents to be audited.* The first step is to select the service agents to be audited. This could be based on a

Figure 9.11 Service agent audit phases

specific anomaly or suspected fraud case, or KPIs defining the service agent performance in terms of warranty control and repair efficiency, such as frequency of repair close to the end of the warranty period, average cost per repair, frequency of labor-only repairs, or high deviations from the normal failure type distribution.

2. *Prepare the audit.* Additional data analysis besides the triggering anomalies, selection of the issues and areas to be verified, questions and data requests to be sent to the service agent before the audit, and communication with the service agent.

3. *Execute the audit.* On-site verification of the issues identified, analysis of all the evidence gathered during the visit, discussion of the identified performance gaps and potential remedies with the service agent.

4. *Devise an action plan.* The service agent proposal on improvement plan with corrective and preventive actions. The warranty provider will decide upon what type of actions the findings call for—demanding refunds, demanding improved performance onwards, deauthorization of the service agent, or legal actions.

5. *Follow up.* Continue with reporting and analytics, as well as follow-up visits, to ensure that the suspected behavior no longer exists.

For the audit, the service agent should be required to do the following:

- Keep and maintain a reasonable system with transactional and other records related to the warranty services delivered to the warranty provider and its customers. The records should include, but not be limited to, customer and customer product information, service activities conducted, parts used, costs charged from the customer, the warranty provider, and other parties, spare parts ordering and usage, and scrapped products.

- Store replaced parts and products in such a way that product or part with a given serial number can be easily located. For those products and parts that are not serial numbered, keep them in monthly buckets so that their volume can be easily counted.

- Make such records, products, and parts available for the warranty provider's inspection and audit at any time—for example, for 12 or 24 months after the warranty claim has been submitted.

■ Provide any other information on service agent's operations, like capacity, service instructions, tools, and personnel used.

■ Allow the warranty provider to interview any of the service agent's current and former employees.

■ Allow the warranty provider to audit any of service agent's subcontractors.

▼ Number of Claims Exceeding Service Capacity

 CASE STUDY

A service agent submitting substantial amount of claims was audited. It was identified that the capacity of the repair equipment would not have been sufficient to handle the reported repair volume, even if the equipment had been running 24/7. The service agent claimed that it could handle the volume, because it was more efficient than other companies. The service agent employee was then requested to show how efficient it was. The duration was measured using a timer. The repair took as long as in any other company. As a result, the service agent had to admit that the reported claim volume was not possible.

Mystery Shopping

Mystery shopping is a general approach used by market research companies and companies assessing their own performance to gather specific information of products, services, and customer experience. In service agent fraud management context, it means that the warranty provider (or a third-party representative) pretends to be the customer returning a product for warranty service. Then the service agent actions and behavior are monitored during the service visit. Service agent claims are crosschecked against the servicing provided once the claims have been submitted to the warranty provider.

Typically, mystery shopping serves a wider purpose than fraud control, such as customer experience, diagnostics thoroughness and validity, effectiveness of service, and utilization of any cross-selling/upselling[3] opportunities in the customer dialogue. In fraud control, check these cases:

■ If product (or failure) is out of warranty, is the customer invoiced, and is the service agent issuing a claim to the warranty provider?

▪ If product is in warranty, are the service activities and parts used the same as the ones that are claimed?

Customer Verification Calls

The main purpose of customer verification calls is typically to check the customer satisfaction with the service provided. Their results should be tightly integrated with warranty control. Those results can be used to verify the following:

▪ The customer exists (detect fictitious claims).

▪ The customer has had a product issue and has dealt with the service agent (detect fictitious claims).

▪ The issue has been correctly recorded in the claim (detect inflated claims).

▪ The service activities and parts used were the same as claimed (detect inflated claims).

▪ Product and failure were in warranty (detect double-invoicing).

NOTES

1. Goodwill repairs can be justified in specific situations. This can be the case, for example, if a fault fixed during the warranty period repeats soon after the warranty period has expired.
2. The expected distribution depends on the volumes and serial number generation algorithm. We recently did a warranty data analysis on a company where the low numbers were distinctively more likely than the high numbers.
3. These refer to sales strategies to an existing customer. Cross-selling refers to suggesting related products and services (accessories for the product in service) and upselling to suggesting additional features or more expensive models (proposing an extended warranty or an upgraded model for the product in service).

CHAPTER 10

Fraud Management with Other Parties

hapters 8 and 9 discussed how the warranty provider can manage customer and service agent fraud. In this chapter, we focus on how the warranty provider can manage fraud resulting from the following three parties in the service chain:

- Sales channel
- Warranty administrator
- Units within the warranty provider organization

In all of these cases, the warranty provider is the victim of fraud. We follow a format similar to that used in Chapters 8 and 9.

SALES CHANNEL FRAUD MANAGEMENT

Chapter 6 discussed the following methods used by the sales channel to defraud the warranty provider:

- Unauthorized goodwill service
- Creation of fictitious claims using serial numbers from sellable products
- Sales of warranty assets
- Charging extended warranty costs from the OEM

In the two first cases, the sales channel can also be acting as a service agent or in collusion with a service agent. Methods to detect and prevent these kinds of fraud were described in detail in Chapter 9.

In the following we discuss methods to detect and prevent sales channel fraud using the following elements from the warranty control framework.

- Contracts
- Entitlement
- Claim validation
- Analytics
- Material returns
- Service network management

Contracts

Although the warranty provider's, or, more specifically, the manufacturer's, negotiating position with the sales channel may be weak, the warranty provider should have a set of rules in its contract with the sales channel to protect against fraud, abuse, and or sloppiness of sales channel. The recommended contractual terms include:

- Issuing a proof of purchase with serial number and date of purchase when a product is sold
- Compensation for receiving products from end-customers and forwarding them to repair, and compensation for product or part replacements
- Sales channel's responsibility on entitlement when it acts as a return channel for end customers
- Sales channel's responsibility to verify the original purchase price before a refund is given from a sales receipt, another document or sales channel registers.
- Specific checks the sales channel is required to do when conducting entitlement (See customer warranty terms and conditions in Chapter 8.)
- Sales channel responsibility when entitlement has been done carelessly and it is later detected that, for example, the claim relates to out-of-warranty or customer damaged-product, or no fault is found
- Requirements on replacement products to be given to the customers (e.g., the replacement product cannot be a competitor product in the same price category)
- Sales channel responsibility to return the defective, replaced product to the warranty provider
- Archiving and delivery of proof of purchase, sales receipt, extended-warranty certificate, photographs, or other evidence related to warranty status, purchase price and the defect

Entitlement and RMA

Like the service agents, sales channel may be the party that conducts the entitlement. And like the service agents, sales channel can conduct fraud at the expense of the warranty provider. Sales channel can replace out-of-warranty products or allow such products to enter the service chain at warranty provider's expense. Similar methods that are applied with service agents can also be applied to sales channel:

- Sales channel is required to strictly follow the entitlement process defined by the warranty provider (in the contract).

- Sales channel is only allowed to handle the product after the end-customer has obtained an approval (RMA) from the warranty provider.

Claim Validation

Although service agents are the primary source of warranty service claims, sales channel also provides services for customers and charges these costs to the warranty provider. Similar controls that were introduced in Chapter 9 for service agent claims also need to be applied to sales channel claims to the extent relevant. Unless the sales channel is acting as a service agent, sales channel claims are typically related to costs of warranty handling, and replacements and refunds given to the end customers.

Analytics

Several analytics methods are available to control sales channel fraud. Many of the analytics methods applicable for controlling customer and service agent fraud can also be applied to control claims from sales channel. For example, the following analytics can be used to detect sales channel fraud:

- Unauthorized or excess out-of-warranty and goodwill service can be detected by comparing the ratio of out-of-warranty and goodwill (see Chapter 9, Analytics, Detection of Out-of-Warranty Servicing).

- Benchmarking of failure rates (or replacement or refund rates) in different sales channels allows outliers to be detected. High failure rate might, for example, indicate a sloppy entitlement process that allows customer-damaged products to be replaced or forwarded to service. It may also be a sign of fictitious replacements. An example of the application of failure rates in controlling the sales channel is given below.

CASE STUDY

Controlling Sales Channel Failure Rates

A warranty provider selling sports equipment applies failure rates to claims received from the sales channel. Controls on those retailers who are only reporting a limited number of claims are relaxed. Basically, all replacements are accepted and the defective products do not need to be returned. Only if the volume of defective products increases above a threshold are tighter controls applied.

- Benchmarking of customer-damage ratios across products originating from different sales channels based on the reporting done by service agents allows detection of sloppy or intentionally leaking sales channel entitlement process.

- Matching claims reported by the sales channel versus that received by the service agents can be used to detect fictitious claims. If the number of shipped products reported by sales channel exceeds the number of received products reported by service agents, it is possible that sales channel is reporting fictitious claims.

- Matching replacements reported by the sales channel versus defective products received by material returns operations can be used in a similar way as the previous method to detect fictitious replacements.

- Fictitious claims created by the sales channel using serial numbers from sellable products can also be detected by using age analysis and serial number distribution, as discussed in Chapter 9. Deviations from that expected is an indicator of potential fraud.

Material Returns

The sales channel can do replacement fraud in two ways:

- Out-of-warranty or customer-damaged products are replaced at warranty provider's expense to improve customer satisfaction.

- Fictitious replacements or refunds may be reported to obtain compensation in the form of money or replacement products.

To ensure that the returns really happened, sales channel should return the defective products. This allows the warranty provider to:

- Ensure that the product reported to be replaced is not fictitious—that is, that a defective product exists.

- Verify the serial number of the product to ensure that the replaced product is the one it was reported to be. Otherwise, out-of-warranty products could be reported using serial numbers of in-warranty products.

- Technically analyze the products for customer damage and no-fault-found.

The sales channel is compensated only after the warranty provider receives the defective product.

CASE STUDY

▼ Implementing Requirement to Return Replaced Products

Implementing a requirement to return defective products is one of the key activities applied in projects aimed at reducing warranty fraud. We have often observed a significant drop in the replacement volumes overnight after the implementation of return requirements. The drop in the volumes can be 40 to 70 percent.

CASE STUDY

▼ No Material Returns for Defective Musical Instruments

The distributor imports and sells high-quality musical instruments. When there are defects, the manufacturers deliver replacement products to the distributor without delay. Return of defective instruments is normally not required. However, some of the manufacturers require photographic evidence of the defect. From distributor's point of view, the model works smoothly, but lack of requirement to return products could be abused by fraudulent distributors.

Service Network Management

The sales channel acts as a part of the service network—for example, when conducting entitlement, replacements, and handling of defective and repaired products. Audits and, in particular, mystery shopping can be an effective way to close the gaps in warranty controls. The issues verified by an auditor acting as a customer can include the following:

- Is a proof of purchase with a serial number and a date given for products sold?

- For serviced products, does the sales channel verify proof of purchase? What is done if it is tampered with?

- Does the sales channel verify the existence of defect and if it is caused by customer damage?

- Does the sales channel verify the original purchase price before giving a refund (relevant only if the refund value is charged from the warranty provider)?

- How easily is goodwill service granted?

- Is the replacement unit given to the end customer a model approved by the warranty provider?

- What type of warranty service is claimed from the warranty provider and the customer in the following cases?

    - Product is out of base warranty (is the warranty provider charged under base warranty or under an extended warranty, even when an extended warranty does not exist?).

    - Product is in warranty (are both the warranty provider and the customer charged for the service, for example, when the warranty is just about to expire?).

Checking the warranty service claims and comparing them with the activities done in mystery shopping can confirm or eliminate the suspected issues identified by claim validation and/or analytics.

WARRANTY ADMINISTRATOR FRAUD MANAGEMENT

Chapter 6 discussed warranty administrator fraud and the following methods in which the warranty provider can be defrauded:

1. Consciously not doing entitlement, claim validation, or material returns control properly to earn extra income or to minimize own effort

2. Applying inflated prices in calculation of service agent compensation

3. Approving invoices that exceed the claimed amount

4. Generating and approving fictitious claims to fictitious companies

The following sections deal with methods that can be used for controlling warranty administrator fraud. Many of these are based on industry leading practices used in purchasing and finance operations of various sectors.

Controls on Master Data Changes

Service Agent (Vendor) Master Data

Manipulation of service agent master data allows fictitious service agents to be added and fictitious claims to be processed, resulting in payments to bank accounts used by the fraud perpetrator. Alternatively, justified payments may be directed to false bank accounts.

Creation and maintenance of service agent master data (i.e., vendor master data) can be controlled in the following ways:

- Allow only authorized people to create or change service agent master data. These people should not be involved in
  - Making contracts or buying services from service agents
  - Warranty service claim validation
  - Processing payments to service agents
- Use a documented request for master data creation and update.
- Allow changes in service agent master data to come into effect only after management approval.
- Keep log files of all changes made to master data so that what, when, and by whom the data have been changed can be tracked.
- Verify existence of the service agent and company details utilizing public registers.
- Frequently report summary of changes done in service agent master data.
- Verify that a contract for each service agent exists and there are no discrepancies between service agent contract and master data records, especially with regard to recently added or changed data.
- Actively maintain master data and remove inactive service agents.

Price Data

The warranty provider maintains service price lists in its systems either to:

- Verify that the prices charged by the service agents are correct or

- Calculate compensation based on the activities reported by the service agents.

Manipulation of these prices allows payments to exceed the amount agreed in the contract.

Most of the controls available for service agent master data changes can be applied also for price changes. Additionally, use of standardized price lists and cost elements is recommended (within a geographical area with similar cost level) to minimize the possibility of service agent–specific price adjustments. Analytics can be used to highlight price list differences between service agents. This allows the detection of service agents who have higher price figures than the others.

Entitlement and Authorization Controls

A warranty administrator working in the RMA process can work in collusion with a customer, a service agent, or sales channel to authorize fictitious repairs and product replacements. Furthermore, excess amount of out-of-warranty repairs (e.g., under goodwill approval) can be granted. When the service agent needs an authorization for specific repairs, the warranty administrator can grant them even when it is not justified. Instead of seeking financial benefit, the warranty administrator may give unnecessary authorizations out of sloppiness.

Several methods can be applied to prevent such cases:

- Communicate and document the control procedures to be followed by the warranty administrators.

- Register the approval decisions and record the calls between the warranty administrator and the customer or the service agent.

- Monitor the amount of approvals given by each warranty administrator. Inform the warranty administrators about monitoring practices and further actions. In addition to monitoring approvals by the warranty administrator, monitor service agent and customer level (when relevant) approvals.

- Take action if the amount of authorizations exceeds a threshold or there are suspicious authorizations, as illustrated by the following case.

RMA for Printer Repairs and Replacements

CASE STUDY

A global printer manufacturer applied an RMA process to give approval for warranty repairs and product replacements. Especially, replacements of ink cartridges were under strict control. Warranty administrators working in the contact center were able to authorize replacements. However, approvals given by the administrators were carefully monitored. If the approval ratio of a warranty administrator exceeded the threshold, management was quick to react and give feedback. Also, calls were monitored among other things to verify that pre-agreed control questions were applied during the customer call. Warranty administrator performance had a direct link to his or her compensation.

- Use job rotation to prevent situations where the same warranty administrator continuously gives authorizations for specific service agents or (high-volume) customers.

Validation and Analytics Controls

Within the validation and analytics processes, pending claims can be falsely approved, a blind eye turned to the signs of fraud, and action not taken even when fraud is obvious. The methods available to control warranty administrators doing validation and analytics include the following:

- Automate claim validation in such a way that results cannot be manipulated without controlled and traceable procedures.
- Document policies for handling pending claims and for conducting warranty analytics. This includes the rules based on which customers or service agents are selected for detailed analysis and which analytics methods are applied in the analysis. This prevents employees working in analytics from not analyzing certain customers and service agents.
- Segregate duties so that the same person is not doing validation and analytics. As a result, validation can identify signs of issues that need to be answered through analytics. Analytics again can observe issues that have been ignored by validation.
- Rotate duties so that the same person is not predictably and continuously validating or analyzing claims from the same service agents.

- Establish an audit trail to validation decisions. Keep a log of who has approved or rejected claims, and when and why.

- Report approval ratios by warranty administrator, by service agent, and by category of pending claims. For example, this could include cases where a warranty administrator on average rejects same percentage of claims as other administrators, but approves higher percentage of claims from certain service agent(s).

- Archive analytics results in such a way that they cannot be manipulated.

- Verify validation decisions, analytics results, and actions taken by another warranty administrator or by a supervisor.

- Communicate on crosschecks and monitoring practices to the warranty administrators.

Payment and Credit Note Controls

The payment value to the service agents and the other parties in the service chain may not match the approved claims or there may not be approved claims at all. Invoices can be paid twice and there can be a failure to process credit notes. To prevent manipulation done in the warranty administration phase, the following methods can be used:

- Number invoices or self-billing documents sequentially.

- Segregate payment value calculation (if self-billing in use) and the payment transaction.

- Establish an invoice/payment approval step for payments before they can be processed.

- Set up controls and reconciliation to ensure that the same invoices are not paid multiple times.

- Control manually created payments during the payment run.

- Establish an audit trail to all payment and credit note transactions. Keep log data on what transactions are done, when, and by whom.

- Ensure that when a service agent has already been paid for a set of claims and issues with these claims are later found in analytics, auditing, or through other methods, these issues are systematically logged.

- Ensure that logged issues are systematically processed, credit notes are raised, or a documented decision not to raise a credit note is done.

- As discussed under validation-related controls, ensure the payment value matches the value of the approved claims. In addition to preventing mismatches between the value of approved claims and the payment, this prevents the payment of invoices where claims do not exist at all.

- Keep track of credit notes requested from the service agents and that they are settled.

Material Returns Controls

Failure to control returned materials provides several opportunities for fraud. Materials can be registered as received, although nothing has arrived. As a result, customers can receive replacements for nonexistent products and service agents be compensated for parts that were never used. Although parts are received, the shipment may be incomplete, the products and parts may not be diagnosed, or observed fraud may be ignored.

To control the issues, a set of procedures is needed:

- Segregate counting and logging of received materials from claim validation handling pending claims that are approved once materials are received.

- Reconcile quantities of materials registered to be received with pending claims approved after material receipt.

- Document date and time of goods receipt, quantity and serial numbers of the goods when available, and the person who has received the goods.

Additional controls can be implemented—for example, to verify that diagnostics results are not manipulated and certain service agents are not excluded from sampling.

Background Checks

In addition to process-related controls, it is important that background checks are done for warranty administrator candidates to identify applicants with criminal records. Possible conflicts of interest also need to be looked at. This is the case e.g., when a warranty administrator or his or her relative owns or works for a service agent or a (major) customer.

WARRANTY PROVIDER FRAUD MANAGEMENT

Chapter 6 discussed warranty provider fraud and discussed the following two methods of fraud, where warranty provider's own organization is the actor and another part of the organization is the victim of fraud:

1. Cost avoidance through unjustified cost transfer
2. Increased sales through abuse of warranty offering

Sales, service, and country organizations were identified as the actors conducting fraud, the motivation being to meet performance targets and to obtain personal bonuses.

Like the contracts with the service network, internal policies can be applied to define the costs— a country organization can tag as warranty costs and charge from product lines. This eliminates the gray area between chargeable and nonchargeable costs. Internal audit teams can then monitor conformance with these policies.

Organizational units can also be compared against each other and units with the highest costs identified and more closely analyzed. In addition to indicating high service network costs, high costs charged from a product line can also be a sign of inflated internal cost transfers. In both cases, actions are required.

Abuse of warranty offerings to promote sales can be prevented through company guidelines on cost accounting and by adjusting KPIs applied when measuring performance of sales teams. Controllers can then monitor conformance with these guidelines.

CHAPTER 11

Structures Influencing Warranty Fraud

With Maximilian Kammerer

n Chapter 5, we discussed warranty management in general, and in Chapters 7 to 10, we discussed in detail the methods to detect and prevent warranty fraud. For crafting and implementing suitable strategies to reduce warranty fraud and the associated costs, the manufacturer needs an effective process and a proper organizational structure. This in turn requires a holistic view of the customer service process and the service organization that takes into account the key factors, when and where to influence warranty. In this chapter, we take that view and discuss the ways to influence warranty management in general and warranty fraud management in particular through the processes and organization of a company.

In the following sections, we will first discuss an effective service process that looks at the different relevant factors. We then look at the organizational structure and issues such as the roles and responsibilities of different units, the mindsets, ethics, and attitudes, and their impact on warranty fraud reduction. To improve warranty fraud management, companies need to compare their service processes and organizations with what is proposed in this chapter. Without this, the manufacturer cannot achieve the goal to reduce, and hopefully eliminate, warranty fraud. This will then be the focus of Chapter 12.

EFFECTIVE SERVICE PROCESS

In general, avoiding warranty fraud is often seen as a reactive task of the after-sales service organization, although the root causes for warranty fraud are already initiated far earlier in the overall service process. In Chapter 5, we discussed the product life-cycle perspective on warranty management and the key warranty-related decisions in the early phases of product life cycle. Product serviceability and determination of the product's ability to record and store key performance and usage information are set during the front end, design, and development phases of the product life cycle.

This includes, for example, product performance counters and indicators as well as sensors and detectors for malicious damage, accidental damage, and liquid damage in combination with ways how to access and utilize the information recorded. To achieve this, a fully transparent after-sales network between participating stakeholders and a visualized end-to-end system is needed. Apple's Global Service Exchange (GSX) system and associated service guidelines and governance principles is a representative sample.

New technologies such as video and audio analysis, as well as smart big data analytics, are creating additional transparency in the process. This can prevent fraud from happening or at least reduce its likelihood.

Ideally, service and warranty management should go along the value creation process and be addressed in all phases of the product life cycle.

Figure 11.1 shows the phases involved in the service process from the product life-cycle perspective. Like the product life cycle discussed in Chapter 5, the service process involves several phases and subphases. Service planning and realization take place in the early phases of the product life cycle and service operations, and support is important during the later phases of the product life cycle. We now discuss the various elements of the figure and the role of each element in warranty fraud management.

Service Planning

Making decisions and design choices, which have an impact on warranty (fraud) management, should start in the first two phases of the service process. At this phase, the basic service components, delivery opportunities, and technical requirements for serviceability and service transparency are determined. The earlier in the process these can be configured, the easier it is to avoid gaps in the warranty management process and fraud avoidance. The general definition of the service strategy for a product is heavily influencing the number of "opportunities" for warranty fraud and misuse of extended warranty programs, like identification of the product and associated owner/user during warranty cases, and the overall interaction between the manufacturer, the service agent, and the customer.

Service planning includes two main phases, (i) service design and (ii) service engineering, each of which has two subphases, as shown in Figure 11.2.

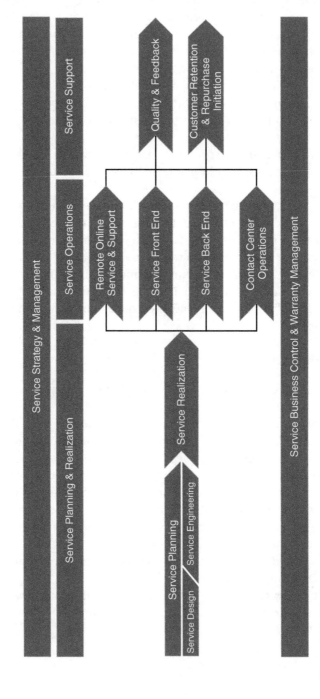

Figure 11.1 Effective service process

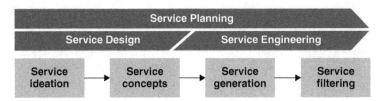

Figure 11.2 Process steps in service planning

Service Design

Service ideation

In this subphase, one looks at the services associated with products. While determining the overall service network for a product, it needs to deal with the following questions:

- What are the general market and customer needs or expectations for the services, and what should the subsequent customer experience design look like?

- How can new serviceability innovation[1] be integrated and be ready when the product gets launched?

Service concepts

In this subphase, decisions relating to the general design of service and serviceability are made. All the technical requirements (e.g., sensors, product performance counters, etc.), which are later on impacting the serviceability of a product and providing opportunities for fraud detection, need to be carefully considered. The general service concept influences service data availability and transparency, as well as certain service levels and service delivery design.

Service Engineering

Service generation

In this subphase, serviceability solutions, prototyping and solution testing are carried out in close collaboration with the product hardware and software engineers.

Service filtering

In this subphase other requirements that cannot be resolved internally (by the unit responsible for service delivery) are addressed. Here the final strategic fit takes place as well as a check of new service design against external requirements and limitations (e.g., legal check), how later collected product service data could be utilized without violating privacy and confidentiality, etc. At this time the first detailed verification of possible gaps in service design, which would allow fraudulent behavior from the customer, channel, or service delivery side, need to be addressed.

Service Realization

Service realization includes three subphases, (i) service portfolio planning, (ii) service capability planning, and (iii) service go-to-market, that are sequentially linked as shown in Figure 11.3.

Service Portfolio Planning

Here the service engineers and warranty cost "owners"[2] are looking at delivery of services and associated financial planning. In this phase the most critical topics for later warranty management are determined—such as service levels and desired differentiation from competition—for example, turnaround times, repair or replace decisions (for the entire product or a subassembly), logistics like home pickup service or provision of loaner products, which are costly items, too. Based on the service levels, the KPIs for warranty management are decided, together with the warranty compensation model for service agents and other parties, and potential incentive/penalty schemes for the service and channel partners. The impact on fraud detection and fraud avoidance needs to be considered when planning these measures. An additional item in this phase is the calculation of the pricing for out-of-warranty service and potential positioning of additional added value extended-warranty offerings, like coverage of accidental or liquid damage, warranty extensions, and insurance programs.

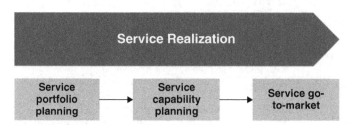

Figure 11.3 Process steps in service realization

Service Capability Planning

Here all critical factors for service delivery readiness, service value chain integration, service road mapping on a geographical basis, service documentation, new service blueprinting, training and certification requirements, and materials need to be prepared. In parallel, the IT department works on data model adaptation and system integration for any new or changed requirements out of product and service design.

Go-to-Market

In this subphase the operational readiness and setup for service delivery are prepared. All training and certification of service partners and of internal stakeholders is conducted, while the performance management system and associated KPIs for the partners are communicated and setup in the system. The last stage is to upload and activate all system changes and associated data, such as BOM (bill of materials), warranty compensation rates, spare part pricing, and value-added services programs.

Service Operations

After products have been launched, the operation for service and warranty delivery starts. Depending on the chosen service delivery strategy and concept, as well as the serviceability capabilities of a product, there are different ways to influence warranty (fraud). Service operations phase includes four areas, as listed in Figure 11.1. We discuss briefly each of these.

Remote Service and Support

In the past, the majority of service delivery was either via online, contact center, or physical service points. However, the trend is toward on-device remote support and service. There are various applications in the market that allow on-device diagnosis and remote access with issue resolution. Through these applications and associated data submission, as well as the transparency of on-device (mis-) usage, possible root cause for failures and indication for upcoming failures can be identified. The overall trend goes rather toward failure prevention and remote on-device resolution—which will contribute to reduced fraud "opportunities."

Service Front End

Within the service delivery at the physical service front end, there are multiple opportunities to avoid fraud. While fully integrated system and data management allow better transparency, certified staff, clear guidelines, and working instructions are the keys for seamless service transactions, good customer experience, and minimal space for fraudulent activities. Apple is a very good example of how a fully integrated system and clear work instructions are creating a transparent, well-managed, and customer-friendly service process. Additionally, new technologies like video and gesture analysis can support the service staff to indicate any fraud attempts or deviating behavior from customers.

Service Back End

On the service back end side, the main opportunity to detect or avoid fraud is to manage a transparent end-to-end process, where transactions are linked to individual service technicians or work benches and all steps are tracked in the service management system—for example, which technician has performed the repair, what parts were used for the repair, are these logical for the failure type and root cause. Later on, service quality and customer satisfaction are measured by transaction and technician, so that deviations can be identified. In addition to that, big data and predictive analytics can help to identify if more parts than normal are used or a particular technician or service provider is performing outside of the defined guidelines, benchmarks, and KPIs.

Contact Center Operations

Last delivery area is the contact center operations—in general, an area where warranty fraud management could be supported or prevented but not necessarily directly controlled. The contribution is heavily dependent on the overall data transparency and process integration of contact center staff. Here the key point is their competence to identify suspicious claims and queries, as well as to what extent supporting technology like audio, video, and text analytics is implemented and used.

Service Support

Supporting the operational service delivery processes are two sub-phases that provide critical elements to determine fraud attempts and help to further improve the warranty management system itself: (i) quality and feedback and (ii) customer retention and repurchase, as indicated in Figure 11.1. We discuss each of these briefly.

Quality and Feedback

This subphase is mainly looking at service quality—measured in service performance and customer satisfaction, product quality feedback from field to manufacturing, and R&D (research and development)—and the defective product and material diagnostics/analytics as the key ways to identify warranty fraud based on material misusage, malicious damage, and other irregular transactions. Additionally, regular quality assurance audits and recertification programs help to permanently control and improve the overall warranty process.

Customer Retention and Repurchase Initiation

This subphase deals with customer retention. Here the opportunity to support warranty fraud management is obviously limited, as apart from trade-in programs and take-back solutions no real service transaction takes place. The only real opportunity is to identify customers that have been flagged as "suspicious" due to transactions with malicious damage, fraud attempts, or other deviating behavior.

SERVICE ORGANIZATION

To answer the question of how to create the "perfect" after-sales service organization—the best answer is, there is none! Each service organization needs to be integrated into the overall product creation and contribute at all steps. In terms of the organizational responsibilities, the driving factor is, how early in the product creation process are the people responsible for warranty and delivery functions involved. In many cases this happens too late to influence the main warranty fraud drivers or to apply routines for warranty fraud prevention.

Just like the service process should be aligned with the product creation process, it is of utmost importance to align the service organization according to the service process. The organizational setup is dependent on the global operating model (centralization/decentralization) of the company and the internal positioning of the service organization. In the past, service was more often positioned close to supply chain management and operations. The current trend is going now toward product management, sales, and marketing. The reason for that is the increasing importance of customer experience management and the overall consumer design and stakeholder integration together with product life cycle management. An example of a service organization aligned with the process is shown in Figure 11.4.

Service Planning and Realization

Service planning and realization is responsible for the activities from service ideation to service go-to-market. In addition to the design- and engineering-related activities, it also ensures the service readiness before the launch, with related training and qualification.

Service Network Management

Service network management is responsible for the physical service front-end and back-end network design and operations, including service agent vendor management, service supply chain management, and technical engineering.

Customer Support Operations Management

Customer support operations management is responsible for contact center operations management, field service planning and scheduling, customer-facing online support platforms (including social

Figure 11.4 Aligned service organization

media, in-device support, and other online support) and knowledge management.

Warranty Administration and Control

Warranty administration and control is responsible for the entitlement, validation, and control points starting from the customer claim and ending with the service compensation allocated to the right stakeholders. In case there are outsourced partners involved in the entitlement, warranty administration is responsible for monitoring and controlling the correctness of the entitlement done by external parties.

Back-Office Support

Back-office support includes all functions needed for the service organization to operate, not directly related to service delivery, such as quality, finance, human resources, customer retention, environment and sustainability, and governance (legal, compliance, auditing etc.).

Roles and Responsibilities

Defining roles and responsibilities or a mandate around "Who is finally responsible to manage warranty cost and to minimize fraud?" is a long-lasting debate within organizations. On one hand, the service department is the designated lead on warranty cost and subsequent fraud management. On the other hand, most service departments are not at all in the right position to influence fraud avoidance or to create the right technical, process, governance, or strategic capabilities, which would allow end-to-end transparency and impact. Most service leads are getting involved too late into the product development cycle or strategic product positioning process to contribute meaningful input for R&D or material sourcing. At the same time, many partners in the service network are in one or another way linked to sales channels, which finally might not allow straightforward warranty controls, fraud prevention, and appropriate consequence management with repair or other channel partners.

What works in several industries is that whoever owns warranty management and associated cost drivers must have the end-to-end mandate to influence warranty cost drivers and to close any process, system, and governance gaps that "allow" fraud to happen. This setup requires new thinking about the management of the overall service of a business so that a new approach to service delivery, cost management, and fraud avoidance could happen.

Service Mindset, Ethics, and Attitude

One aspect of warranty (fraud) management is the overall mindset, which "allows" fraud or fights against it. In companies with a strong service mindset, strong values, and work ethics, fraud is relentlessly prosecuted, independent of potential negative impact on sales or existing business relationship. Any kind of tactical or strategic excuse for ignoring fraud attempts is weakening the mindset and opening opportunities for fraud to happen. Fraud "management" should be a part of the overall companies' governance and leadership principles and should not leave any room for interpretation or escape.

Governance, Transparency, and Code of Conduct

Company's governance, transparency, and code of conduct should reflect the clear direction to prosecute any attempt of fraud in a strict and transparent way. Most companies have this in their company values and stated explicitly in all commercial contracts with suppliers and delivery channel partners. The governance principles are supported by the following:

- Additional implementation of regular audits
- Compliance checks
- Changing responsibilities for managing fraud-sensitive business areas

NOTES

1. Serviceability of a product describes the ease with which the product can be maintained and repaired.
2. Warranty cost owner refers to the organizational unit that is responsible for warranty cost within a company.

CHAPTER **12**

Implementing a Warranty Control Framework

What should a manufacturer do to improve its warranty fraud management capabilities? Naturally, this depends on the current status of the capabilities, and this in turn determines the type of improvement initiative that is appropriate. We look primarily at the service agent and customer fraud scenarios. However, the approach is applicable to other cases and setups as well.

The typical structure of any warranty control improvement initiative includes the following steps:

1. Assess the current situation.
2. Craft an improvement plan.
3. Define policies and rules.
4. Build the capabilities.
5. Deploy the change.

The following two issues need to be taken into account:

- Business case considerations
- Challenges in implementation

These are important, as improving warranty control and tackling warranty fraud is difficult and needs to be financially justified. We discuss the steps and the issues in a warranty control improvement initiative in this chapter and conclude with recommended principles for achieving a successful warranty transformation.

ASSESSING THE CURRENT SITUATION

Like with any roadmap, the manufacturer needs to know the current situation and the desired targets in order to develop a plan for a successful warranty control transformation. When assessing the current situation, key questions need to be addressed:

- Is there evidence or suspicions of fraudulent behavior?
- What are the potential root causes and motivations for suspected fraud?
- How can one prevent or mitigate these issues?
- What is the status of the current warranty control framework?
- Is there global or regional consistency?

- Is there transparency over the warranty process and warranty costs?
- How do the after-sales service processes and service organization support warranty fraud management?
- Is the claim data quality and consistency providing sound basis for proper warranty data analysis?
- What arrangements and incentive schemes exist with the service agents and other parties in the service network?

Addressing these questions to understand the current situation involves a three-stage approach.

The first stage involves the assessment of the current situation against the warranty control framework introduced in Chapter 7 and the service process and organization introduced in Chapter 11. This includes customer, service agent and other contracts, customer entitlement process, service agent claim validation process, material returns process, service agent management approach, approach for supplier recovery from part manufacturers and distributors, and warranty management systems and analytics capabilities, as well as the end-to-end service process and organization.

The second stage includes analyzing warranty claims data to find potential fraud. A sample of the current claim data is taken and validated against the company warranty rules, finding cases that have been accepted although having violations against the set rules, and gaps and anomalies that need to be explained.

As a result, potential suspect cases are identified and the quality and content of the claim data are validated. Also, the consistency of the claim data received from the service agents is verified.

If fraudulent or suspect claims are identified, they are discussed with the corresponding service agents and the first corrective actions can be implemented. If anomalies are large, the current state analysis can already include audits of selected service agents. For those service agents where the share of suspect or rejected claims has been high, the tighter controls started during the assessment project should continue to be applied. Savings from these cases can often fund the rest of the improvement activities.

The third stage includes the assessment of the whole service agent management approach. What could be the motivational elements for fraudulent activities? are the existing compensation and incentivization schemes directing the service agents to the right behavior? What is the culture and ethical conduct across the country organizations and across the service agents?

CRAFTING AN IMPROVEMENT PLAN

Based on the findings of the current situation, the target situation is defined, and a gap analysis and an improvement plan for warranty control can be created. The contents of this plan depend on the gaps identified. The activities involved can be divided into:

- Defining the policies and rules
- Building the capabilities
- Deploying the change

To justify the investment, a business case is needed. It should define:

- Cost estimates and prioritization for the improvement initiatives
- The estimated savings potential of the quick wins as well as the long-term solution

Often, there are immediate benefits and low-hanging fruit that can be captured and should be planned for. These improvements include:

- Immediate improvements in the claim validation process
- Immediate analytics improvements
- Short-term service agent audits

DEFINING POLICIES AND RULES

The foundation for solid warranty management comes from defining the right warranty policies and rules for customers and rules for the service agents that are to be applied globally:

- The terms and conditions applied in the entitlement of customer warranty claims must be very clear.
- The rules for claim reporting, acceptable claims, reporting of data, and other factors need to be properly addressed in service agent contracts.

There can be local differences, but it is desirable to strive for as much global and regional consistency as possible.

There should be a global guideline on the service agent management approach, including the motivational aspects and incentivization schemes. Some elements can be flexible and adjusted to the local business practices, but the main thrust should be the same.

It is important to think through the changes in the policies, processes, and data formats and try to get them right the first time before launching them. There can be hundreds and thousands of service agents whose contracts need to be changed and who need changes in their own systems and processes to accommodate the new requirements. Making incremental changes one after another can cause significant additional costs—costs of making changes and testing the outcome of each change and then implementing in the various nodes in the service network.

 Incremental Updates to the Process

CASE STUDY

A consumer products manufacturer defined a new claim validation approach and built an intermediate system solution to support the process, requesting more data from the service agents. Piloting the new process and learning on the way, they had made several changes in the claim data format. The constant changes were very painful for the service agents in the pilot scope and caused a lot of friction before the format was stabilized. Learning from that, the company decided to wait with the subsequent change ideas and collect them together into one release before the regional and global implementations took place.

BUILDING THE CAPABILITIES

Quite often, we see companies thinking about software solutions when enhancing their capabilities in warranty management. In our opinion, software is an important element but should not be the starting point. A well-thought-out process flow, organizational structure, and roles and responsibilities, as discussed in Chapter 11, should form the basis for the improvement projects as well as for the requirements for the software solutions.

The first step is typically to look at the overall service process and organization and the needed changes. Then design and build an improved claim validation capability. The effort depends on the current claim validation setup and the gap to the target state. Will it be distributed or centralized, executed in-house or outsourced? What are the skills and motivation of the validators? If there are changes in the organizational setup, can they be planned and executed over time as the new concepts are deployed to the service network?

The next step is to enhance the analytics capabilities—If there is a generic analytics or Six Sigma team, it is a good start, but it should be complemented with the contextual understanding.

Other capabilities may also need to be enhanced. An auditing team may need to be established and an auditing approach defined. Material returns may require the definition of new processes and the selection of a partner to run the receiving end of the material returns operations. If a supplier recovery process is not in place, supplier negotiations and establishing the process are needed.

Once the basic process and organization are in place, it is time to look at the systems side:

- Can we live with the current solutions we have?
- Can we enhance them?
- Should some of them be replaced?
- What are the most relevant solution options for us?
- How do they fit with our overall systems architecture and IT strategy?
- What warranty data are collected at different phases of the process?
- What is the balance between simplicity and data coverage?
- How do we ensure high-quality claim data, especially regarding fault and symptom data?
- Is there a data warehouse where all key information needed for analytics is available on serial number level, such as from design, manufacturing, distribution, entitlement, and service systems?
- What are the most important other functional areas that the warranty solution should integrate with?
- Where are the current installed base data located?
- How accurate are they?
- Do we need to invest in a data cleansing effort?

- ▓ Will the installed base solution stay the same, and how will it integrate with the warranty management solution?

- ▓ When can we get the required improvements into the IT development roadmap?

Also, the current product design should be looked at. Are there technical and usage data collection and delivery capabilities in the product development that are not used in warranty control? Are there sensors and usage meters that produce downloadable or real-time data? Are there other usage-related mechanical limiters? What are the new features to be fed into the product development pipeline from the warranty control perspective?

DEPLOYING THE CHANGE

A warranty transformation including fraud management is primarily a large-scale change management effort. Like in any major initiative, strong and visible management commitment is crucial. Compared with other major global initiatives, there are two additional complicating factors:

- ▓ The change involves people outside the warranty provider's own organization (in a global manufacturing company, we may be talking about thousands of external companies being involved).

- ▓ The initiative typically includes additional controls, increased effort for all service agents and naturally a reduction in income, and a threat to business continuity for the fraudulent ones. For many of them, this is bad news.

Conveying these messages is difficult and can be unpleasant. Typically, also the local service organizations in different countries might not be comfortable with the changes. In the worst case, some individuals in the warranty provider's organization may be part of the scheme. In all cases, the local organization must take responsibility for the new actions and face the reactions from the service agents, many of whom have been their business partners for a long time. So we are talking about a major change management initiative and need to treat it accordingly. This type of deployment needs to be driven, not merely managed. It requires strong management sponsorship and accountability for the results. People in the warranty provider's service organization need to be held accountable for taking the difficult actions and conveying the unpleasant news to one or more of the parties in the service chain.

A communications and change management plan is needed to support the process. The plan should address these questions:

- What are the key messages? Why are we doing this? What is changing? What does this mean to people involved? What is the timeline of the change?

- Are contract negotiations needed? What is the cycle for renegotiating using the previous contract term as the starting point?

- Which service agent negotiations are done one-by-one and which are done collectively in larger groups?

- What are the modes for the initial communications?

- Who should be involved in the communications and negotiations?

Also, internal communication is very important. Often, the local customer service organization is used to owning the relationship with the service agents and might get quite nervous if the global organization is messing around with its service agents.

The new warranty control framework may include changes in the daily processes and the IT systems. The changes need to be trained in to the respective people in the service organization. Are there any new data integration requirements with the service agent systems? How should they be piloted, and when is the go-live for the new system? What is the pace that different service agents can adjust to the new structure?

Since the topic is very sensitive and can be taken negatively, the pace and mode of service agent negotiations and local organization involvement is very important, as depicted in the following two examples.

▼ Tension between Headquarters and Country Organizations

CASE STUDY

A global consumer products manufacturer improved its warranty analytics and claim validation processes and was very eager to find a service agent who would be caught with major fraud. The initial analysis revealed a number of cases outside the warranty rules and also a number of suspect cases. There was some tension between headquarters and the local customer service organizations. The central organization took an aggressive approach in the service agent negotiations and wanted to get refunds on the historical claims. Most service agents felt that "the rules are now changed and they are happy to comply with them onwards." The whole process took a lot of time and energy from both sides, and in the end the warranty improvement project was stopped, because it had too negative impact on service agent satisfaction.

 Determined Actions Set an Example

CASE STUDY

A manufacturer found out several service agents involved with diverse fraudulent activities during the pilot of the new validation process. During the first pilot region they terminated three service agent contracts and escalated the cases to the company legal department for further actions. In these cases, the evidence was overwhelming and the severe actions were used as an example both for the service network and their own organization.

BUSINESS CASE CONSIDERATIONS

Unless a company is already running a tight process (with no gaps) with the right controls and analytics, the business case for improved warranty fraud control should be quite compelling. Building the required capabilities and making a global change, including own people and people in other companies (e.g., service agents), is a major effort and should not be taken too lightly. The initial savings can be high, but the key thing is to ensure that there is an effective warranty control capability, which, instead of staying stagnant, is continuously improved upon over time.

The initial business case for the implementation phase comes from the reduced warranty cost. The value of the ongoing capability includes some further cost reductions, but comes mainly from sustaining the reduced cost level as shown in Figure 12.1. It happens quite easily that during the improvement project the attention is high and the first savings are significant, but over time the savings start degrading as the fraudulent parties learn the mechanisms the warranty provider uses to control its costs and invent new methods that did not exist earlier and therefore were not uncovered during project's execution phase.

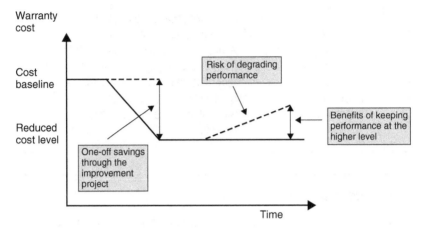

Figure 12.1 Warranty fraud management benefits

IMPLEMENTATION CHALLENGES

Why is it so difficult to manage warranty fraud and take actions in suspect cases? We have identified nine factors that need to be taken into account and dealt with when engaging in a warranty control framework implementation:

1. *The whole subject is very sensitive.* People are very reluctant to admit that this might be an issue for them. For most people it is very natural to want to believe the best of others, especially in cases where we have long-term relationships with them and have learned to trust them. Taking action or even taking up the discussion is quite sensitive and something most people feel quite uncomfortable with.

2. *Most often there is lack of waterproof evidence of fraud.* Even if the statistical analysis suggests that there is something clearly wrong, people may feel it is difficult to act upon.

3. *Unclear or inconsistent contracts leave too many claims in the gray area.* Intuitively, they may be wrong, but they are not violating any rules in the contract.

4. *There is lack of proper systems support for claims transactions or warranty analytics.* Many companies are still relying on very old legacy warranty management solutions with missing functionality and controls, forcing claim validators to spend most of

their time in manual routine activities and too little time in digging deeper into more complex cases.

5. *Lack of standardized warranty offerings and service transactions also complicates matters.* This makes it more difficult to automate the claim handling and more difficult for the validators to remember the differences between the warranty offerings.

6. *There may be political or structural factors reducing the negotiation power of the warranty provider against the service agent.* For example, the service agent is also a channel partner, a key customer, or has tight links to the local government in certain countries.

7. *Unfortunately, there is always the possibility that the warranty provider's own employees are involved with the fraudulent activities.* This will make internal change resistance even stronger and getting the agreed actions forward even more difficult.

8. *Warranty fraud management skills are difficult to find.* A combination of service and warranty understanding and analytical skills are needed for analytics. Discipline and attention to detail are needed for claim validation, often over a very high volume of cases.

9. *Building a capability once is not enough to thrive in this hide-and-seek game.* Fraudsters don't stop—they just invent new ways when their earlier methods have been detected. In the same way the warranty management organization needs to have the curiosity to find new anomalies and promote a culture and attitude for continued improvement.

ACHIEVING THE TRANSFORMATION

This chapter has discussed the structure and challenges in global warranty transformations. In our experience, the following principles work well:

1. Ensure visible management commitment and support. Engage them in the key communications activities.

2. Ensure senior management participation in the team to be able to drive the change and push through also unpleasant activities and handle the more tricky service agent discussions.

3. Track the results and confirm them with warranty business controlling—the initiative should be largely self-funding.

4. Build the warranty analytics team to contain both warranty business skills and analytical and modeling skills. Ensure the team is eager to find new things and look for continuous improvement as opposed to merely producing a set of standard reports.

5. Ensure anomalies are acted on and clarified promptly.

6. Do not accuse anyone or any party of fraud with only suspect cases. Clarify extraordinary aspects and ensure you have the facts.

7. Involve different regions in the global warranty control framework definition. Trying to implement a concept defined in one location is bound to create resistance in the other regions. ("Our local circumstances are different; this will not work for us" is the most common feedback we have heard in any global deployment we have been involved with.)

8. Look at all aspects of the change:

Do different stakeholders know what is expected?

Do they understand why this is done?

Are they willing to make the change?

Do they know how to make the change?

Are the processes ready for the change?

Is the infrastructure in place for the change?

Following these principles will take the manufacturer on the right path to reducing warranty fraud.

CHAPTER **13**
Epilogue

arranty fraud is a significant issue causing multibillion-dollar losses for the manufacturers and the other warranty providers every year. Warranty fraud is carried out not only by customers and service agents but also by sales channel and warranty administrators. Warranty providers themselves might also indulge in fraud. A multitude of methods are used to carry out (individually or in collusion) warranty fraud.

We had three primary goals for this book:

- Increase the awareness and understanding of warranty fraud.
- Provide concrete and practical methods for effective warranty fraud management.
- Provide a holistic approach to implement these methods.

In this book, we have proposed a warranty fraud taxonomy using a three-dimensional characterization: (i) the actor, (ii) the victim, and (iii) the motivation and methods used in carrying out the fraud. Based on this classification, we have discussed over 50 methods of fraud. However, the list is not complete, as there are many unknown methods and fraudsters are continuously inventing new methods.

We have discussed a number of methods to detect and avoid the different types of warranty fraud conducted by different actors, either acting alone or in collusion. These include dozens of contractual rules, and around 100 entitlement checks, validation rules, and analytics methods. These, together with proper processes and organizational setup, form the framework for warranty fraud detection and avoidance. A right combination of practices is needed, as none of them is effective in isolation. Policies, processes, people, and systems are needed. These methods not only should deal with tackling known fraud types but must be capable of identifying anomalies that point to signs of unknown modes of fraud. Even when the methods used by the fraudulent parties to conduct warranty fraud are known and the methods to manage known issues are implemented, this is not enough. Continuous development is needed as fraudulent parties also continuously improve their techniques. In several occasions, we have observed that improvement of warranty fraud controls can rapidly reduce warranty fraud and overall warranty costs. However, over time the fraudsters learn the control methods and adjust the way they do fraud. Gradually, the warranty costs start to rise again.

One after-sales director summarized the situation as follows: "When we develop new analytics methods to control warranty fraud, our service agents hire mathematicians to circumvent our controls." People fighting warranty fraud can never rest!

Although significant improvements can be achieved with these methods, there is still room for improvement, and many questions need to be addressed in the future:

- How can visibility be improved on what has actually happened to the product in the hands of the customer and in the service?
- How can organizations detect small-scale fraud that stays below the radar screen of available detection methods?
- Are there better ways to control customer fraud that is often one-off in nature and beyond the reach of analytics?
- How can analytics be automated to reduce dependence on expert skills when interpreting results?
- How can organizations better quantify the probability of fraud given the available analytics results?
- How can organizations establish structures and incentives that reduce the conflict of interest between different parties, thus reducing the motivation for fraud and the need for controls?

We foresee several opportunities to improve existing approaches, tools, and methods for fraud management. There is a need for academic research on the topic. We discuss these issues briefly.

OPPORTUNITIES TO IMPROVE WARRANTY CONTROL

New technologies and wider adoption of existing technologies can improve fraud control. Smart, connected products can already collect and provide valuable data and enable companies to move into predictive maintenance. As a result, the required service activities are largely known in advance. This provides new opportunities for warranty fraud management. Smart, connected products can also help in answering the following questions:

- When was the product taken into use (the start of warranty period) and what is the subsequent usage history?
- To what kind of environment has the product been subjected (e.g., are the temperature limits exceeded)?

▪ Has the product been altered (e.g., hacking of car software to increase power)?

▪ Have the usage mode and limits been exceeded (e.g., driving a truck with flat land service contract excessively in mountainous areas)?

▪ Has the product been maintained as required (e.g., required oil changes done)?

▪ Who has serviced the product since taken into operation (authorized service agent or not)?

▪ Has the customer damaged the product (e.g., mobile phone that has been dropped or with liquid damage indicated by sensors)?

▪ Within the limits of privacy, where has the product been at each point of time (e.g., has the product been at service agent location at the time of repair)?

▪ What parts have been replaced, and what are their serial numbers (have the reported parts really been changed)?

▪ Do the details of the warranty service claim match the diagnostics data read from the product (has the charged labor cost been inflated by charging a higher cost service activity, have all the required service activities been done, or has something been skipped to save effort)?

As discussed in Chapter 11, automatic face and gesture analysis can support the service staff to indicate the possibility of fraud by, or deviating behavior of, customers requesting warranty service. Matsumoto et al. (2011) suggest that facial behaviors, gestures, body movements, voice and speech characteristics, heat emanation from their faces and heads, pupil dilation, and gaze direction can be used to evaluate truthfulness of individuals. Additionally, spoken words can be recorded and their verbal statements and style analyzed. They suggest that when motivated people lie, clues to deception emerge and appear as leakage across multiple channels. Naturally, such technologies must be implemented with care in order not to trigger negative customer reactions.

Analytics is another area that provides opportunities for improved control. Although a rich variety of analytics methods have been developed, there is still room for more advanced and automated analytics. Targeted analytics methods focusing on individual types of fraud can be combined to provide a complete picture of fraud done by a (major) customer or a service agent. Interpretation of the analytics results can be improved to reduce the dependence on experts to detect fraud. Statisticians are needed to further develop the analytics methods originating from the findings of practitioners. For example, analytics methods can be improved not only to identify signs of fraud but also to calculate the probability of fraud given the available data.

New insights can be gained from other industry sectors, such as insurance and health, where similar fraud occurs. In both cases, there are two or more parties. An example in the insurance context is the insurance cover for automotive vehicles for collision damage where the service agent (panel beater) charges excess amount (fraud against the insurance company) or does not do the repair to the standard required (fraud against the owner of the vehicle). An example in the health context is doctors and hospitals overcharging or carrying out unnecessary tests (fraud committed against the insurance company covering the patient).

NEW RESEARCH INTO WARRANTY FRAUD

As mentioned in Chapter 1, warranty has been studied by researchers from many different disciplines leading to theories of warranties and building models (descriptive and mathematical) to gain new insights into different aspect of warranty. The models are also useful in evaluating different options and deciding on the optimal option.

In contrast, warranty fraud has received very little attention from researchers. Since warranty fraud involves many different parties with different goals and objectives, game theory is an appropriate framework to study the different issues.

Appendix C gives a brief introduction to game theory. It can be used to build models to address several issues. We list two of them:

1. The behavior of fraudster under different terms of contract. How will different incentives and penalties terms affect the level of fraud?

2. A proper cost–benefit analysis of different monitoring schemes that the warranty provider can use to detect fraud and to decide on the best one.

Models to study these issues require (i) an interdisciplinary approach (from various disciplines such as law, economics, psychology, engineering, statistics, operational research, etc.), and (ii) a good understanding of stochastic modeling.

The agency theory deals with the outcome of the relationship between two players—principal and agent, where the principal delegates to the agent tasks to be executed. The relationship involves a contract. The two have different goals, and the contract should deal with various issues such as monitoring, risk, penalties, moral hazard (faced by both parties), and the role of information. Appendix B gives a brief introduction to the agency theory and lists the issues. The agency theory is appropriate for the study of service agent fraud.

There is a lot of scope to study warranty fraud using concepts, model formulation, and techniques from game theory and agency theory. One of the authors (Murthy) is working on new research on a model where the service agent defrauds by overcharging some of the claims in an uncertain manner and the warranty provider uses an inspection scheme to detect the fraud. The model gives the optimal strategies for both the warranty provider and the service agent and how these change with the parameters of the model (e.g., penalty if caught).

Detailed Claim Data

This appendix describes detailed list of data fields to be included in warranty service claim reporting and the reason why each field is needed. Not all of these fields are needed in every company, as the need for claim reporting varies across industries and, for example, due to differences in warranty policies. Also, additional data fields may be needed in some companies due to company-specific requirements.

Serial number

Unique identifier of the product item. Key information for determining warranty and repair warranty status, preventing fictitious claims, and deriving other information about the item from warranty provider's own databases. If products are lot numbered, lot number is reported instead of the serial number.

Product type or model

If a product in question is not serial numbered, the product ID is the second best alternative to obtain information about the product. It allows warranty providers to derive information about product's configuration and possible repair activities, for example. However, warranty status cannot be validated and fictitious claims cannot be determined with product ID. This is unnecessary information if unique serial numbers are in use and product ID can be derived through serial number. However, in some companies, product ID and serial number together form a unique ID.

Customer ID or customer name and contact information

This information allows the customer to be identified, contacted for verification purposes and customer location to be verified.

Service agent ID

Identifier of the service agent as a company and location of service if service agent operates in multiple locations. This information is the basis for paying to the right service agent and the verification of volumes by service agent location.

Repair order number

Unique identifier of the warranty service event within a service agent company. This information allows detection and rejection of claims erroneously or intentionally sent twice.

Technician ID

Identifier of the service agent employee who has conducted the repair. This allows verifying technician with a list of authorized employees, detecting anomalies in repair volumes by technician, and linking signs of fraud or other excess billing with individual technicians when fraud is conducted on the level of an individual.

Customer symptom description and code

A free-format text description of the problem from customer's point of view and a code categorizing the problem based on warranty provider's categorization. Description is used in text analysis to detect fictitious claims. Symptom data can also be compared to repair data to find mismatches and anomalies.

Service activity ID

Defines conducted service activity and is the basis for compensating service agent for labor and possible other costs covered by the service activity. Distribution of service activities, for example, can be used to detect inflation of labor costs. If invoicing is not service-activity based, hours worked can be reported instead or in addition to service activity.

Failure/fault description and code

A free-format text description of the defect and the source of the issue from technician's perspective and a code categorizing the defect based on warranty provider's classification. Like the symptom data, this information can be used for text analysis and identification of mismatches and anomalies by comparing it to the other elements of repair data.

Spare parts used

Part codes of the parts used based on warranty provider's coding standards and part quantities. If spare parts are serial numbered, the serial number of the original and the new part are reported. If other materials are used, they are also reported. Parts usage is a key element in calculation of service agent compensation. In fraud analytics, parts usage can be used for comparing it with usage by other service agents, for example. If the actual device is replaced, the part code and the serial number of the new device must be reported. In addition to compensating the service agent, this allows the new device to inherit the warranty of the original device.

Part location

For each part: This information can be used, for example, in the cases where the same part can be used in multiple locations within the product's configuration. The location identifier indicates which of the parts has been replaced.

Software version

Identifies the old and new software versions in case of a software update.

Physical presence identifier

A code that can only be obtained when product is physically available or data can be read from the product. The data can be used to prevent part of the fictitious warranty service claims, as a claim cannot be reported without getting additional information from the product.

Date information

This includes date of failure, date and time of receiving the product to service, date and time of completing the repair, and date and time of returning the product back to the customer. The data can, for example, be used to verify fulfillment of service SLAs and to identify abnormalities in the distribution of repair dates.

Area code, distance traveled, travel time, and/or customer repair location

Used in field service context to indicate the distance traveled by the service agent. This is one of the cost elements used as a basis for service agent compensation. At the same time, the cost is controlled by measuring technician's travel distances and costs by day and comparing these with other technicians and service agent companies.

Date of purchase or installation

Date when the item has been purchased, installed, or taken into use. This information can be used to verify warranty validity and reject out-of-warranty repairs. These dates can also be compared to manufacturer's registers on the dates when the same item has been shipped from factory or distribution center to identify abnormal deviations.

Usage

The figures indicating usage, such as mileage or running hours. In two-dimensional warranties, this is another determinant of warranty validity. Consequently, it can be used to reject out-of-warranty claims or adjust compensation levels when they depend on usage. The distribution on reported usage figures can be analyzed to detect abnormal distribution, for example, overpresence of mileage just below out-of-warranty threshold.

Freight

Information about freight costs related to repaired item, such as when the item is shipped back to the customer. The data can, for example, include weight, volume and destination, and/or logistics service provider ID, and waybill number. This information is one of the bases for service agent compensation. Shipment weights and volumes, for example, can be compared with product weight with packaging and shipment details in benchmark population.

Authorizations

Codes related to various repair authorizations. This includes RMA authorization and authorization code for goodwill out-of-warranty repairs and authorizations for high-cost repairs. The data can be used to, for example, prevent rejection of out-of-warranty repairs and to monitor ratio of repairs with specific authorization.

Costs

Costs related to various cost elements—namely, labor, parts, travel, freight and handling. In some cases, warranty provider requires the service agent not only to report costs to be covered by the warranty provider, but also proportion of the costs covered by the customer and possible other parties when costs are split. Cost information is only needed when service agent compensation is not calculated by the warranty provider, but based on information received from service agent. This approach, however, is not recommended.

Additionally, supplementary data can be requested with the claim:

Photograph

Picture or multiple pictures of the defective device can be used to verify the identity of the product, verify if it was damaged by the customer, and reduce fictitious claims through image recognition.

Self-diagnostics data

Product self-diagnostics results before and after the repair can be used to verify the plausibility of repair details provided with the claim.

Sensor data

Like diagnostics data, the data set can be used to verify plausibility of reported repair data. Another application is to detect customer-damaged products claimed under warranty.

Proof of purchase

A copy of the proof-of-purchase document or extended-warranty certificate is requested, for example, to prevent claiming of out-of-warranty repairs and to allow authenticity of proof-of-purchase document to be verified.

Sales receipt

A copy of sales receipt or other document showing the customer purchase price might be needed to prove that the refund given to the customer has not exceeded the purchase price.

Agency Theory

The figures and text in this appendix are adapted from Murthy and Jack (2014), pp. 85–86, with the permission of Springer.

gency theory attempts to explain the relationship that exists between two parties (a principal and an agent) where the principal delegates work to the agent, who performs that work under a contract. This is exactly the case where one is looking at service agent fraud. The warranty provider is the principal delegating the warranty servicing to a service agent.

Agency theory is concerned with resolving two problems that can occur in principal–agent relationships. The first issue arises when the two parties have conflicting objectives, and it is difficult or expensive for the principal to verify what the agent is actually doing and whether the agent has behaved appropriately. The second issue is the risk sharing that takes place when the principal and the agent have different attitudes to risk (due to various uncertainties). Each party may prefer different actions because of their different risk preferences.

The different issues that are involved in agency theory are indicated in Figure B.1 and discussed briefly in this appendix.[1]

Moral hazard
This refers to the agent's possible lack of effort in carrying out the delegated tasks and the fact that it is difficult for the principal to assess the effort level that the agent has actually used.

Risk
This results from the different uncertainties that affect the outcome of the relationship. The risk attitudes of the two parties may differ,

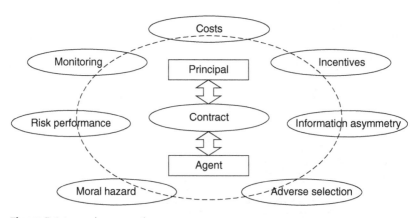

Figure B.1 Issues in agency theory

and a problem occurs when they disagree over the allocation of the risk.

Monitoring

The principal can counteract the moral hazard problem by closely monitoring the agent's actions.

Costs

Both parties incur various kinds of costs. These will depend on the outcome of the relationship (which is influenced by various types of uncertainty), acquiring information, monitoring, and on the administration of the contract.

Incentives

This refers to the means through which the principal can motivate and influence the behavior of the agent. Incentives can be either positive (reward) and/or negative (penalty).

Information asymmetry

The overall outcome of the relationship is affected by several uncertainties, and the two parties will generally have different information to make an assessment of these uncertainties.

Adverse selection

This refers to the agent misrepresenting their skills to carry out the tasks and the principal being unable to completely verify this before deciding to hire them. One way of avoiding this is for the principal to contact people for whom the agent has previously provided service.

Contract

The key factor in the relationship between the principal and the agent is the contract that specifies what, when, and how the work is to be carried out and also includes incentives and penalties for the agent. This contract needs to be designed taking account of all the issues involved.

NOTE

1. For more on agency theory, see Eisenhardt (1989) and van Ackere (1993).

Game Theory

The figures and text in this appendix are adapted from Murthy and Jack (2014), pp. 80–85, with the permission of Springer.

A game consists of three elements: the players (the decision makers who participate in the game), their strategies (the plans for each player describing what they will do in any situation), and the payoffs they receive for all combinations of strategies.

In any game, an action is the decision that a player makes at a particular point in the game, whereas a strategy specifies what actions the player will take at each point in the game. A solution concept is a technique that is used to predict the outcome (equilibrium) of the game. It identifies the strategies that the players are likely to play in the game.

Game theory problems may be classified in a number of different ways. The timing of actions by the players and also the number of periods during which games are played lead to different solution approaches. In some games, the players may choose their actions simultaneously, so that no player knows exactly what the others have done when they make a decision. Alternatively, in games with sequential timing, the players choose their actions in a predetermined order. These two situations are termed *Nash games* and *Stackelberg games*, respectively.

Some games take place during a single time period, whereas others occur over multiple time periods and the actions taken by the players in each period affect the actions and rewards of the players in subsequent periods. These two situations are termed *static games* and *dynamic games*, respectively.

To describe a game, it is also important to specify the information available to each player. In a game with complete information, all elements of the structure of the game are known to all players, whereas in games with incomplete information, some players may have private information. In a game with perfect information, all the players know exactly what has happened in the game prior to choosing an action. Imperfect information implies that at least one of the players is unaware of the full history of the game. Another important assumption of game theory is that the players will always act rationally (choose their best actions/strategies).

Finally, games may be either cooperative or noncooperative. In a cooperative game, the players communicate with each other to coordinate their strategies and, most importantly, make binding agreements. This type of game can be formulated as a multiobjective optimization problem. In a noncooperative game, the players may communicate, but binding agreements are not made.[1]

Two-Player Games

The two players involved are denoted P_1 and P_2, and the sets of possible actions for these two players are Γ_1 and Γ_2, respectively. These action sets may be either finite or infinite. The objective functions (expected profits in the case of a risk-neutral player and the expected utility functions in the case of a risk-averse player) for the two players are $J_1(x;y)$ and $J_2(x;y)$ for $x \in \Gamma_1$, $x \in \Gamma_2$. Note that both of these functions may also contain parameters that are fixed and cannot be controlled by the players.

Nash Game

We assume that each player selects a single action without knowing the particular action chosen by his or her rival. This effectively means that the two players P_1 and P_2 choose their actions simultaneously and have equal decision-making power. This power configuration is shown in Figure C.1. $P_1 \leftrightarrow P_2$ indicates that P_1 and P_2 make their decisions simultaneously.

In such a game, the players' strategies are just the actions they choose, so the terms *actions* and *strategies* will be used interchangeably. The most well-known and widely used solution concept for this static game is called *Nash equilibrium* (NE). An NE is a set of strategies (strategy profile) for the two players such that no player has an incentive to change his or her strategy unilaterally given the strategy chosen by the other player.

Stackelberg Game

Here, P_1 chooses an action $x \in \Gamma_1$ and then P_2 observes x and chooses an action $y \in \Gamma_2$. P_1 is termed the *leader* with P_2 the *follower*. P_1 has more decision-making power than P_2, and this is indicated in Figure C.2. Power is defined to be a player's ability to move first in the game. $P_1 \rightarrow P_2$ indicates that P_1 makes a decision before P_2.

Figure C.1 Nash game decision structure

Figure C.2 Stackelberg game decision structure

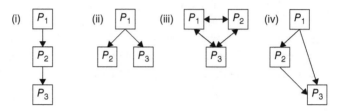

Figure C.3 Alternative decision structures in three-player static games

Multiplayer Games

We now focus on three-player, noncooperative static games with the players involved being denoted P_1, P_2, and P_3. In this case, there are many possible decision scenarios (power structures), some of which are shown in Figure C.3. Games with more than three players produce even more scenarios.

In Figure C.3, if P_i has more decision-making power than P_j, then this is represented by $P_i \rightarrow P_j$, implying that P_j makes a decision only after observing the decision made by P_i. $P_i \leftrightarrow P_j$ indicates that P_i and P_j have equal decision-making power and so make their decisions simultaneously.

NOTE

1. For more on game theory, see Chatterjee and Samuelson (2001), Osborne (2002), and Watson (2008).

Glossary

Actor A person, a company, or an organizational unit involved with fraudulent activities. Also called player, fraudster, perpetrator.

Analytical claim scoring Scoring method indicating the likelihood of fraud of each service agent and claim.

Assisted self-service A service approach where the service organization assists the customer to solve the issue.

Base warranty Limited manufacturer warranty, provided by the manufacturer producing the product to the customer buying the product, as a part of the product sale.

Business-to-business Business where the customer is a business entity.

Business-to-consumer Business where the customer is an individual person.

Claim validation Control done by warranty provider to verify validity of warranty service claims received from service agents and sales channel.

Cost per claim Average cost per claim (Total repair, replacement, and refund cost /Total number of claims).

Cost per repair Average cost per repair (Total repair cost/Total number of repairs).

Customer Owner and often the user of the product (i.e., not distributor or retailer in this book).

Customer claim Customer warranty claim.

Customer damage A product failure caused by the customer, typically not covered by warranty.

Customer self-service A service approach where customer solves an issue independently without raising a warranty claim.

Customer warranty claim A claim from the customer to the warranty provider to fix a product issue under warranty. Also called the customer claim.

Dumpster diving In this context, obtaining discarded proof-of-purchase documents with serial numbers from point of sales' waste containers and using them to create fictitious warranty service claims.

Entitlement   A process where warranty provider verifies if the customer product is entitled for service under warranty and defines the type of service covered by warranty.

Extended warranty   An extension to the base warranty (extending time, usage or coverage). Can be sold separately or given free-of-charge.

Fictitious claim   Fraud scenario where service agents or sales channel invoices warranty provider for service events that never took place.

Field service   A service approach where technician provides service at customer site.

Fraud   Wrongful or criminal deception intended to result in financial or personal gain (*Oxford Dictionary*, 2015).

Goodwill service   Out-of-warranty service done for goodwill purposes.

Installed base   A measure of the products sold and actually in use. Also, a database storing data about the products sold.

Item   A product, part, or component.

Maintenance service contract   Maintenance service provided against a fee. Close to extended warranties. Also called life-cycle services, service agreements, or operate-and-maintain services.

Material returns   Return of defective products or parts replaced during service to the warranty provider. This allows the warranty provider to control that these items existed and were defective. Material returns also allow reuse and recycling of materials.

Mystery shopping   In warranty context, an approach where warranty provider (or a third-party representative) pretends to be the customer returning a product for warranty service. This allows service agent actions and behavior to be monitored during the service visit.

On-boarding   The process of introducing the product to the customer and helping the customer to use the product.

Open-book pricing model   A pricing model where a service agent and warranty provider agree on the costs that are remunerable and the service agent charges the warranty provider based on the actual costs. The service agent is allowed to add a margin on top of the realized costs.

Part distributor   Part distributor (retailer of components) delivers spare parts manufactured by a large number of part manufacturers, but does not manufacture the parts itself.

Part manufacturer   Part (or component) manufacturer produces the parts and other materials needed in warranty servicing.

Product   An article or substance that is manufactured or refined for sale. Refers both to an individual unit and a class (collection of units).

Remote service   A service approach where a technician solves the product issue using remote connectivity.

Replacement   Replacement of customer product instead of repairing it with a product that typically is identical or similar to the product customer originally had.

Sales and distribution channel   Distributors and retailers responsible for sales and distribution of the products.

Service agent   The party that carries out the actions to rectify the customer problem by repairing or replacing the defective product.

Service agent claim   Warranty service claim.

Service back end   Noncustomer-facing nodes in the service network.

Service front end   Customer-facing nodes in the service network.

Service process   The process for service planning and execution, covering the whole after-sales services. Can also refer to warranty service process, which consists of the servicing activities from a customer warranty issue to the closure of the claim.

Value-based pricing   Pricing model where the service agent compensation depends on the outcome of the service (e.g., product uptime).

Victim   The person or company being the target of and suffering from fraudulent activities.

Warranty administrator   The party representing the warranty provider and responsible for various administrative activities related to warranty claims handling and control.

Warranty accrual   Expense posted in accounting as an estimate of the future warranty liabilities related to current accounting period's product sale, including a change in costs estimated earlier.

Warranty claim   A customer warranty claim or a warranty service claim, depending on the context.

Warranty fraud   Fraud done in warranty service context by actors (fraudsters) acting alone or in collusion to defraud one or more parties (victims) using one or more methods of fraud. Main actors doing warranty fraud are (i) customer, (ii) service agent, (iii) sales channel, (iv) warranty administrator, and (v) warranty provider.

Warranty management system   A system to support warranty management. Often a part of an ERP, a CRM, or a service management system.

Warranty provider   The party responsible for providing warranty service. Warranty provider can be the manufacturer or another party.

Warranty reserve   Warranty accruals accumulated over time but not yet spent constitute the warranty reserve. This reserve is used to cover the costs of servicing when warranty claims materialize.

Warranty service claim   A claim from the service agent to the warranty provider to get compensation for warranty servicing executed on behalf of the warranty provider. Also called service agent claim.

Acronyms

AGMA Alliance for Gray Market and Counterfeit Abatement

AT Agency theory

AUD Australian dollar

B2B Business-to-business

B2C Business-to-consumer

BER Beyond economical repair

BW Base warranty

CAS The Center for Auto Safety

CEO Chief executive officer

COGS Cost of goods sold

CRM Customer relationship management

DAP Dead after purchase

DMAIC Define, measure, analyze, improve, and control

DOA Dead on arrival

ERP Enterprise resource planning

EW Extended warranty

FASB Financial Accounting Standards Board

FMEA Failure mode effects analysis

FTA Federal Transit Administration

FTE Full-time equivalent, full-time employee

GM General Motors

GSX Global service exchange

GT Game theory

HP Hewlett-Packard

IBM International Business Machines

IDC International Data Corporation

IFRS International Financial Reporting Standards

IT   Information technology

LCC   Life-cycle cost

MSC   Maintenance service contract

MTBF   Mean time between failures

NFF   No fault found

OEM   Original equipment manufacturer

PC   Personal computer

PLC   Product life cycle

PLM   Product life-cycle management

PoS   Point of sale

PWC   PricewaterhouseCoopers

R&D   Research and development

RIW   Reliability improvement warranty

RMA   Return merchandise authorization, return materials authorization

SA   Service agent

SEC   Securities and Exchange Commission

SLA   Service-level agreement

SOM   Self-organizing map

SPC   Statistical process control

SUR   Same unit repair

TAT   Turnaround time

TREAD Act   Transportation Recall Enhancement, Accountability and Documentation (or TREAD) Act

UCC   Uniform commercial code

USD, US$ US dollar

References

Accenture Global Services GmbH. 2011. "Warranty Management System and Method." US Patent No. US 07970711. Issued on January 28.

AGMA (Alliance for Gray Market and Counterfeit Abatement) and CompTIA (The Computing Technology Industry Association). 2013. *IT Industry Warranty and Service Abuse: Stealing Profitability! Core Issues, New Solutions and Emerging Threats.* http://www.agmaglobal.org/cms/uploads/whitePapers/CompTIA_WhitePaper-WarrantyAbuse-8%2027%2013.pdf.

AGMA (Alliance for Gray Market and Counterfeit Abatement) and PWC (Price Waterhouse Coopers). 2009. *Service Blues: Effectively Managing the Multi-Billion Dollar Threat from Product Warranty and Support Abuse.*

Apple Inc. 2016. "Your Hardware Warranty. Apple One (1) Year Limited Warranty—Mac, United States." http://www.apple.com/legal/warranty/products/embedded-mac-warranty-us.html.

Apple Inc. 2015a. "Apple Authorized Service Provider Program." https://www.apple.com/lae/support/programs/aasp/.

Apple Inc. 2015b. "Submit Your Proof of Purchase." http://www.apple.com/au/support/service/help/warrantycheck/geo_proofofpurchase.html.

Apple Inc. 2015c. "Form 10-K. For the Fiscal Year Ended September 26, 2015." http://files.shareholder.com/downloads/AAPL/982508604x0x861262/2601797E-6590-4CAA-86C9-962348440FFC/2015_Form_10-K_As-filed_.pdf.

Arnum. E. 2004. "Auto Inspectors." *Warranty Week,* October 5.

Arnum, E. 2012. "Average Warranty Costs per Industry." *Warranty Week.* May 31.

Arnum, E. 2015. Private interview on April 14.

Association of Certified Fraud Examiners. 2014. "Report to the Nations on Occupational Fraud and Abuse." 2014 Global Fraud Study.

BearingPoint. 2008. "Global Automotive Warranty Survey Report."

BestBuy. 2015. "GeekSquad Protection Plan." September 13.

Blank, R. 2014. *Warranty Claims Reduction.* Boca Raton, FL: CRC Press.

Blischke, W. R., and D. N. P. Murthy. 1994. *Warranty Cost Analysis.* New York: Marcel Dekker.

Blischke, W. R., and D. N. P. Murthy (eds.). 1996. *Product Warranty Handbook.* New York: Marcel Dekker.

Blischke, W. R., M. R. Karim, and D. N. P. Murthy. 2011. *Warranty Data Collection and Analysis.* London: Springer Verlag.

Blischke, W. R., and D. N. P. Murthy. 2000. *Reliability: Modeling, Prediction, and Optimization.* Hoboken, NJ: John Wiley & Sons.

Borgia, O., F. De Carlo, and M. Tucci. 2012. "Warranty Data Analysis for Service Demand Forecasting: A Case Study in Household Appliances." In *Advances in Safety, Reliability and Risk Management*, edited by C. Berenguer, A. Grall and C. Guedes Soares. London: CRC Press.

Brennan, J. R. 1994. *Warranties*. New York: McGraw-Hill.

Brennan, S., and J. Barkai. 2011. *Methods and Practices: Warranty Capabilities Maturity Model*. IDC Manufacturing Insights.

Burke, B. 2014. "Setting Standards: Demystifying Warranty Fraud." LinkedIn.

Caterpillar. 2015. www.cat.com.

Cauchi, S. 2014. "Fisher & Paykel's Fine Print, Too Fine, Leads to $200,000 Fine." *Sydney Morning Herald,* December 22.

Center for Auto Safety. 2015. "Secret Warranties." http://www.autosafety.org/secret-warranties.

Center for Automotive Research, 2005. *The Warranty Process Flow Within the Automotive Industry: An Investigation of Automotive Warranty Processes and Issues*. Ann Arbor, MI: CAR.

Chatterjee K, and W. F. Samuelson (eds.). 2001. *Game Theory and Business Applications*. Norwell, MA: Kluwer Academic Publishers.

Chu, J., and P. K. Chintagunta. 2009. "Quantifying the Economic Value of Warranties in the Server Market." *Marketing Science* 28: 99–121.

Cisco. 2007. "Cisco Information Packet—Cisco Limited Warranty, Disclaimer of Warranty, End User License Agreement," and US FCC Notice, July 27, http://www.cisco.com/c/en/us/td/docs/general/warranty/English/SL3 DEN__.html.

Davenport, T. H., J. G. Harris, and R. Morison. 2010. *Analytics at Work*. Boston: Harvard Business School Publishing.

Davis, F. W., and K. B. Mandrodt. 1996. *Customer Responsive Management: The Flexible Advantage*. Oxford: Blackwell Publishers.

Ditlow, C., and R. Gold. 1993. *Little Secrets of the Auto Industry: Hidden Warranties Cost Billions of Dollars*. Moyer Bell.

Djamaludin, I., D. N. P. Murthy, and W. R. Blischke. 1996. "Bibliography on Warranties." In *Product Warranty Handbook*, edited by W. R. Blischke and D. N. P. Murthy. New York: Marcel Dekker.

Eisenhardt, K. M. 1989. "Agency Theory: An Assessment and Review." *Academy of Management Review* 14: 57–74.

Etzion, D., and A. Pe'er. 2013. "Mixed Signals: A Dynamic Analysis of Warranty Provision in the Automotive Industry, 1960–2008." *Strategic Management Journal* 35: 1605–1625.

FASB Technical Bulletin No. 90–1 1990. "Accounting for Separately Priced Extended Warranty and Product Maintenance Contracts." Financial Accounting Standards Board.

Figueroa, F., B. McFadden, G. Oden, R. Ording, A. Pawlowski, P. V. Chowdhary, and K. Thompson. 2009. *Warranty Data Analytics*. Ubiquiti Inc.

Foxall, J. 2015. "Kia's Seven-Year Warranty Success." *The Telegraph*, March 11.

Ford UK. 2015. "Ford New Car Warranties." http://www.ford.co.uk/BuyingandprotectingyourFord/Warranties/New-Car.

Germano, T. 1999. "Self Organizing Maps." Worcester Polytechnic Institute, March 23. http://davis.wpi.edu/~matt/courses/soms/#Introduction.

Gomez, M. 2011. "Massachusetts Man Defrauded Cisco of $15.4 Million, Sentenced to Prison." *San Jose Mercury News*. January 11.

Gordon, W. 2014. "How to Get Free Repairs Without a Valid Warranty." *Lifehacker,* October 24. http://lifehacker.com/5952350/how-to-get-free-repairs-without-a-valid-warranty.

Gracey, K. 2008. "Reseller Caught with Hand in the Cookie Jar." *Macworld Forums*, October 31. http://www.macworld.com.au/forums/index.php?showtopic=2862.

HP. 2015. "2014 Annual Report." Hewlett-Packard. January, http://h30261.www3.hp.com/~/media/Files/H/HP-IR/documents/reports/2015/hpq-annual-report-2014.pdf.

Johnson, T., R. H. M. Dinh, and Y. T. Tan. 2010. "Consumer Abuse Detection System and Method." United States Patent Application 20100312920. Apple Inc., Dec 9.

Köpf, A. 2013. "A Spatial Pooler for Real-Valued Inputs—Normalized Distributed Self-Organizing Map." *Provisio Research* 17 June. http://research.provisio.com/activity/2013/06/17/normalized-distributed-self-organizing-map/.

Kraus, C., and R. Valverde. 2014. "A Data Warehouse Design for the Detection of Fraud in the Supply Chain Using the Benford's Law." *American Journal of Applied Sciences* 11(9): 1507–1518.

Kristensen, G. 2012. "Disclosure of Cheating by Statistical Methods." *Journal of Statistical and Econometric Methods* 1(3).

Matsumoto, D., H. S. Hwang, L. Skinner, and M. G. Frank. 2011. "Evaluating Truthfulness and Detecting Deception." U.S. Department of Justice, Federal Bureau of Investigation, June.

Microsoft Mobile Oy. 2015. "*Manufacturer's Limited Warranty*." Espoo, Finland https://www.microsoft.com/en-gb/mobile/support/manufacturers-limited-warranty/.

Murthy, D. N. P., and W. R. Blischke. 2005. *Warranty Management and Product Manufacturing*. London: Springer Verlag.

Murthy, D. N. P., W. Blischke, S. Kakouros, and D. Kuettner. 2007. "Changing the Way We Think about Warranty Management." *Warranty Week*, June 19.

Murthy, D. N. P., and I. Djamaludin. 2003. "New Product Warranty: A Literature Review." *International Journal of Production Research* 79: 231–260.

Murthy, D. N. P., and N. Jack. 2014. *Extended Warranties, Maintenance Service and Lease Contracts*. London: Springer Verlag.

Murthy, D. N. P., M. Rausand, and T. Østerås. 2008. *Product Reliability*. London: Springer Verlag.

Nagelvoort, M. 2015. PCMI Corporation. Personal interview on September 3.

Oh, H., S. Choi, K. Kim, K., B. D. Youn, and M. Pecht. 2015. "An Empirical Model to Describe Performance Degradation for Warranty Abuse Detection in Portable Electronics." *Reliability Engineering and System Safety*. Amsterdam: Elsevier.

Osborne, M. J. 2002. *An Introduction to Game Theory*. Oxford: Oxford University Press.

Oxford Dictionary 2015. http://www.oxforddictionaries.com/.

Pinder, A. 2013. "Service Contract and Warranty Management." Aberdeen Group.

Pinder, A. 2015. "Returns Management Matters: The Biggest Hidden Secret in the Supply Chain." Aberdeen Group.

Pinder, A., and S. Dutta. 2011. *"Warranty and Contract Management."* Aberdeen Group.

Rai, B. K., and N. Singh. 2009. *Reliability Analysis and Prediction with Warranty Data*. Boca Raton, FL: CRC Press.

Rawes, E. 2014. "Four of the Most Expensive Car Problems." CheatSheet, November 20. http://www.cheatsheet.com/personal-finance/4-of-the-most-expensive-car-problems.html/?a=viewall.

Rowley, S. 2015. "Warranty Reserves, Ford University." March 13. https://credit.ford.com/webcontent/investorcenter/2015_Ford_University_Final.pdf.

Sadgrove, K. 2015. *The Complete Guide to Business Risk Management*. Burlington: Gower Publishing Limited.

Sahin, I., and H. Polatogu. 1998. *Quality, Warranty and Preventive Maintenance*. Boston: Kluwer Academic Publishers.

Sands, A., and V. Tseng. 2009. "Squaretrade Research: One-third of iPhones Fail over Two Years, Mostly from Accidents." SquareTrade Inc. https://www.squaretrade.com/htm/pdf/SquareTrade_iPhone_Study_0609.pdf.

SAS Institute 2015. SAS Institute materials as a part of the content contribution to the book from Bill Roberts.

Swatch 2015. Warranty, Biel, Switzerland, http://www.swatch.com/en/services/warranty.

Thomas, M. U. 2006. *Reliability and Warranties: Methods for Product Development and Quality Improvement*. New York: Taylor & Francis.

Thomas, M. U., and S. S. Rao. 1999. "Warranty Economic Decision Models: A Summary and Some Suggested Directions for Future Research." *Operations Research* 47: 807–820.

Trefis Team. 2012. "Best Buy Continues to Diversify by Selling Geek Squad Services." *Forbes*, October 10. http://www.forbes.com/sites/greatspeculations/2012/10/10/best-buy-continues-to-diversify-by-selling-geek-squad-services/.

The UK National Fraud and Cyber Crime Reporting Centre. 2015. http://www.actionfraud.police.uk/a-z_of_fraud.

Van Ackere, A. 1993. "The Principal–Agent Paradigm: Its Relevance to Various Functional Fields." *European Journal of Operational Research* 70: 83–103.

Verma, S., and C. Rajendran. 2015. *Spare Parts Dispatch Fraud Detection Analysis*. University of Duisburg-Essen, Duisburg-Essen Publications online, Duisburg, Germany

Volkswagen UK 2015. *"Warranty."* http://www.volkswagen.co.uk/owners/warranty/factory.

Volvo. 2015. Volvo Cars press releases, *Volvo Cars Introduces "Pay Once and Never Pay Again" Lifetime Parts & Labor Warranty*, Volvo Car USA, Release ID: 165853, July 8, and *Volvo Cars of Canada Offers Lifetime Warranty*, Volvo Cars of Canada, Release ID: 167805, October 1.

Warranty Week. 2004. "Auto Inspectors." *Warranty Week,* October 5.

Warranty Week. 2012. "Average Warranty Costs per Industry." *Warranty Week,* May 31.

Watson, J. 2008. *Strategy: An Introduction to Game Theory*, 2nd ed. New York: W.W. Norton & Company.

Wu, S. 2011. "Warranty Claim Analysis Considering Human Factors." *Reliability Engineering and System Safety* 961: 131–138.

Index

Note: Page references followed by f and t indicate an illustrated figure and table, respectively.

CPSIA information can be obtained
at www.ICGtesting.com
Printed in the USA
LVHW081250230419
615220LV00009B/29/P

9 781119 223887